Table of Contents

This book belongs to:

____

Pre-Kindergarten Skills Checklist

Understanding Language and Communication

Expressing Themselves: Your child should be able to verbally communicate their needs and wants.
Examples: Saying "I'm hungry", "I want to play", or "I need a nap"

Listening Skills: Your little one should be able to listen to simple instructions and follow them, such as "Please put your toys in the box." Make this a part of your daily routines.
Examples: "Please pick up the teddy bear" or "Put your cup on the table"

Understanding Stories: They should be able to follow along with simple stories and answer questions about them. Reading bedtime stories and discussing them afterward can be a great way to practice this skill.
Examples: "Why was the little bear sad?" or "What did the bunny find?"

Vocabulary: By pre-kindergarten, children should be able to name common objects and describe them using simple words. Start by talking about the things around your house or in a picture book.

Social and Emotional Skills

Sharing and Taking Turns: Your child should understand the concept of sharing and be able to take turns. Board games or shared playtime with siblings or friends can help instill this.
Examples: Sharing a toy with a sibling or waiting their turn on the slide

Expressing Emotions: They should be able to express their feelings verbally and recognize simple emotions in others. Encourage them to talk about their feelings and ask them how characters in stories might be feeling.
Examples: Saying "I'm happy" or understanding a crying friend is sad

Self-Care: Your child should be able to handle basic self-care tasks like washing their hands, using the toilet independently, or putting on their shoes. Regular routines can help develop these skills.
Examples: Washing hands before a meal or trying to tie their shoelaces

Pre-Kindergarten Skills Checklist

Cognitive Skills and Mathematics

Recognizing Shapes and Colours: Your child should be able to identify basic shapes and colours. Flashcards, colourful toys, or simple drawing activities can be a fun way to learn these.
Examples: Pointing out a red apple, a blue car, or a yellow sun; recognizing a circle, square, or triangle

Counting: They should be able to count from 1 to 10. You can practice this together by counting toys, fingers, or steps.
Examples: Counting fingers, toys, or steps

Understanding Concepts: Your child should understand basic concepts like big/small, up/down, in/out. You can illustrate these concepts with objects around the house.
Examples: Comparing a big ball with a small ball, recognizing the dog is 'in' the kennel, or understanding an airplane is 'up' in the sky

Physical Development

Gross Motor Skills: Your child should be able to walk, run, jump, and climb. Fun outdoor games can help develop these skills.
Examples: Climbing a small playground ladder or hopping on one foot

Fine Motor Skills: They should be able to do simple tasks like buttoning their own shirt, holding a pencil correctly, or cutting with safety scissors. Engage them in activities that improve fine motor skills like drawing, colouring, or simple crafts.
Examples: Stacking blocks, drawing a line, or stringing large beads

Remember, every child develops at their own pace and it's okay if your child hasn't mastered all these skills yet. What's most important is to keep engaging them in activities that help them learn and grow while making sure they enjoy the process.

Look at Me!

Look into the mirror. Now draw a picture of yourself.

Print your name.

Colours, Shapes, and Sizes

Colour Review

Colour the crayons.

red

orange

yellow

green

blue

purple

brown

black

The Colour Red

Colour the pictures red.

stop sign

fire truck

apples

heart

Trace the word red.

The Colour Orange

Colour the pictures orange.

carrot

pumpkin

orange

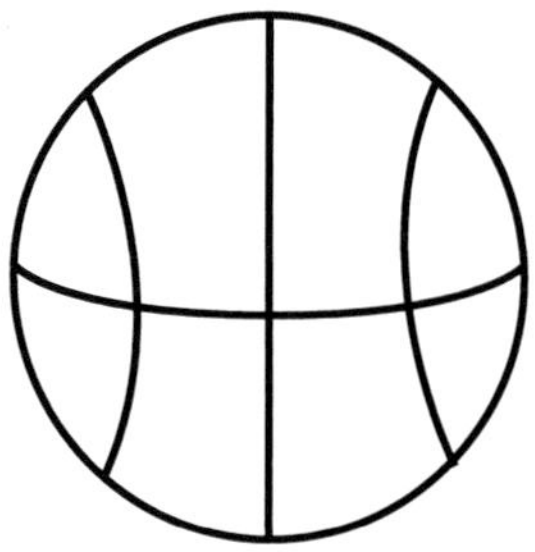

basketball

Trace the word **orange**.

orange

The Colour Yellow

Colour the pictures yellow.

sun

bus

bananas

duck

Trace the word **yellow**.

yellow

The Colour Green

Colour the pictures green.

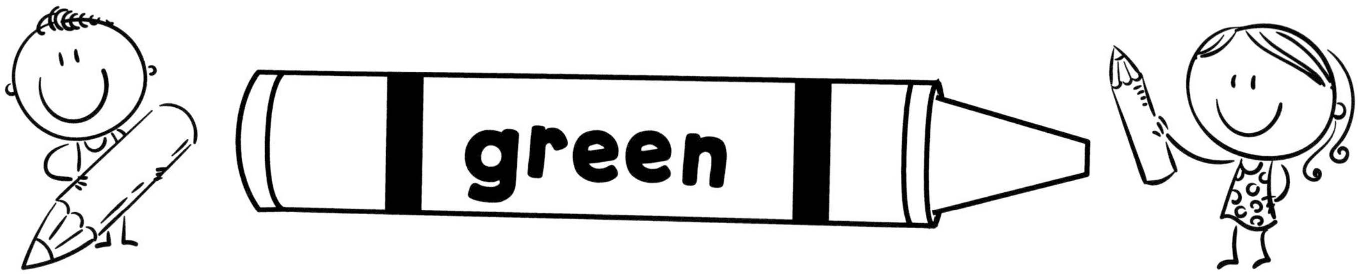

leaf

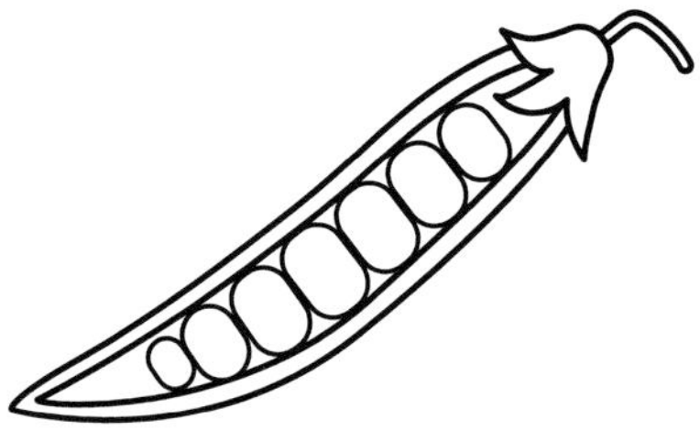

peas in a pod

alligator

truck

Trace the word **green**.

green

The Colour Blue

Colour the pictures blue.

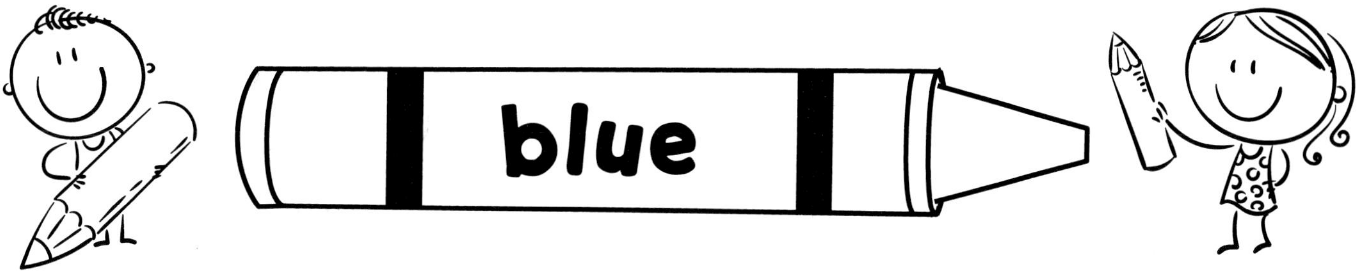

jeans

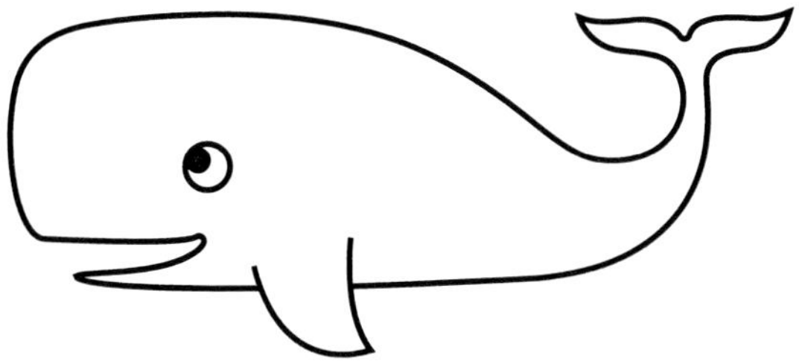

whale

umbrella

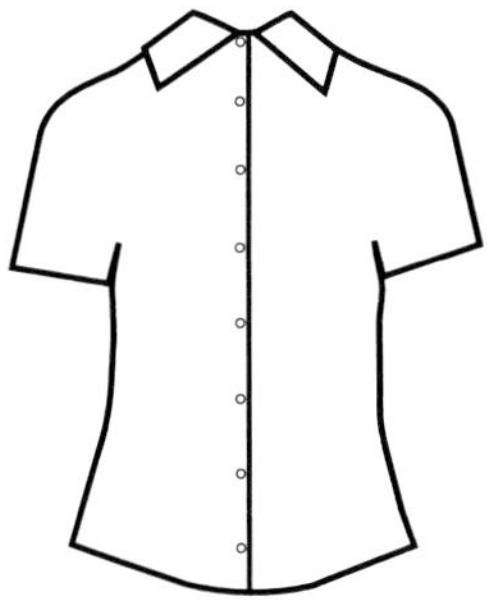

shirt

Trace the word **blue**.

blue

The Colour Purple

Colour the pictures purple.

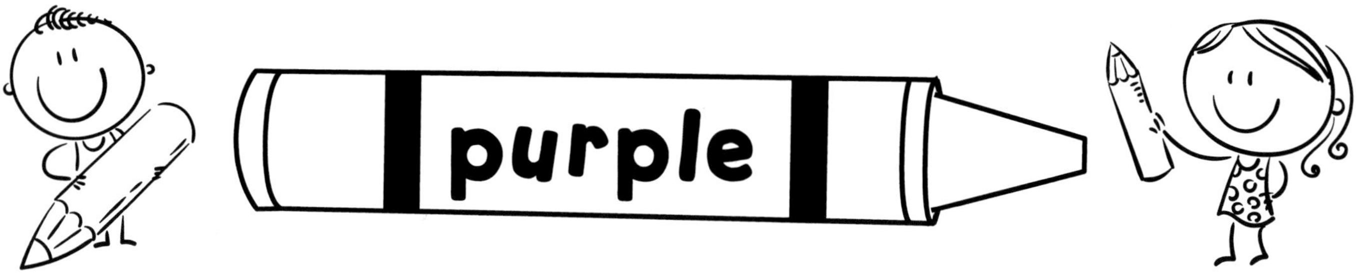

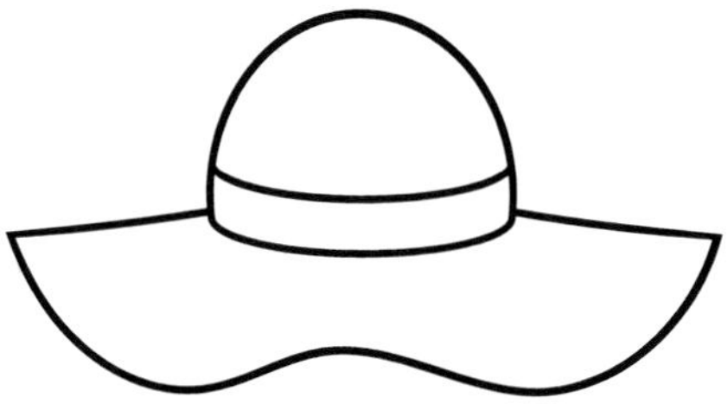

hat

grapes

eggplant

violets

Trace the word **purple**.

purple

The Colour Black

Colour the pictures black.

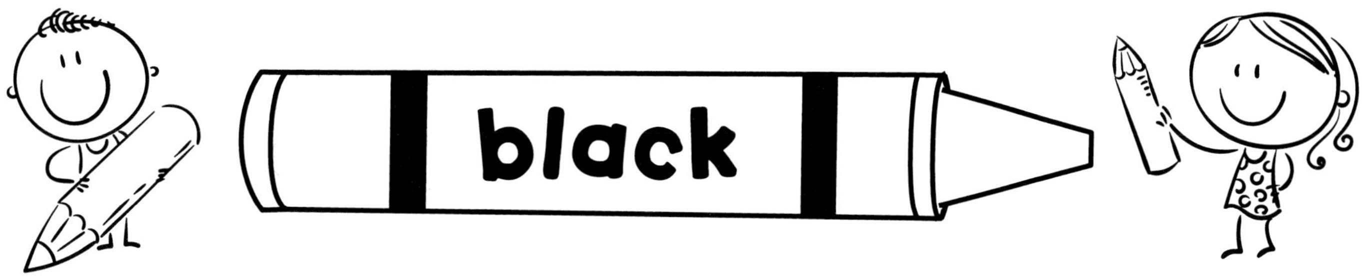

kettle

van

bat

sheep

Trace the word **black**.

black

The Colour Brown

Colour the pictures brown.

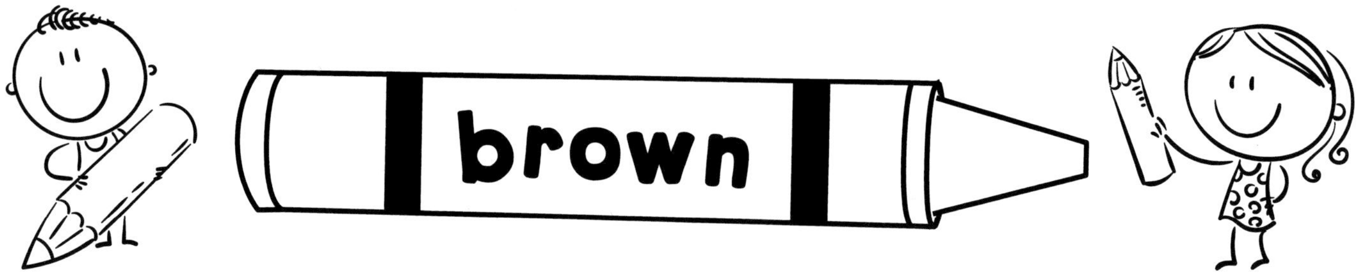

mushroom

dog

potatoes

acorns

Trace the word **brown**.

brown

Colouring Fun

Colour the balloons.

Looking at Circles

A **circle** is a shape that is round. Trace the circle.

Colour the circle red.

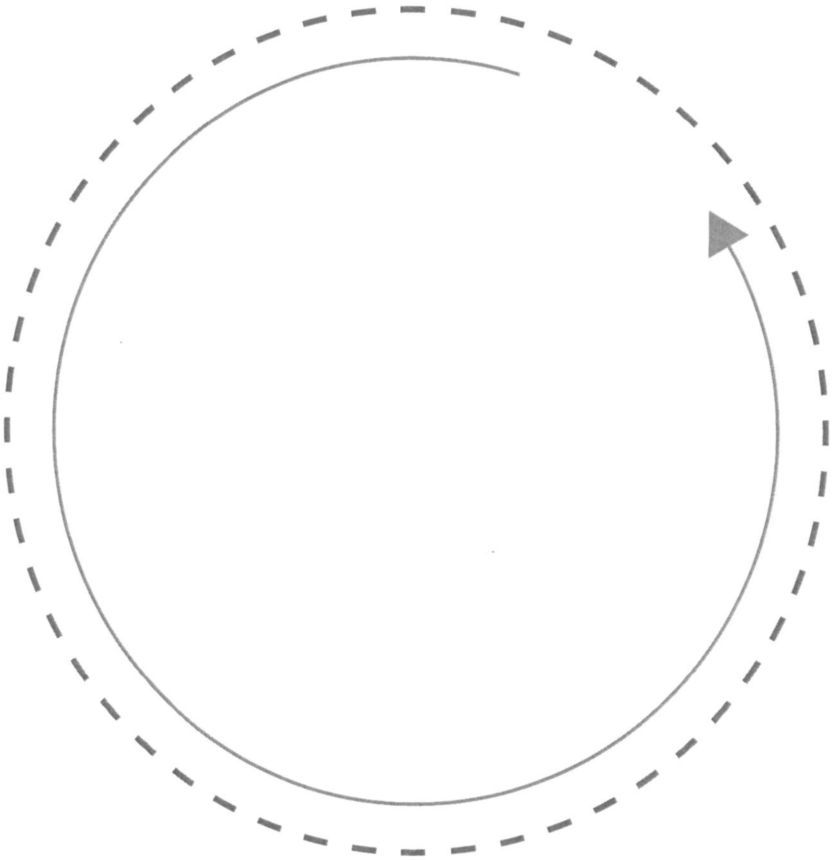

Think About It!

You can find examples of circles all around you!

clock

wheel

Looking at Squares

A **square** is a shape with four equal sides. Trace the square.

Colour the square 

.

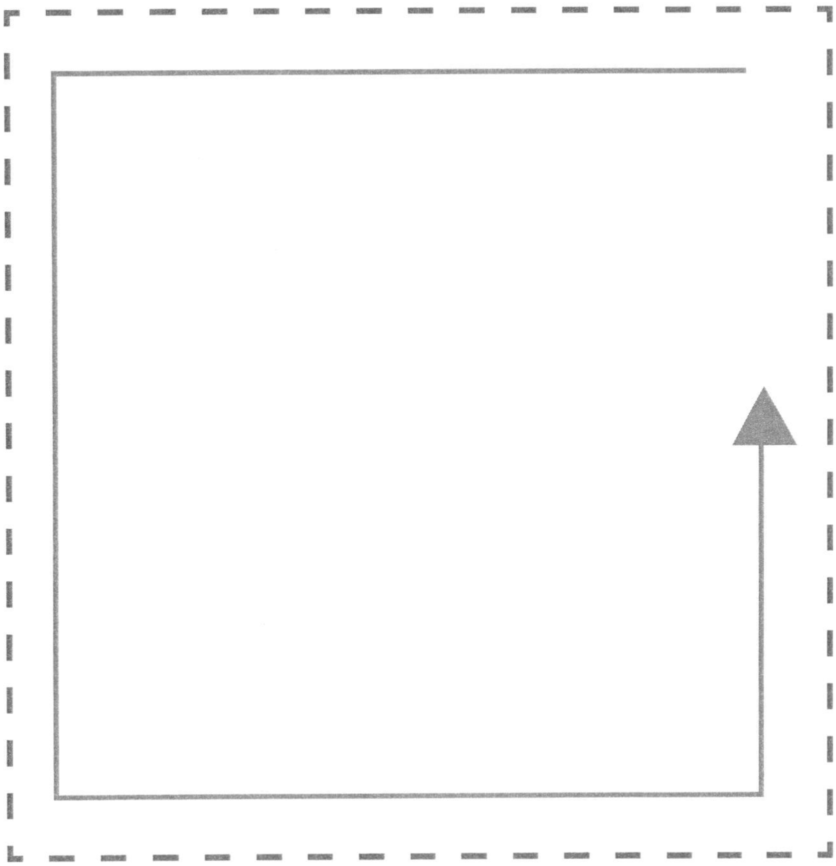

Think About It!

You can find examples of squares all around you!

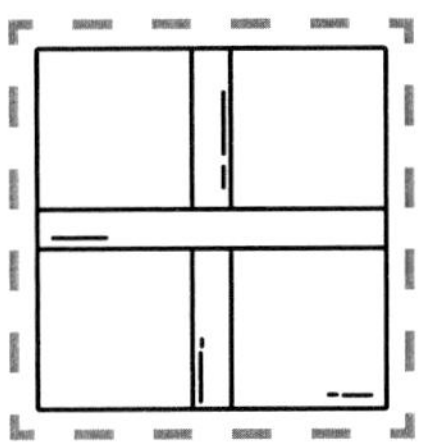

box

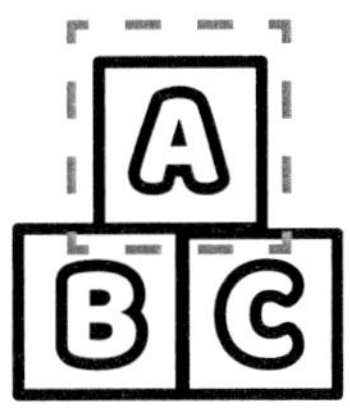

blocks

Looking at Triangles

A **triangle** is a shape with three sides. Trace the triangle.

Colour the triangle green.

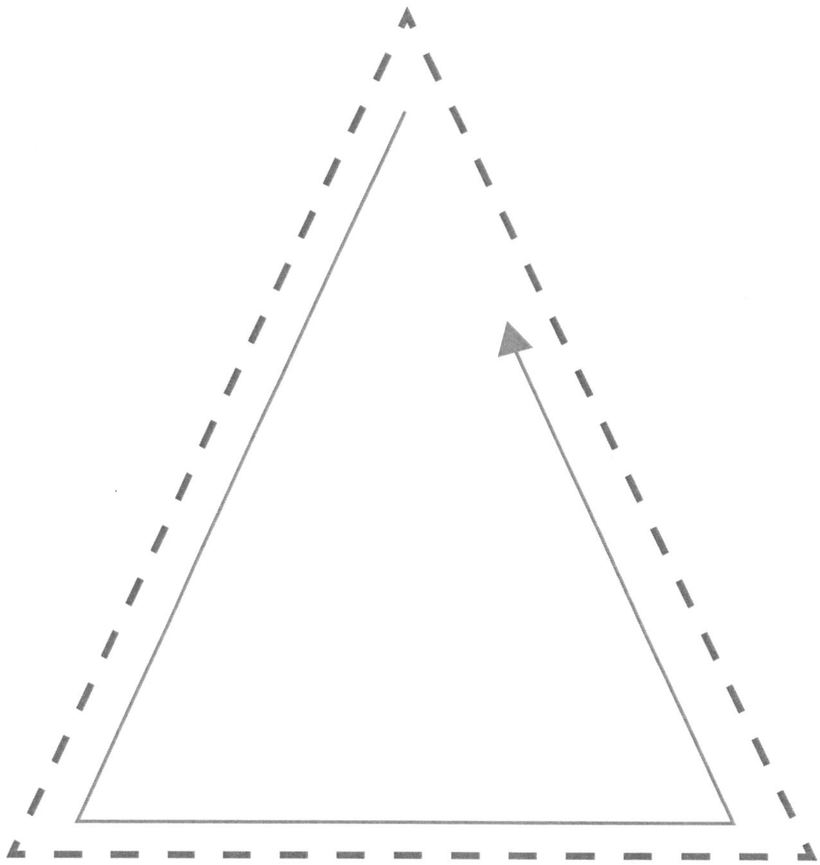

Think About It!

You can find examples of triangles all around you!

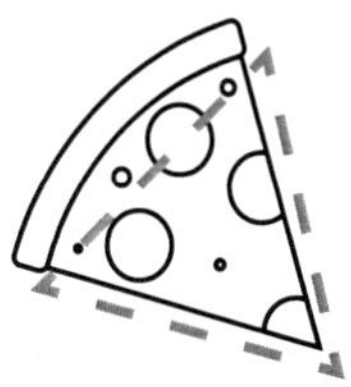

pizza

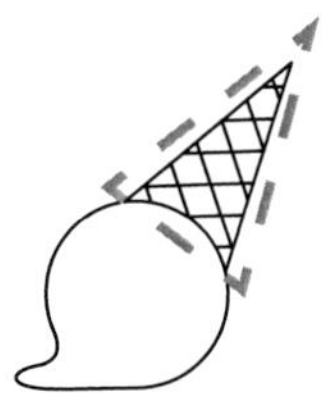

ice cream cone

Looking at Rectangles

A **rectangle** is a shape with four sides. Trace the rectangle.

Colour the rectangle 

.

Think About It!

You can find examples of rectangles all around you!

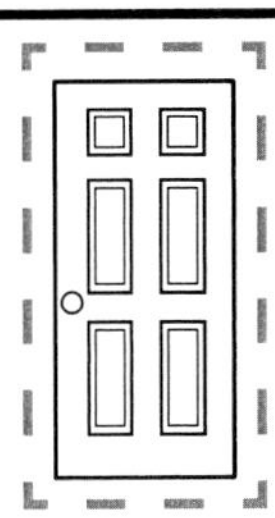

door

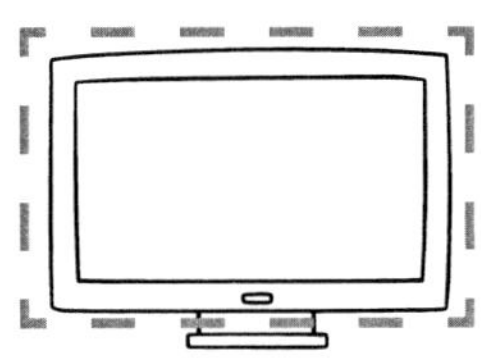

television

Looking at Ovals

An **oval** is a shape. It is round, but a bit longer in one direction.

Trace the oval. Colour the oval 

.

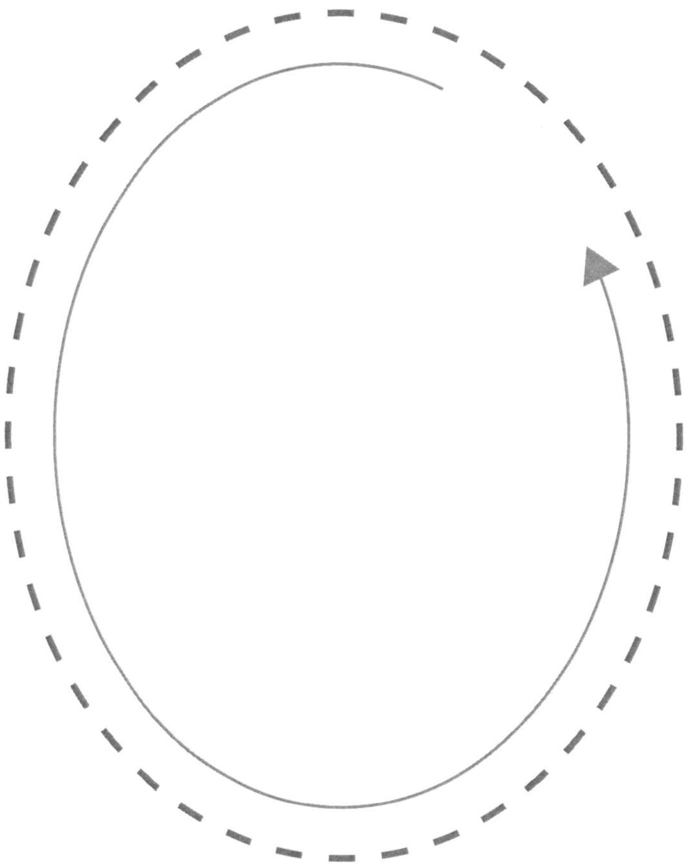

Think About It!

You can find examples of ovals all around you!

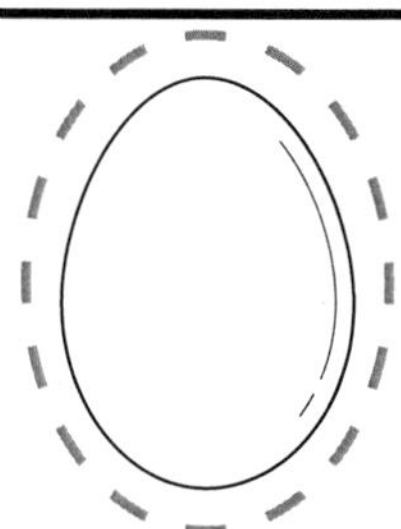

egg

light bulb

Looking at Diamonds

A **diamond** is a shape with four sides. Trace the diamond.

Colour the diamond 

.

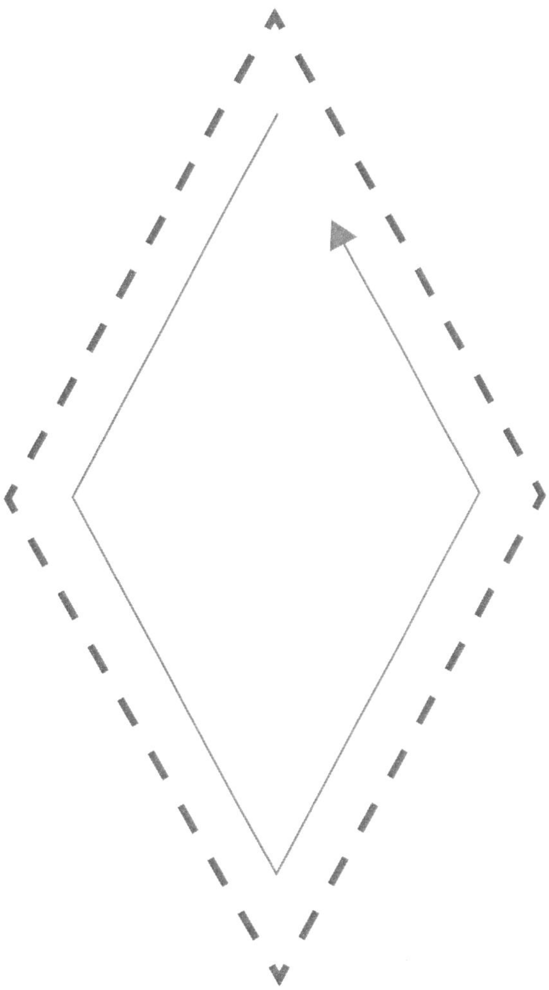

Think About It!

You can find examples of diamonds all around you!

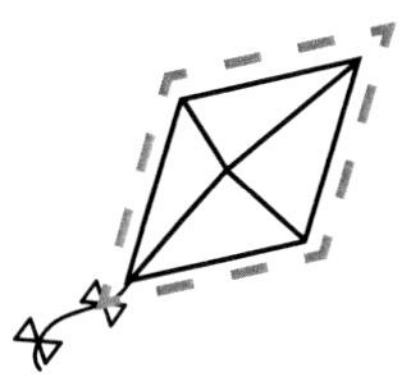

kite

road sign

Shape Matching

Say the name of the shape out loud. Trace the shape.
Draw a line to the matching shape. Colour the shapes.

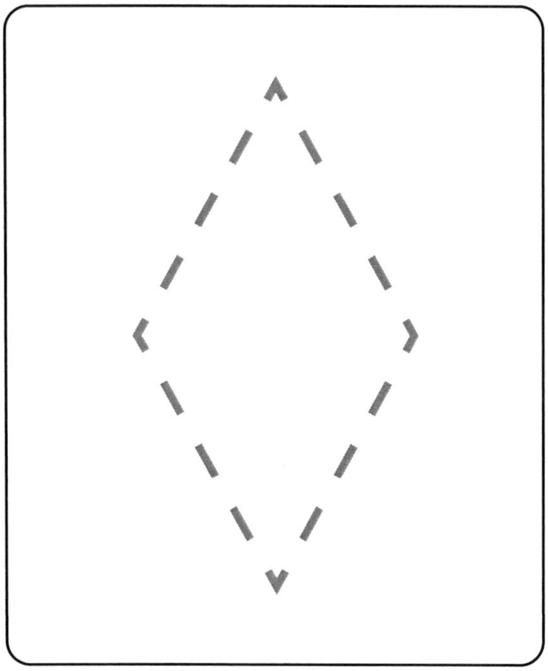

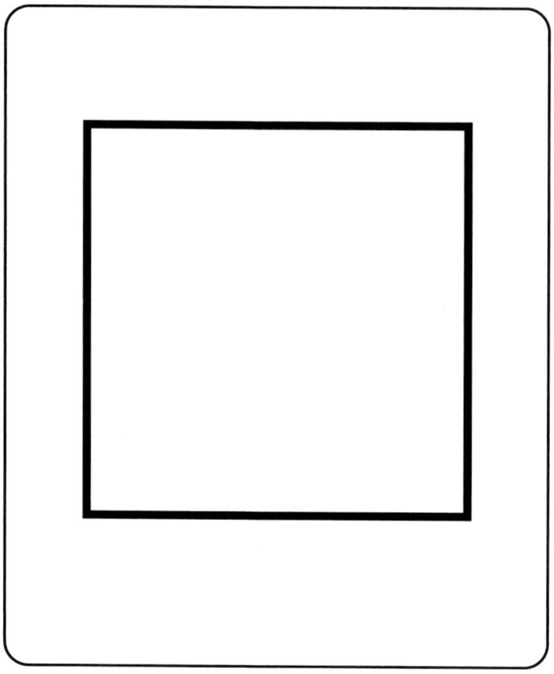

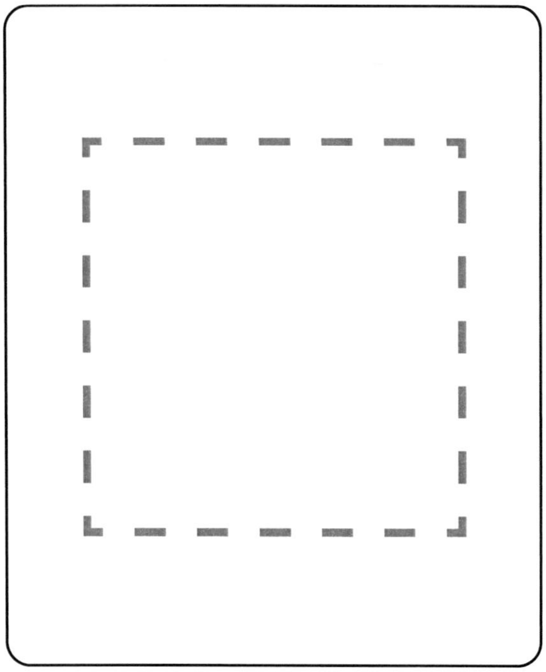

Shape Matching

Say the name of the shape out loud. Trace the shape.
Draw a line to the matching shape. Colour the shapes.

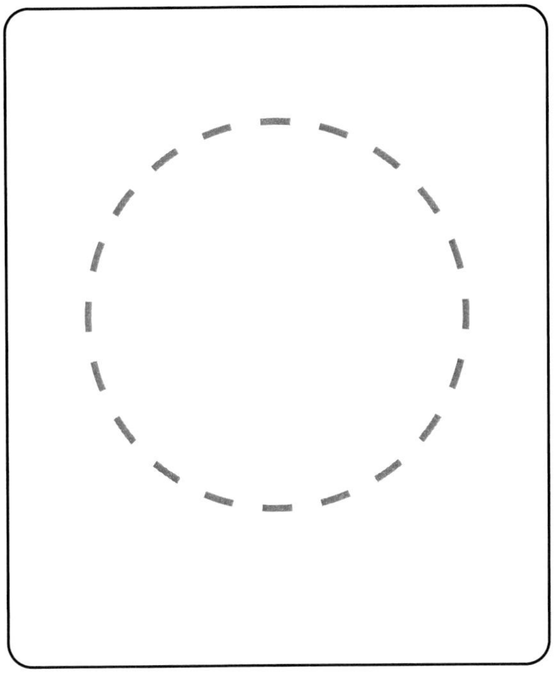

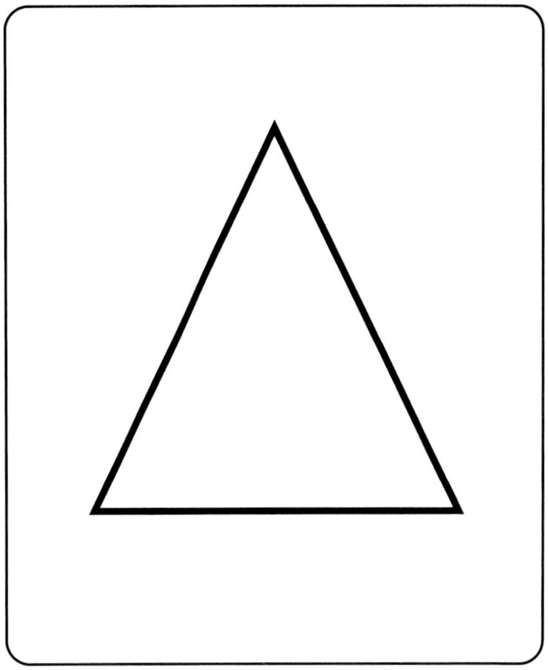

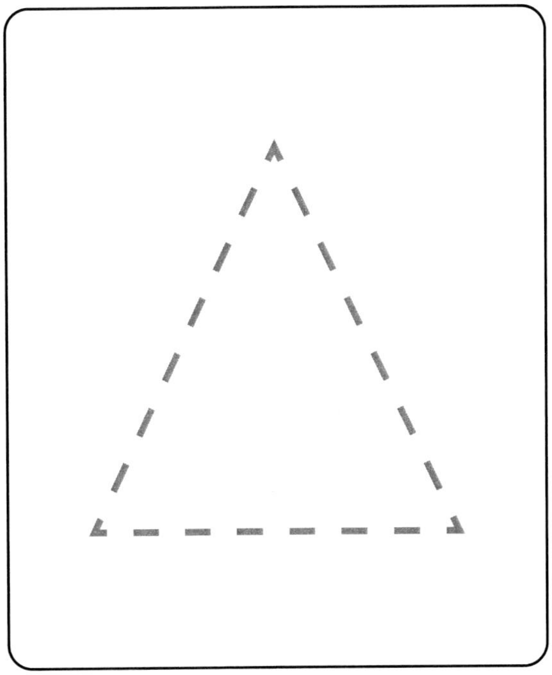

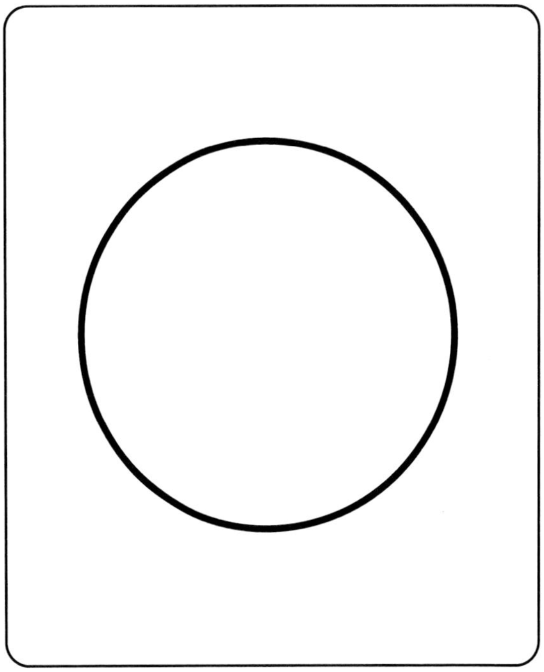

Shape Matching

Say the name of the shape out loud. Trace the shape.
Draw a line to the matching shape. Colour the shapes.

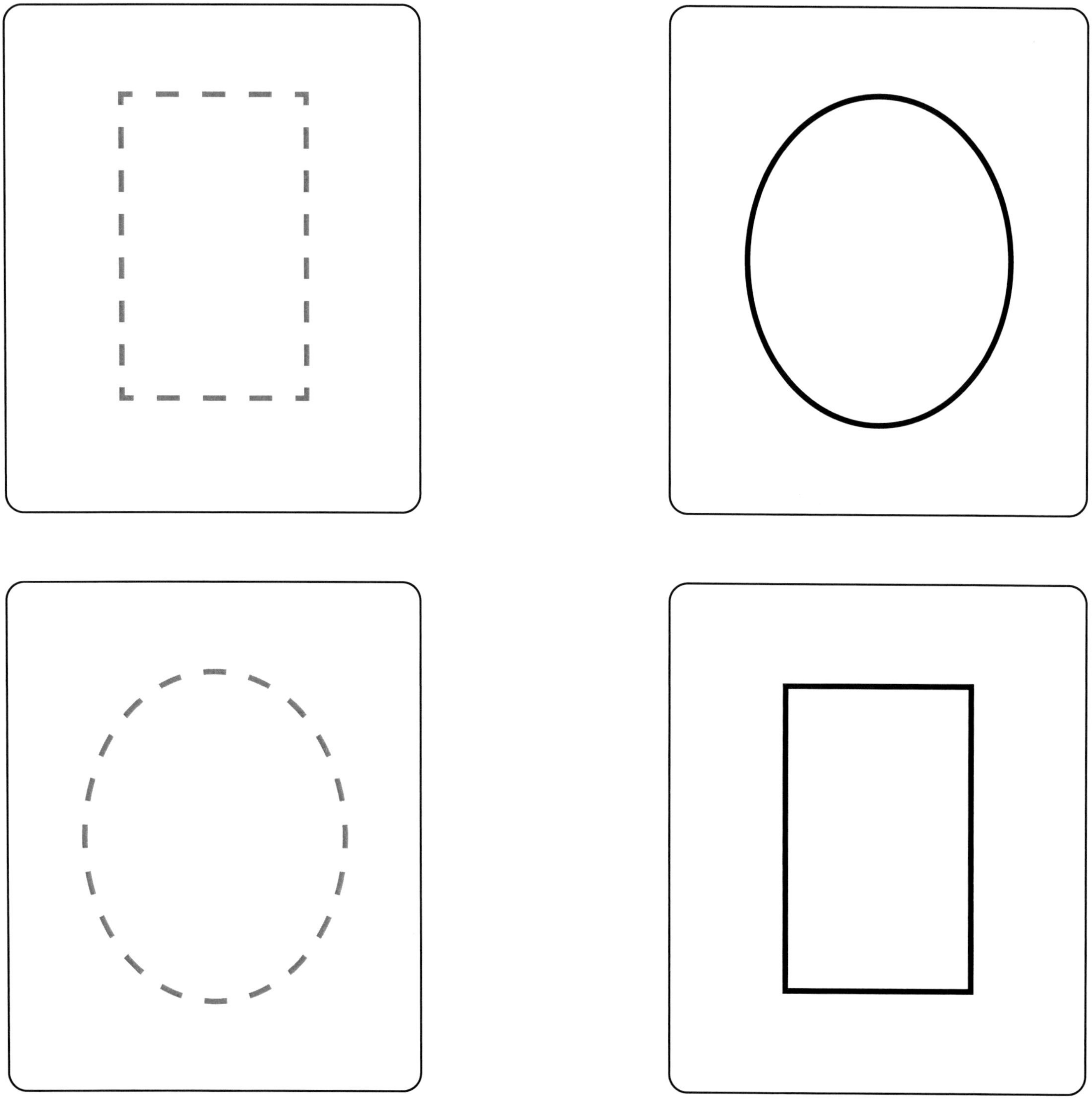

Shape Matching

Say the name of the shape out loud. Trace the shape.
Draw a line to the matching shape. Colour the shapes.

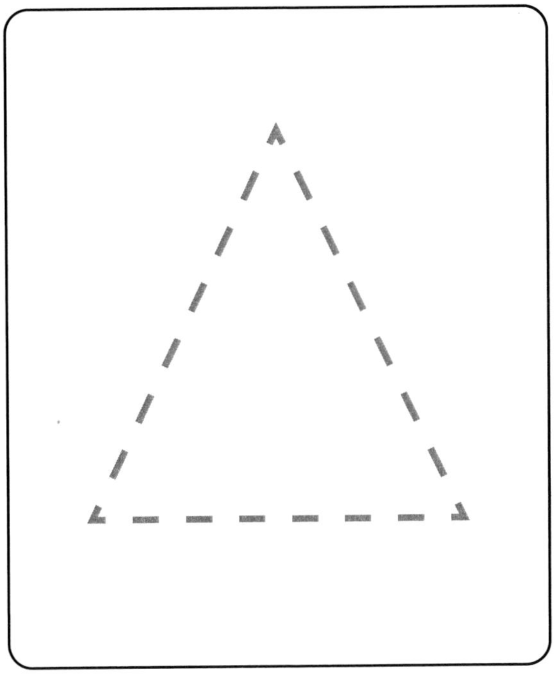

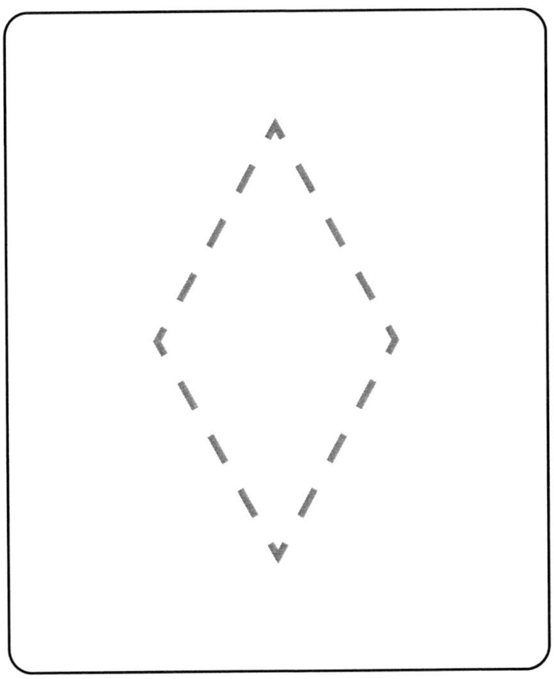

Looking at Shapes

Trace all the shapes.
Use the colour key to colour the shapes.

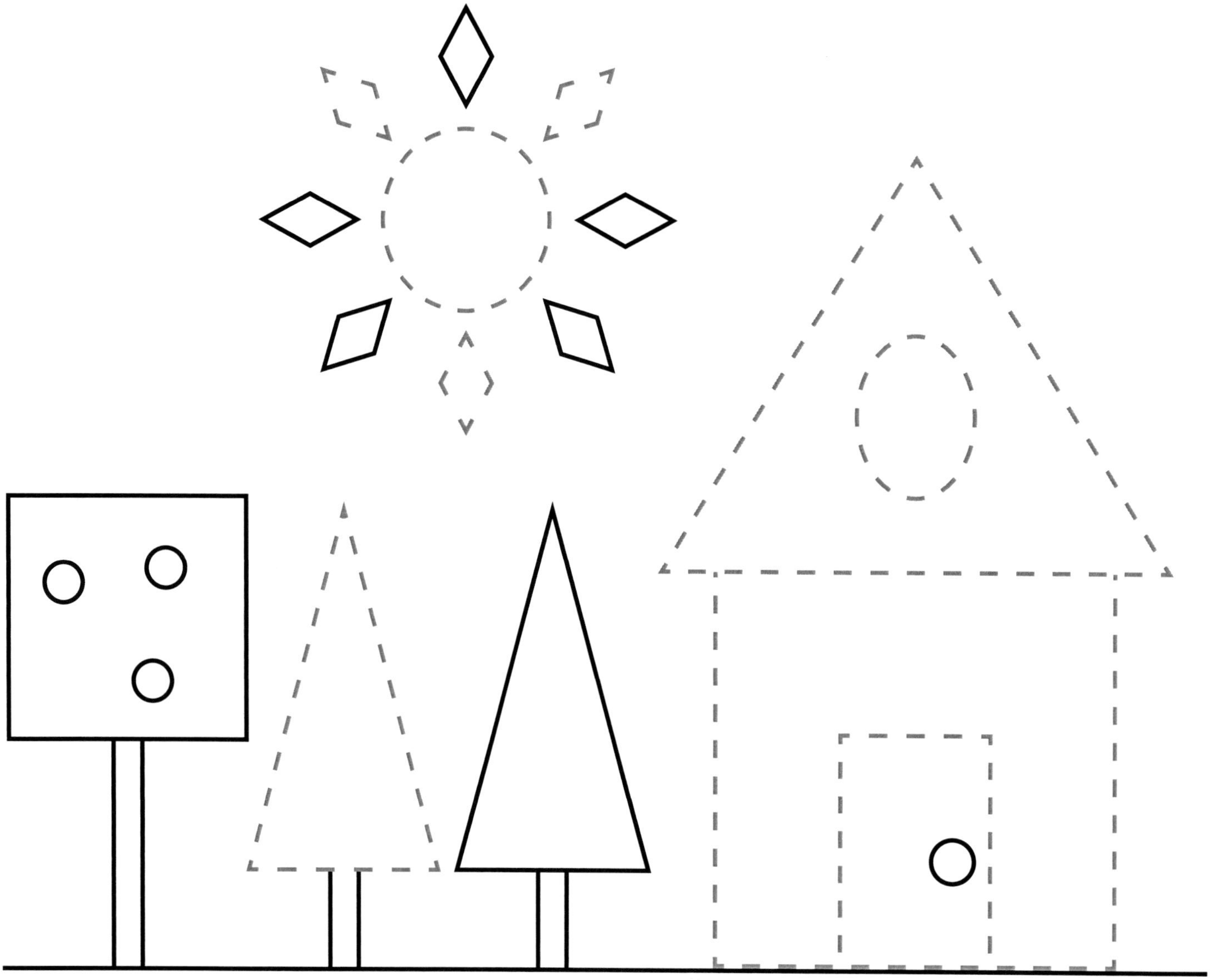

Colour the circles.	yellow	Colour the triangles.	green
Colour the squares.	red	Colour the ovals.	blue
Colour the rectangles.	brown	Colour the diamonds.	orange

Looking at Shapes

Trace all the shapes.
Use the colour key to colour the shapes.

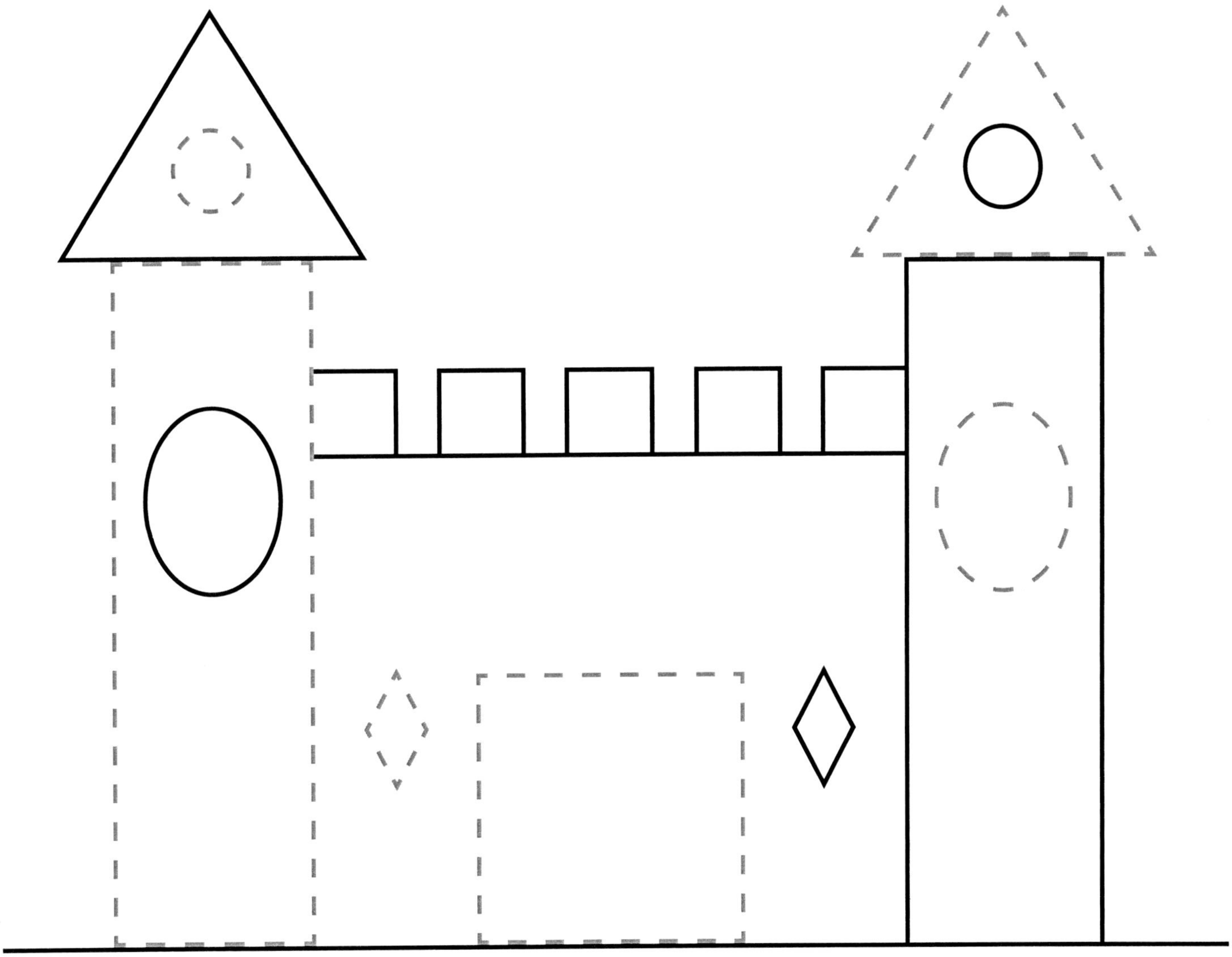

Colour the circles.	red	Colour the triangles.	orange
Colour the squares.	blue	Colour the ovals.	yellow
Colour the rectangles.	green	Colour the diamonds.	purple

Looking at the Same Size

Look at the first picture in the row.
Draw a circle around the shape that is the **same size**.

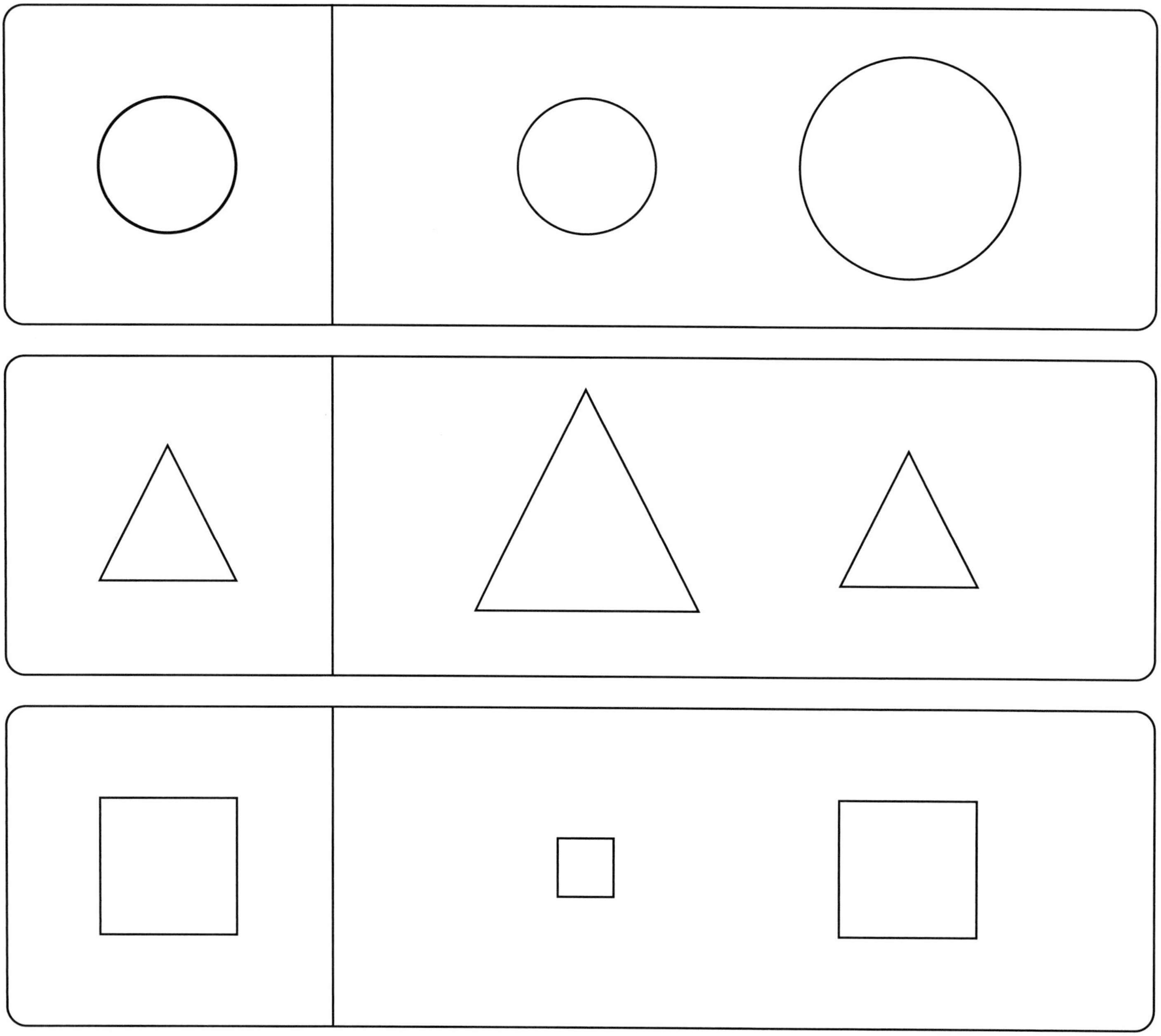

Colour the circles. blue Colour the squares. yellow
Colour the triangles. orange

Looking at Different Sizes

Look at the first picture in the row.

Draw a circle around the shape that is a **different size**.

Colour the diamonds. green Colour the hearts. red

Colour the stars. purple

Drawing Bigger Shapes

Look at the shapes in the row. Trace the **bigger** shape.
Then draw the **bigger** shape. Colour the shapes.

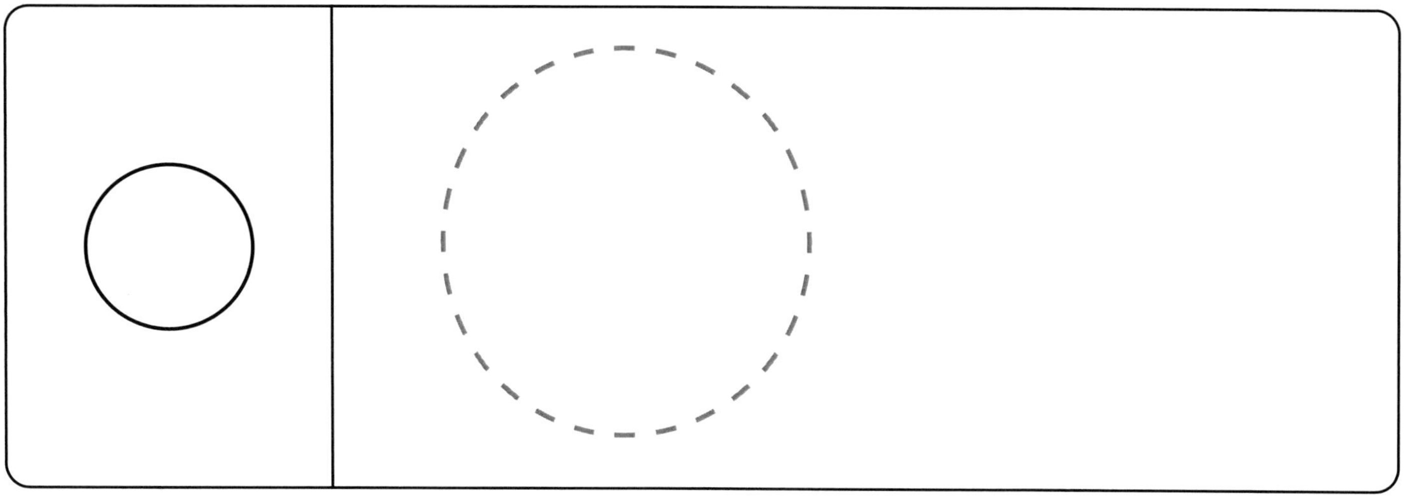

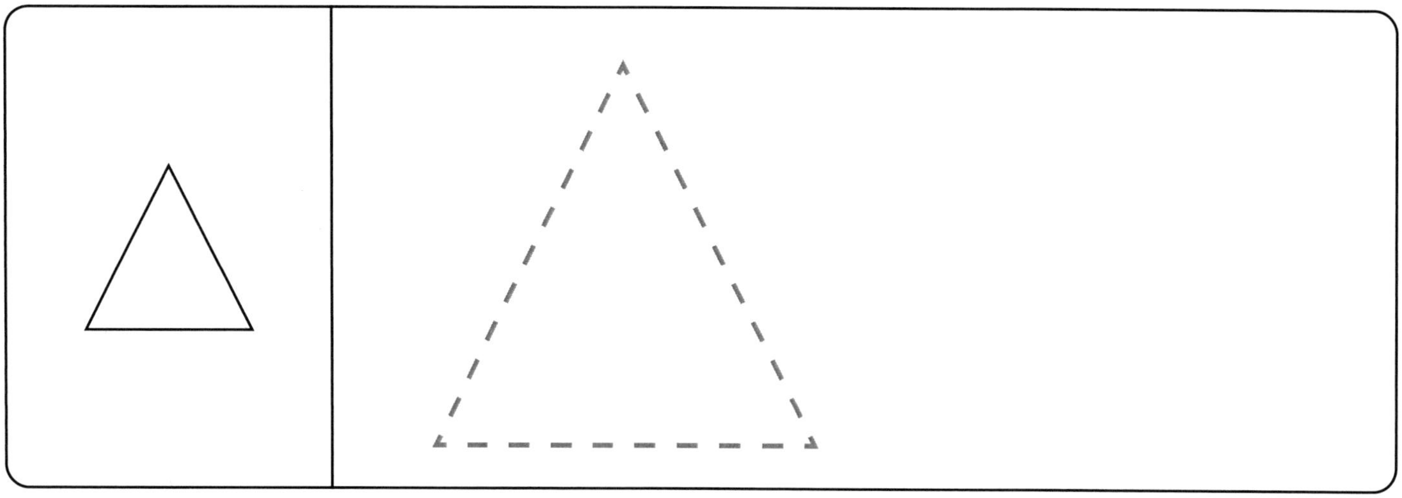

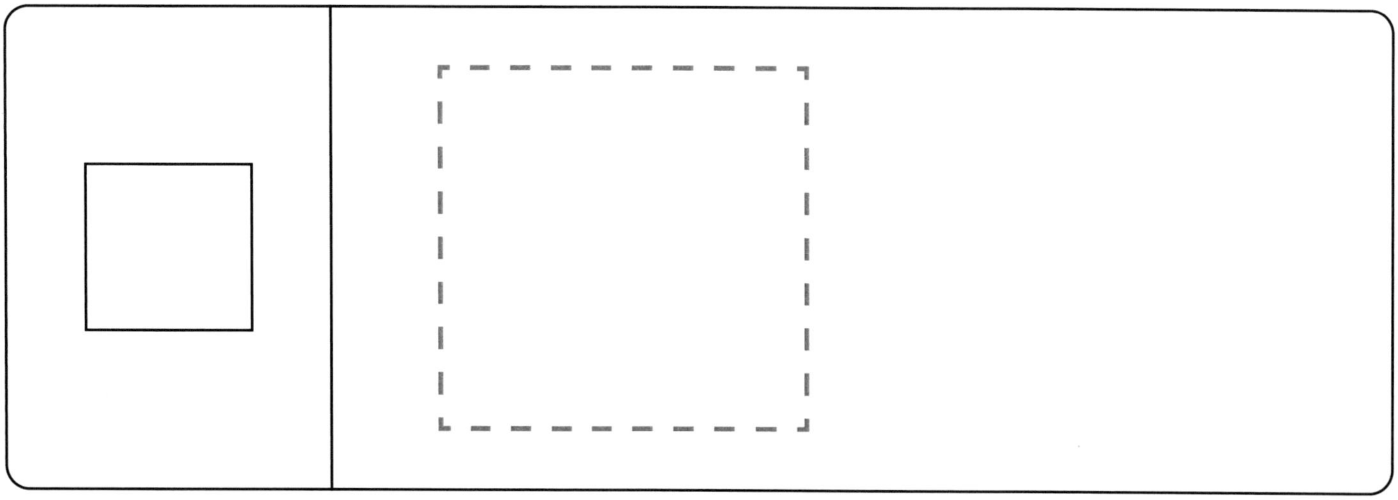

Drawing Smaller Shapes

Look at the shapes in the row. Trace the **smaller** shape.
Then draw the **smaller** shape. Colour the shapes.

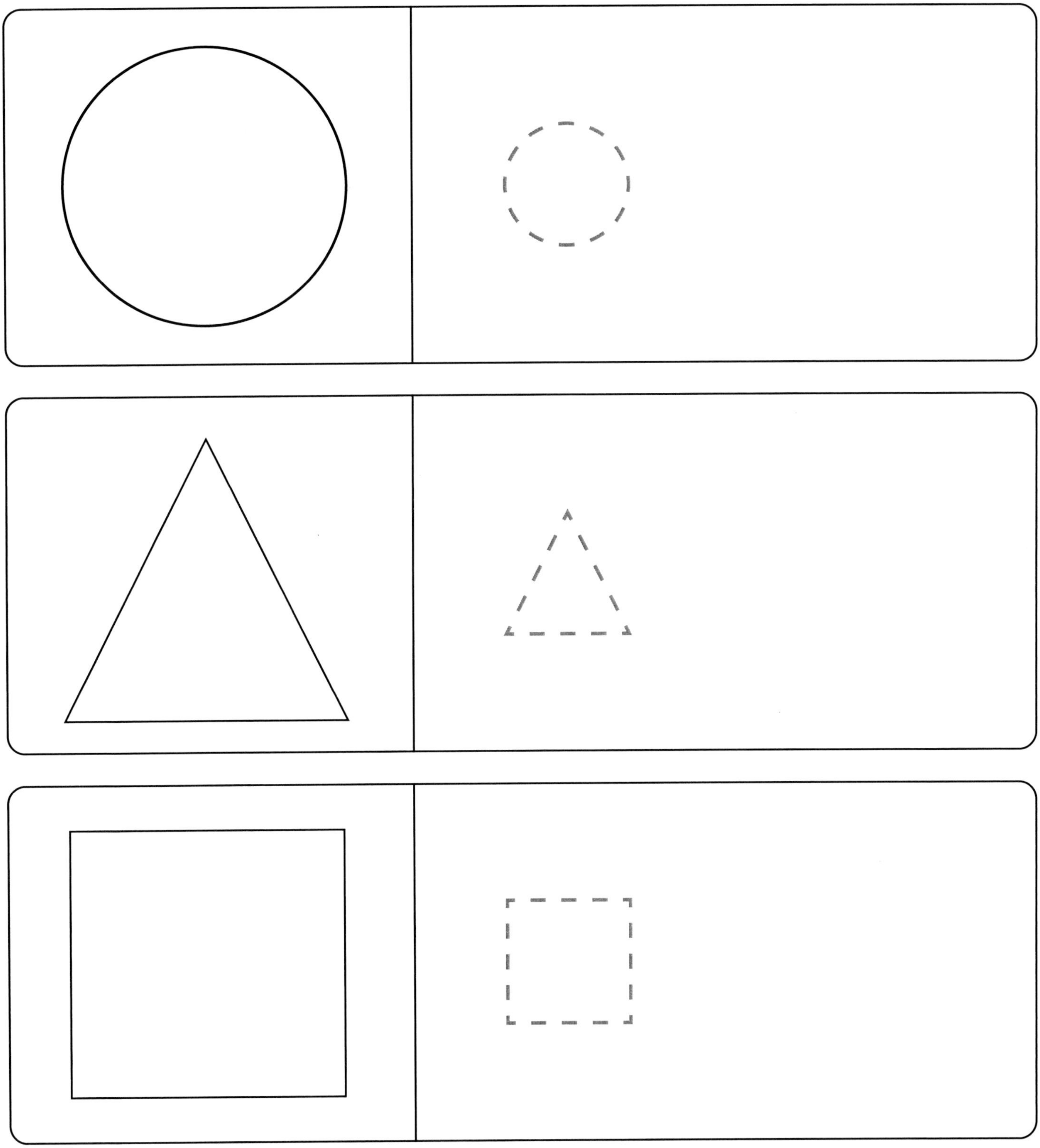

Looking at the Biggest Size

Look at the shapes in the row.
Circle the **biggest** shape.

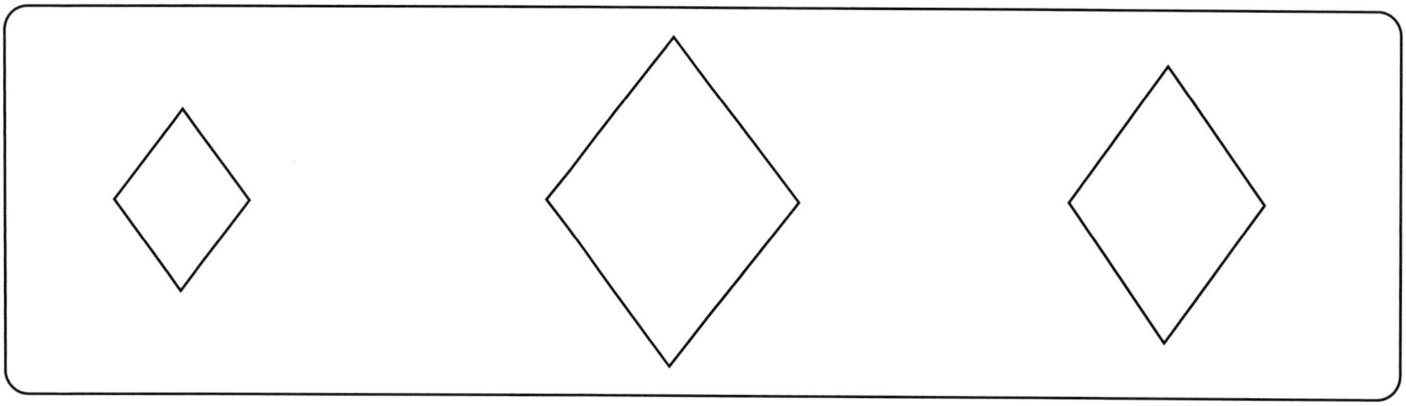

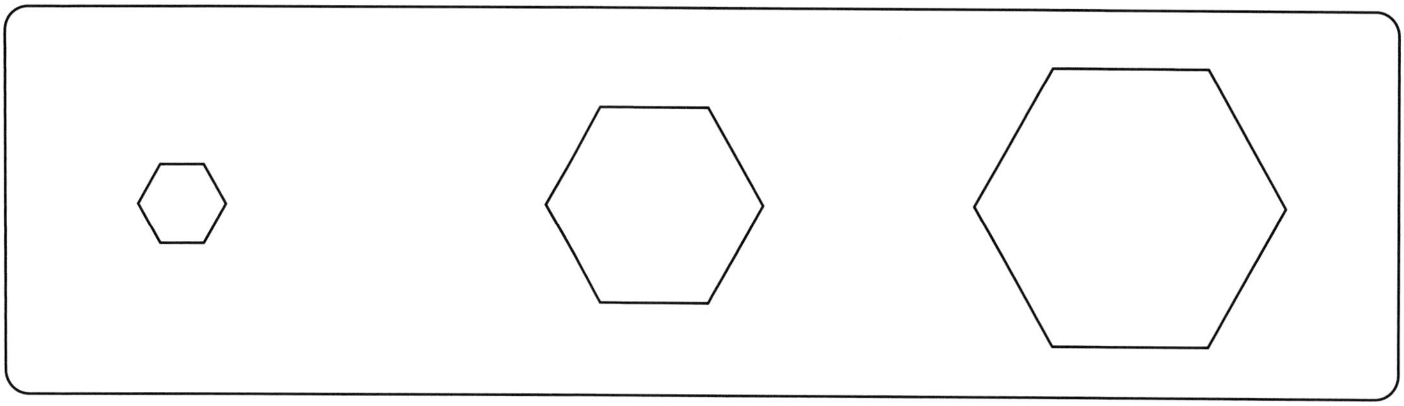

Colour the diamonds. blue

Colour the stars. yellow

Colour the hexagons. orange

Looking at the Smallest Size

Look at the shapes in the row.
Circle the **smallest** shape.

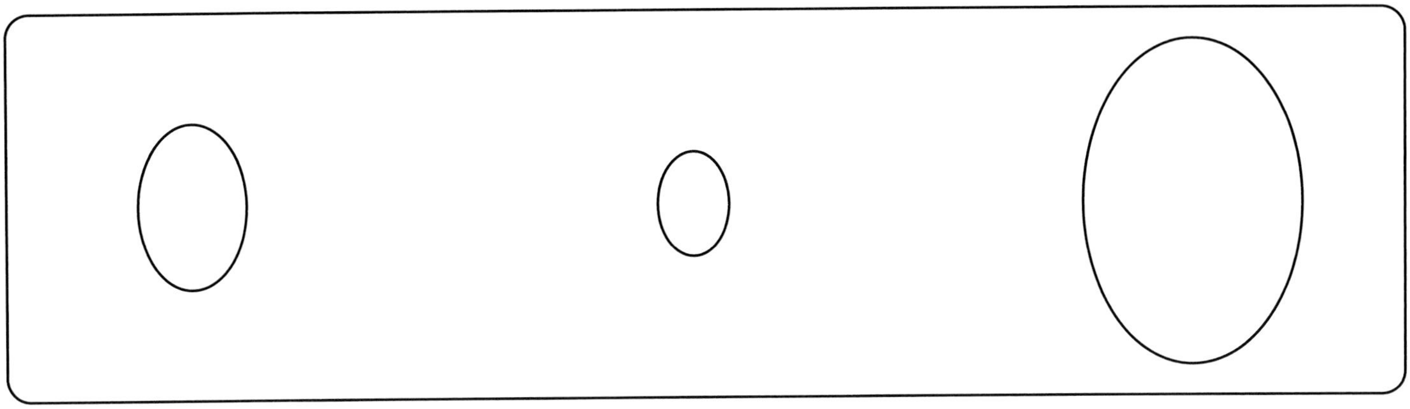

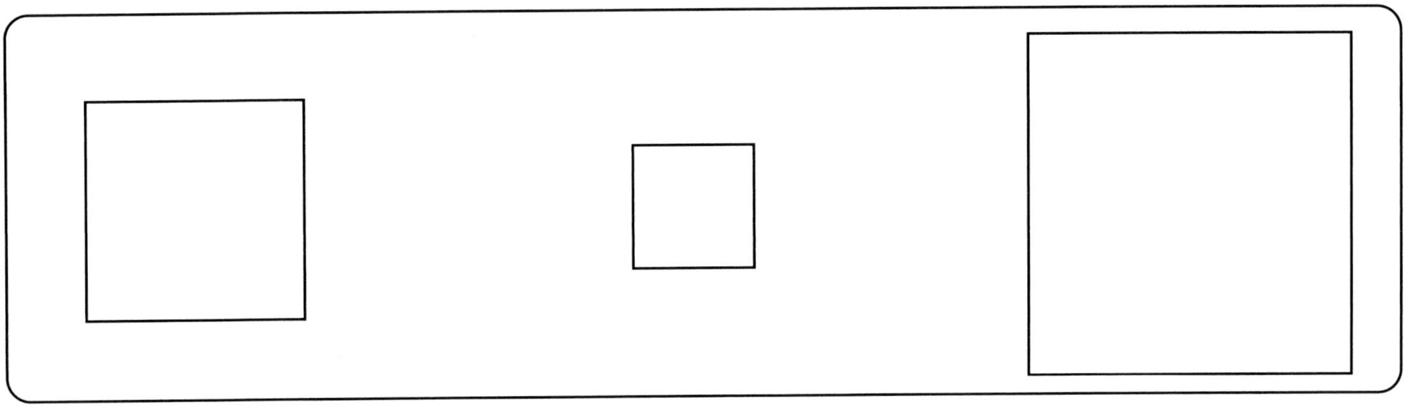

Colour the ovals. green

Colour the hearts. red

Colour the squares. purple

Big and Small

Circle the **big** animal. 

Circle the **big** seashell. 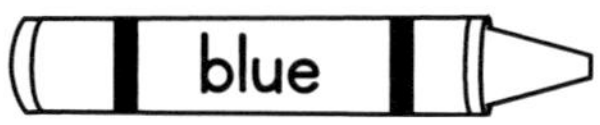

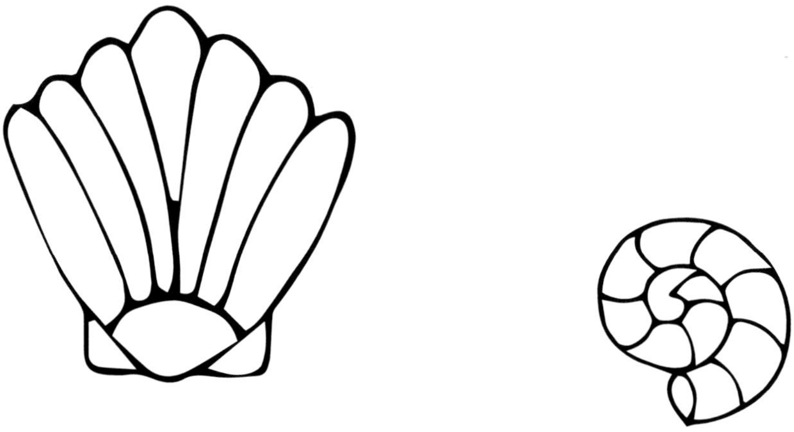

Big and Small

Circle the **big** fish. 

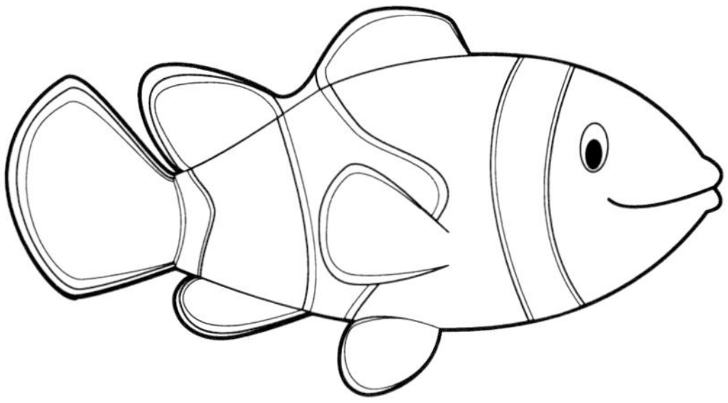

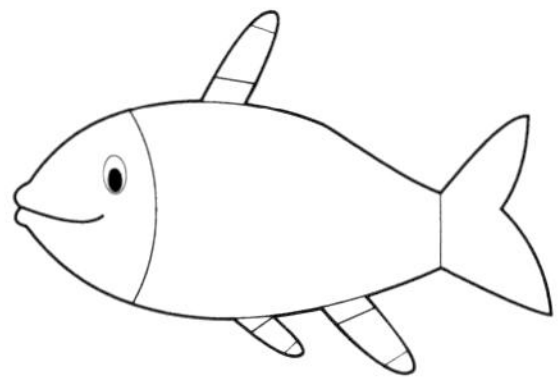

Circle the **big** fruit. 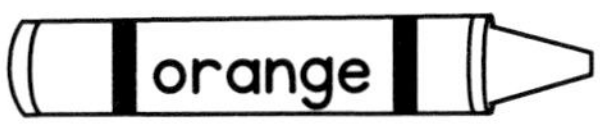

Big and Small

Circle the **small** hat. green

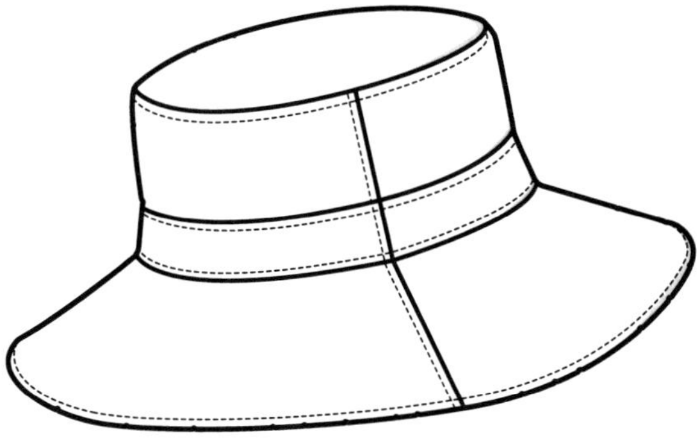

Circle the **small** backpack. red

Big and Small

Circle the **small** animal. (blue)

Circle the **small** ball. (yellow)

Tall and Short

This giraffe is **short**. This giraffe is **tall**.

Circle the **tall** stack in red.
Circle the **short** stack in blue.

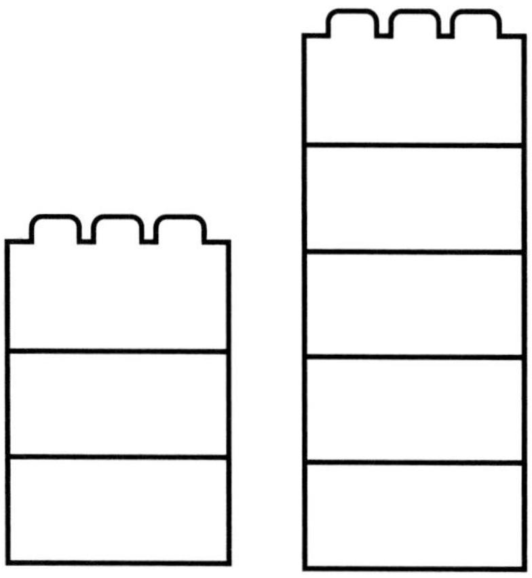

Circle the **tall** flag in red.
Circle the **short** flag in blue.

Alphabet and Printing Skills

Pre-Printing Practice — Straight Lines

Trace the lines below.

Circle your best traced line.

Think About It!

What bug do knights hate?

Dragonflies!

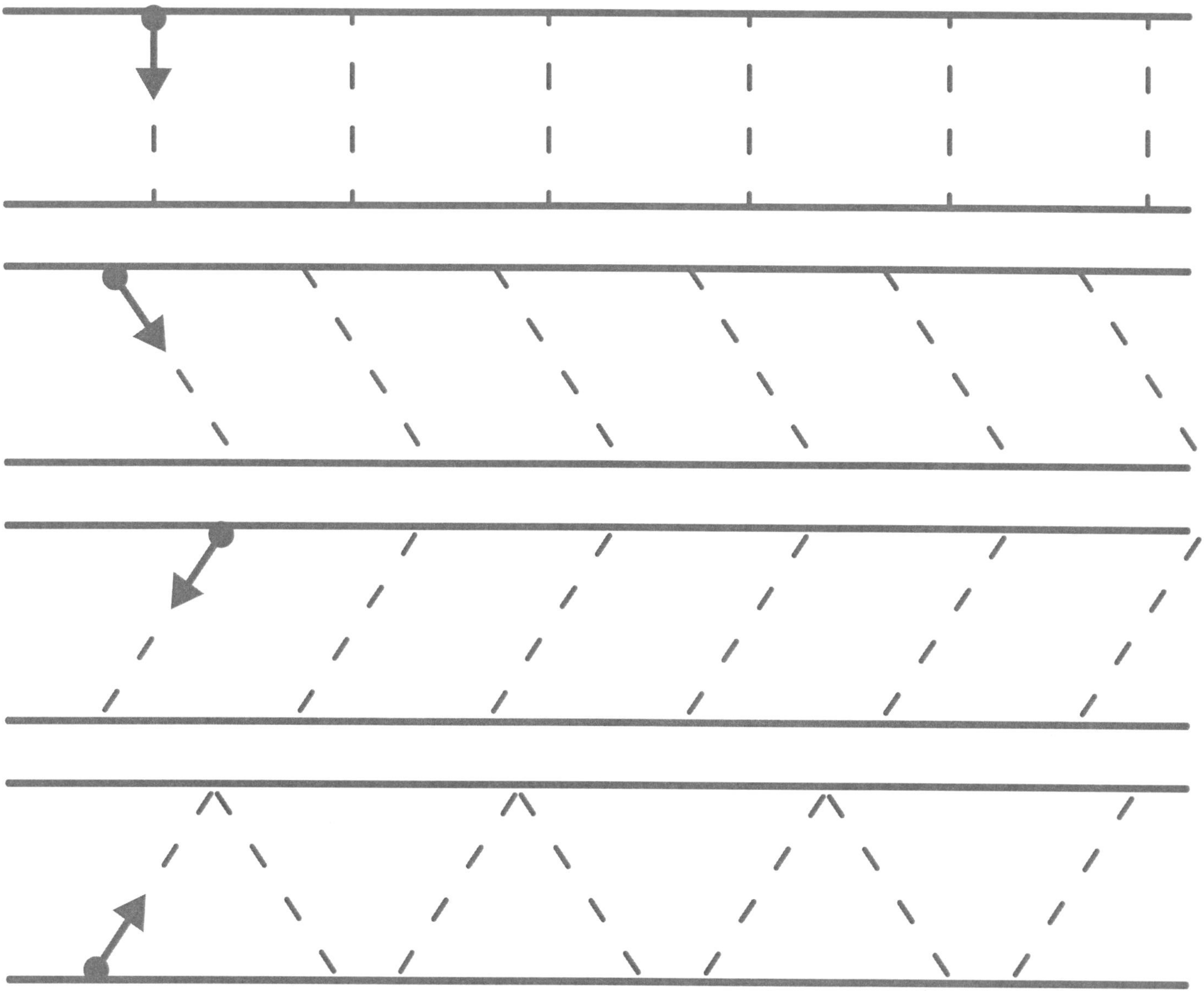

Pre-Printing Practice — More Straight Lines

Trace the lines below.

Circle your best traced line.

Think About It!

Why don't crabs like to share?

Because they're a little shellfish!

Pre-Printing Practice — Rounded Lines

Trace the lines below.
Circle your best traced line.

Think About It!

What's a dog's favourite kind of pizza?
Pupperoni pizza!

Pre-Printing Practice — More Rounded Lines

Trace the lines below.

Circle your best traced line.

Think About It!

What do you call a famous turtle?

A shell-ebrity!

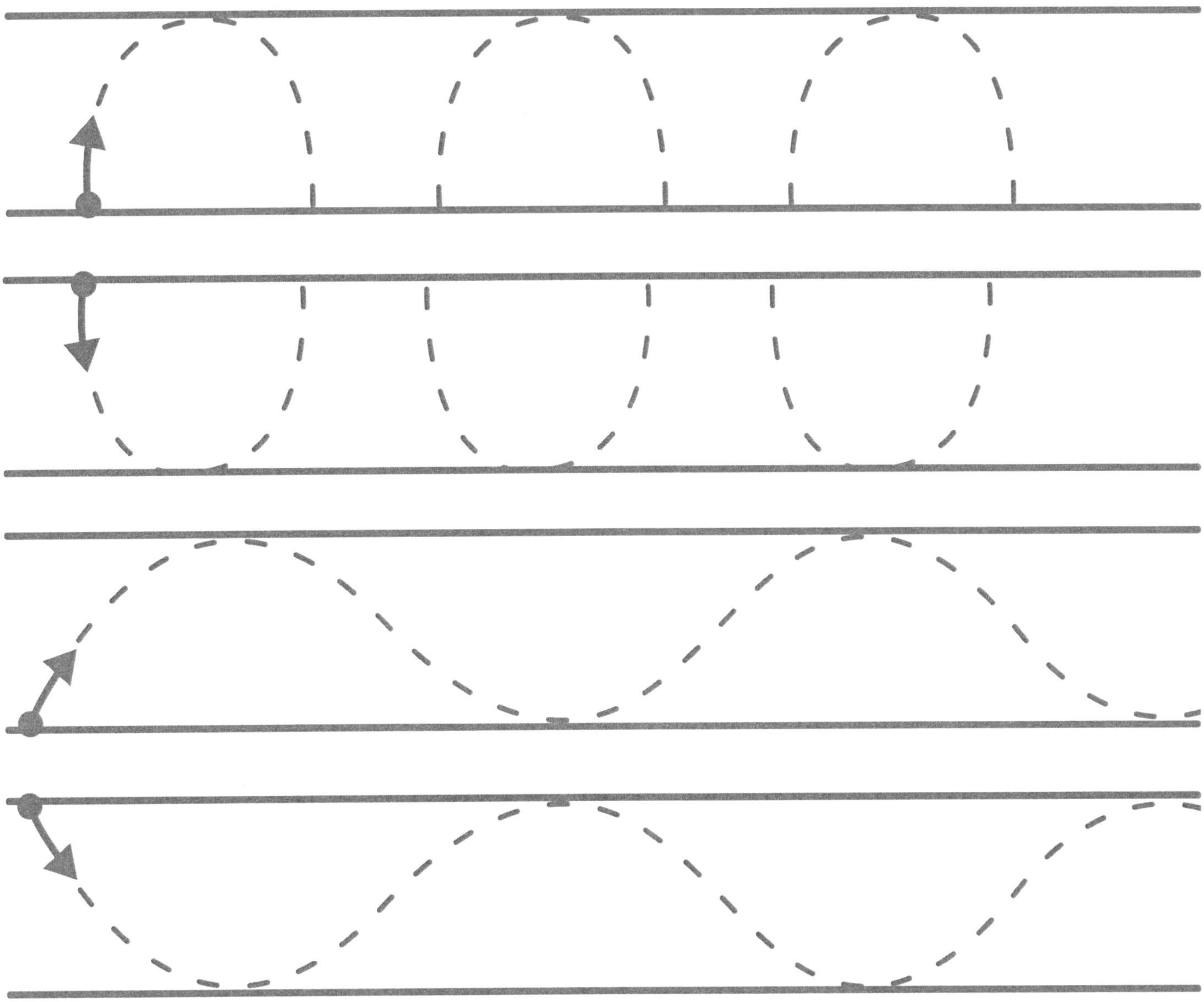

Letter Aa

A is for ant.

Trace and print the letters on each line.
Circle your best letter on the line.

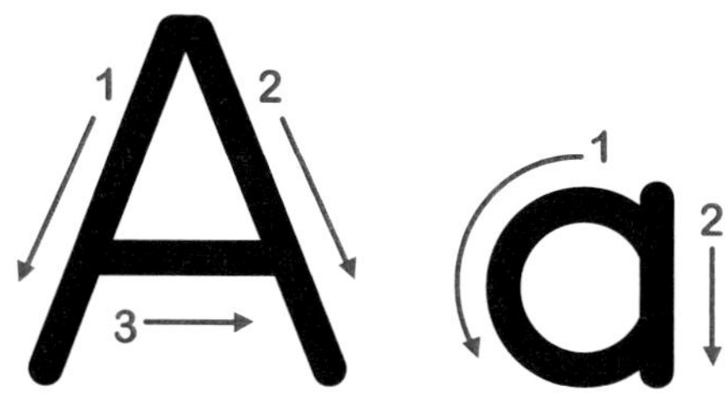

Letter Aa

Colour the apple with a capital A. green

Colour the apple with a lowercase a. red

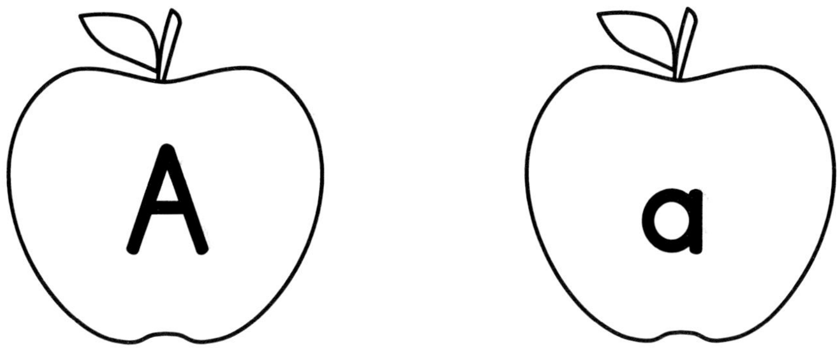

Trace and print the letters on each line.

Circle your best letter on the line.

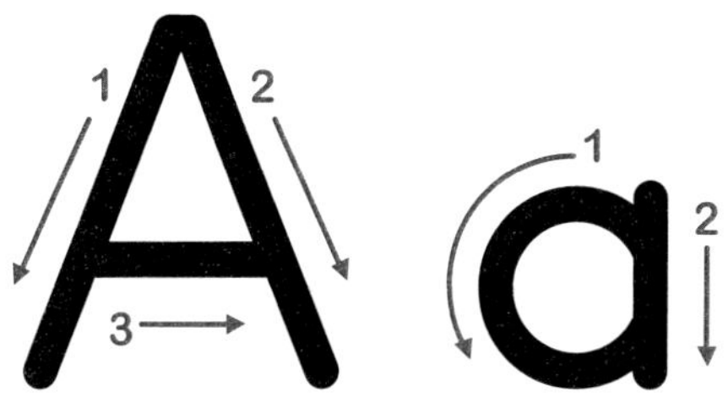

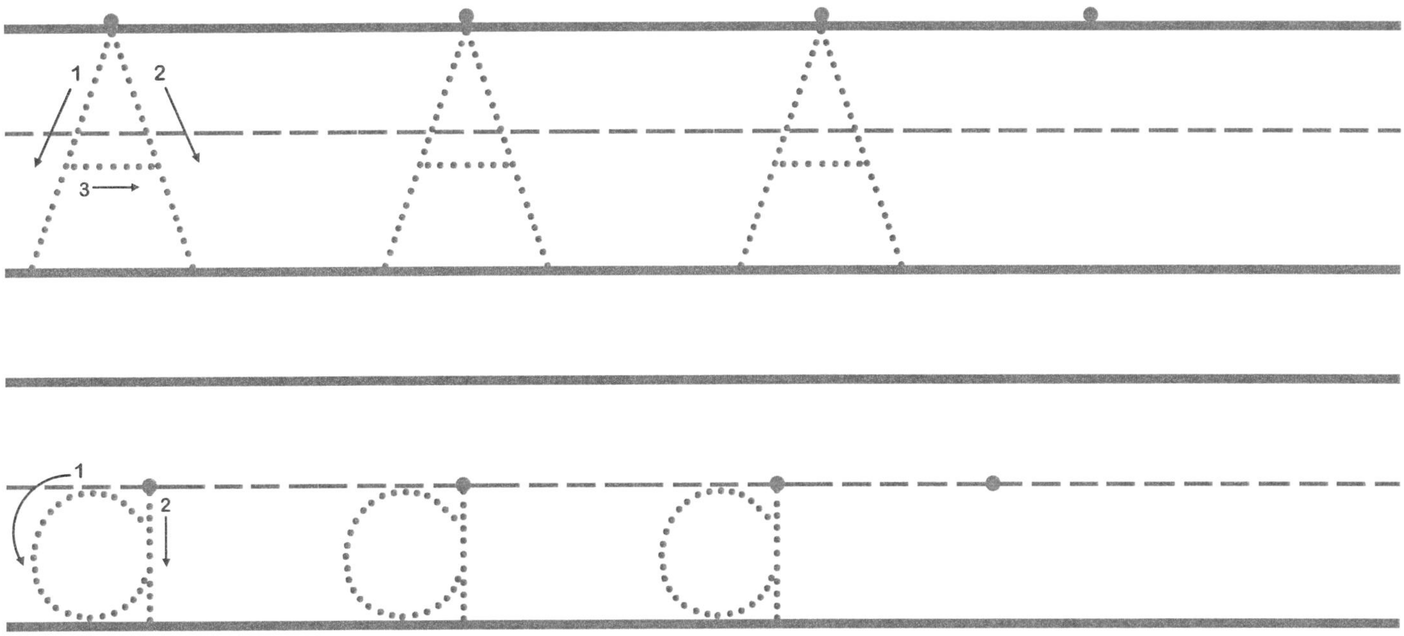

Letter Bb

B is for bee.

Trace and print the letters on each line.
Circle your best letter on the line.

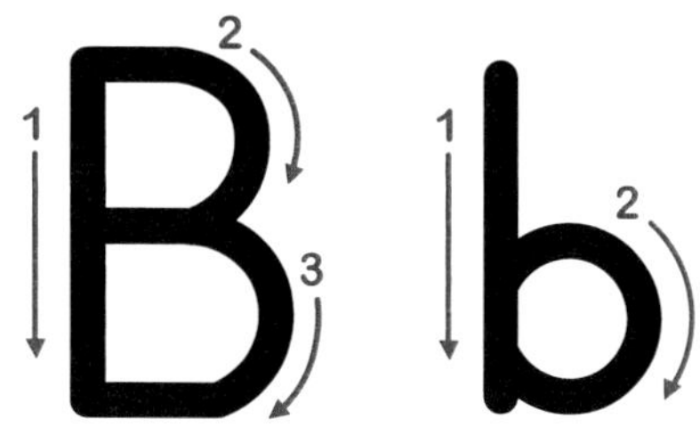

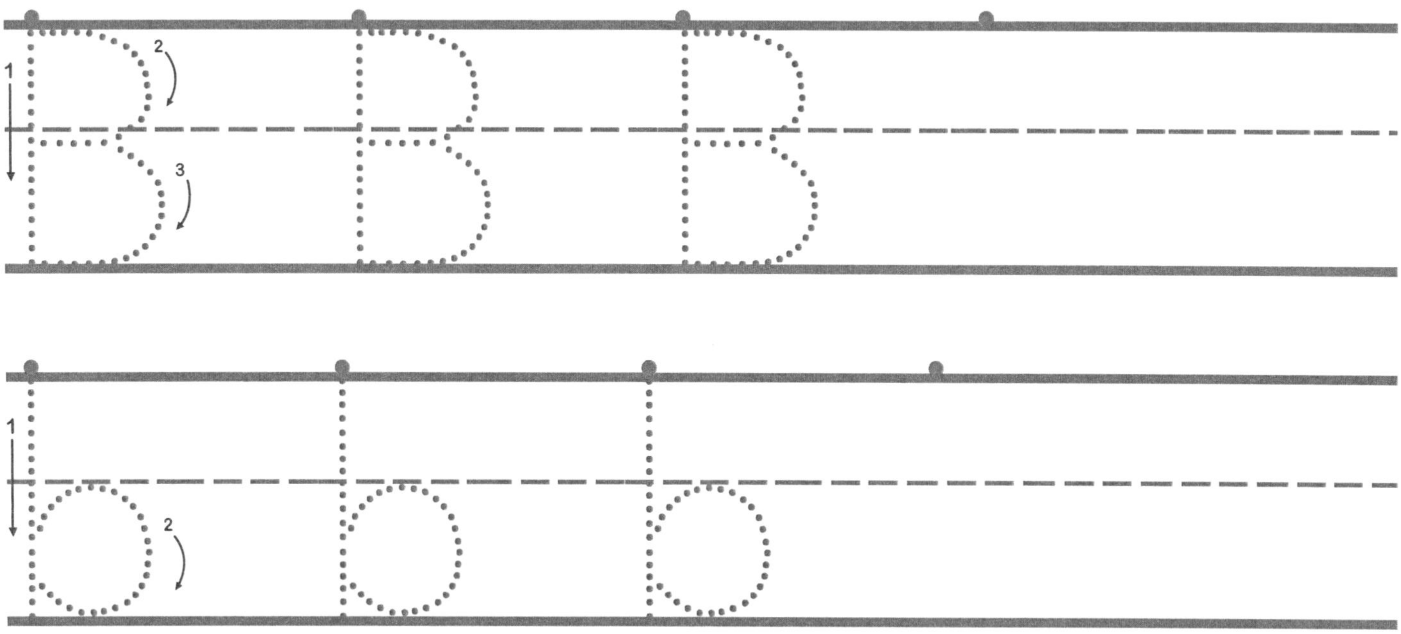

Letter Bb

Colour the book with a capital B. 

Colour the book with a lowercase b. 

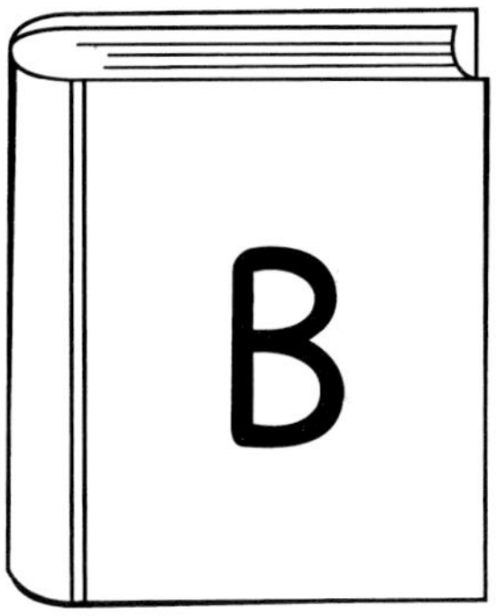

Trace and print the letters on each line.
Circle your best letter on the line.

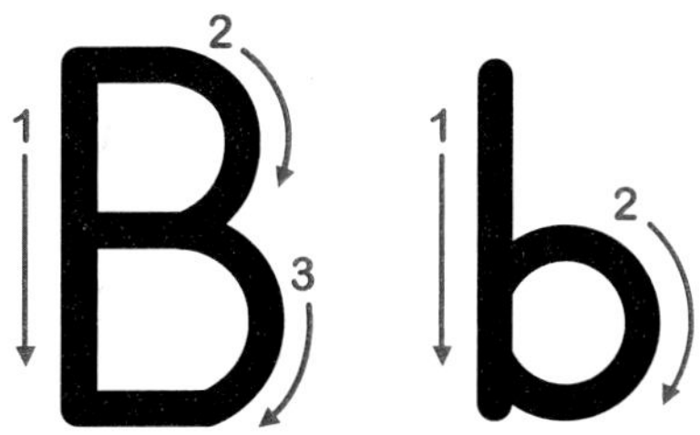

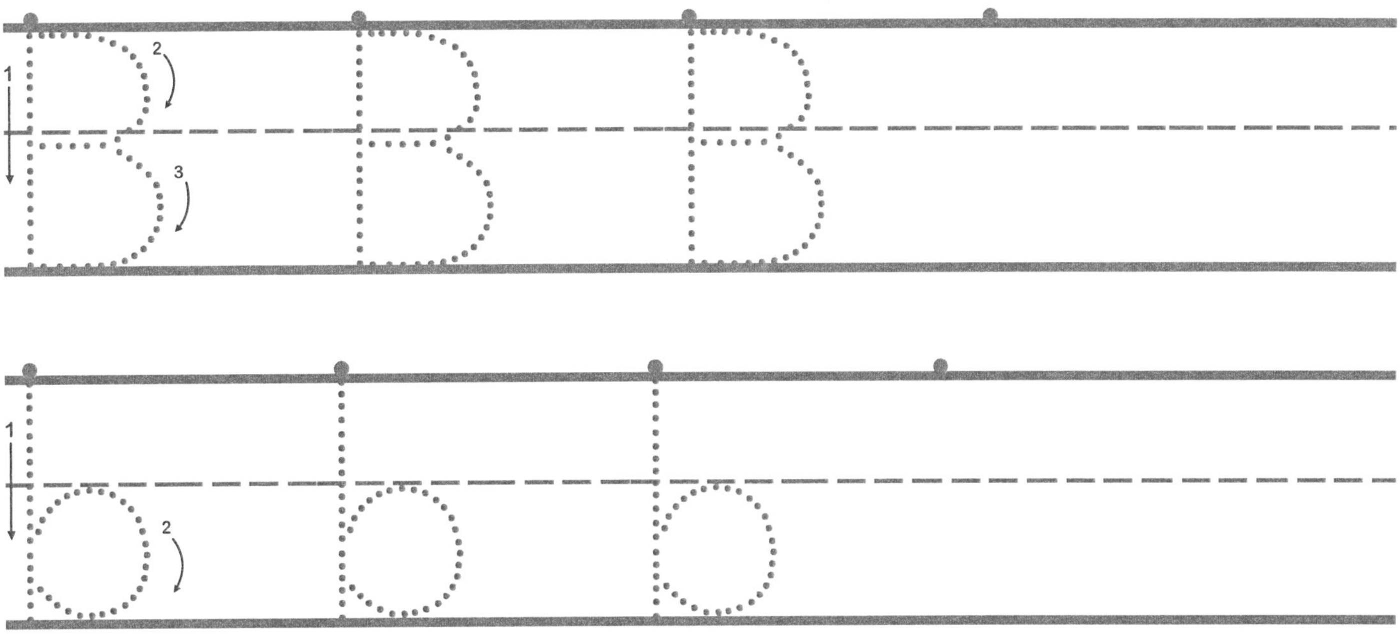

Letter Cc

C is for cow.

Trace and print the letters on each line.
Circle your best letter on the line.

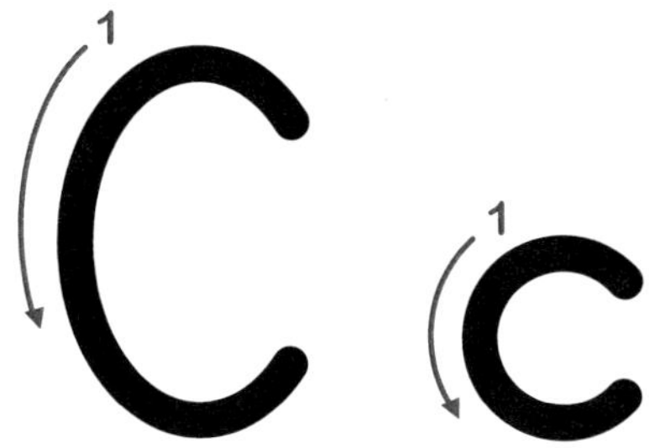

Letter Cc

Colour the cookie with a capital C. 

Colour the cookie with a lowercase c. 

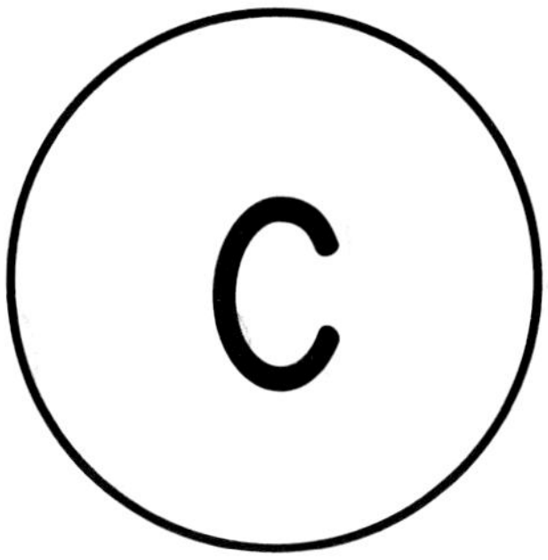

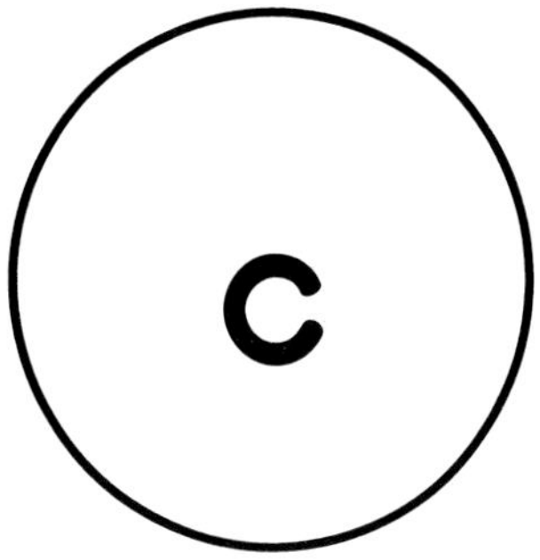

Trace and print the letters on each line.
Circle your best letter on the line.

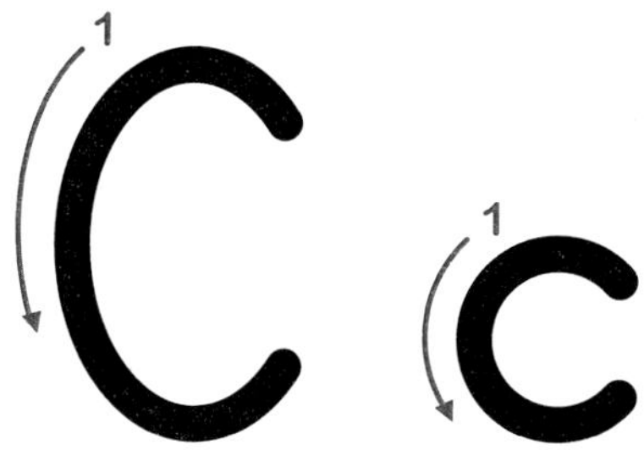

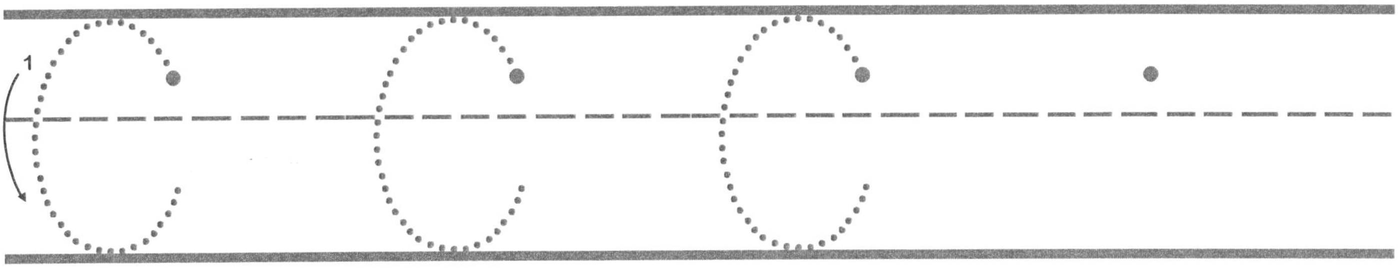

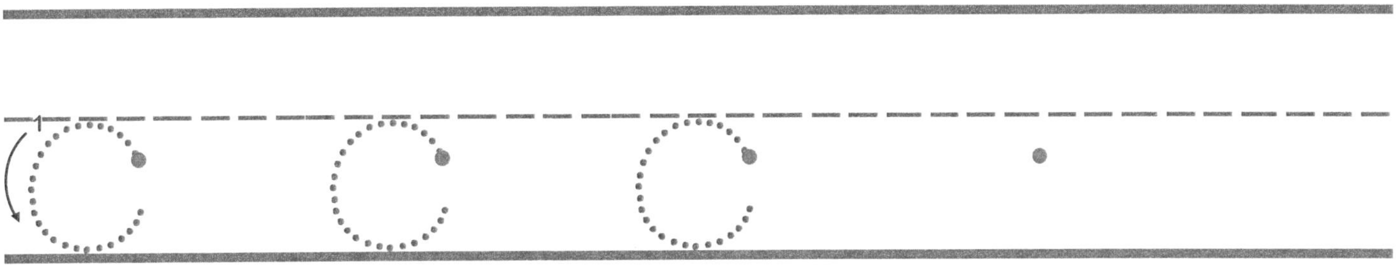

Letter Dd

D is for dog.

Trace and print the letters on each line.
Circle your best letter on the line.

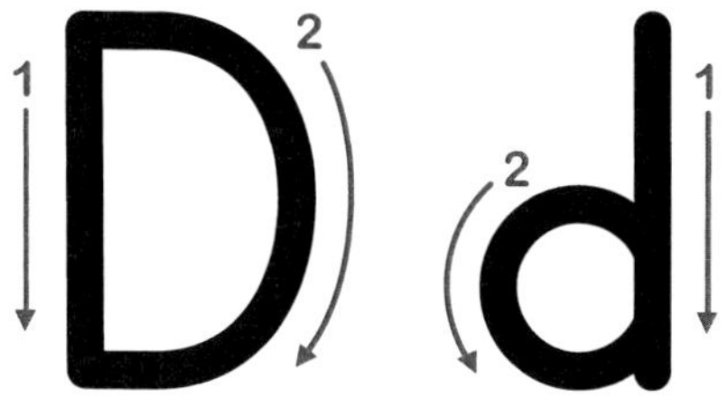

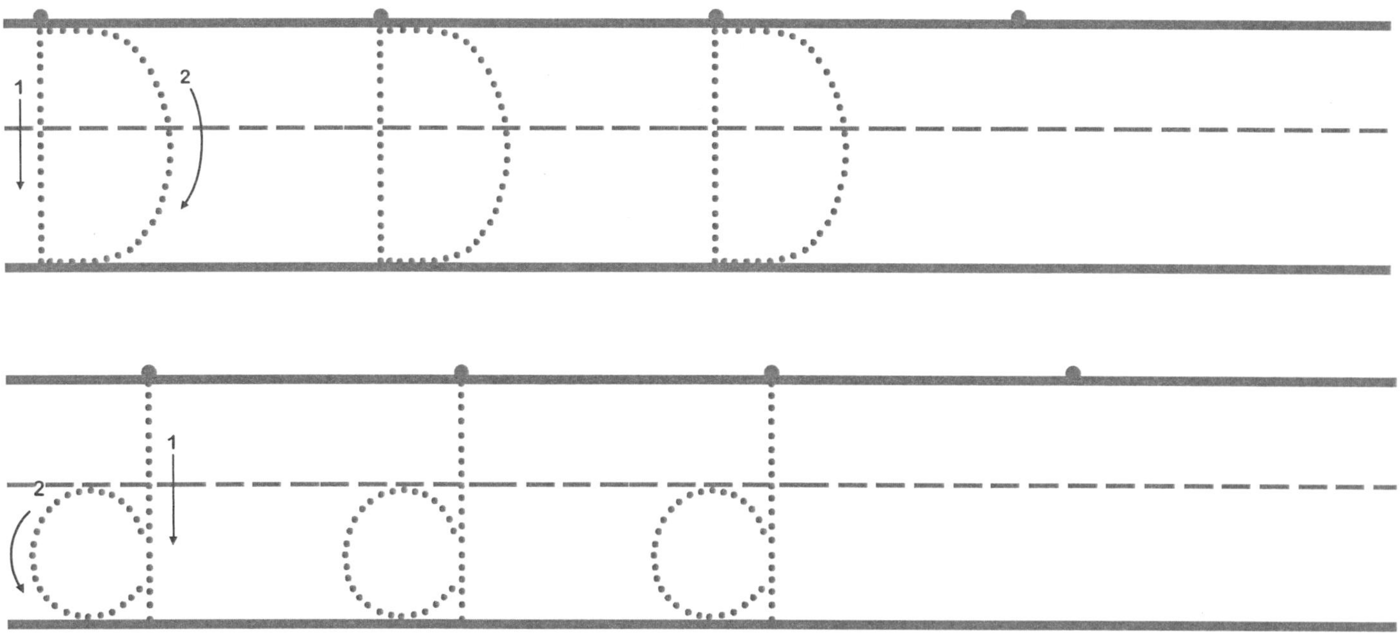

Letter Dd

Colour the drum with a capital D. 

Colour the drum with a lowercase d. 

Trace and print the letters on each line.
Circle your best letter on the line.

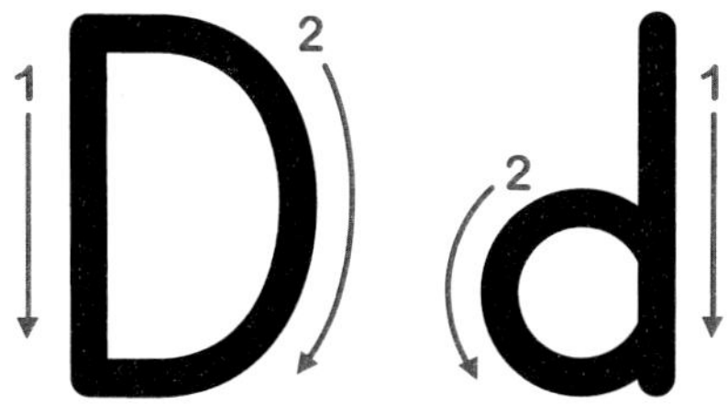

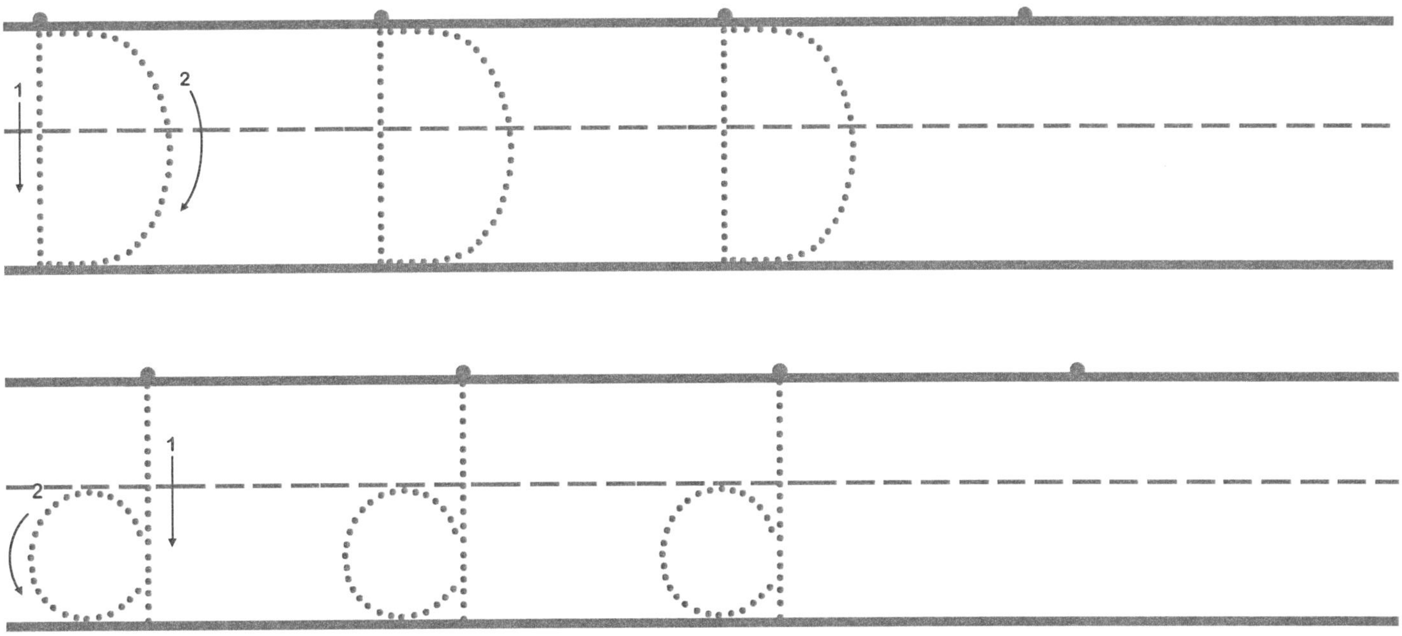

Letter Ee

E is for eagle.

Trace and print the letters on each line.
Circle your best letter on the line.

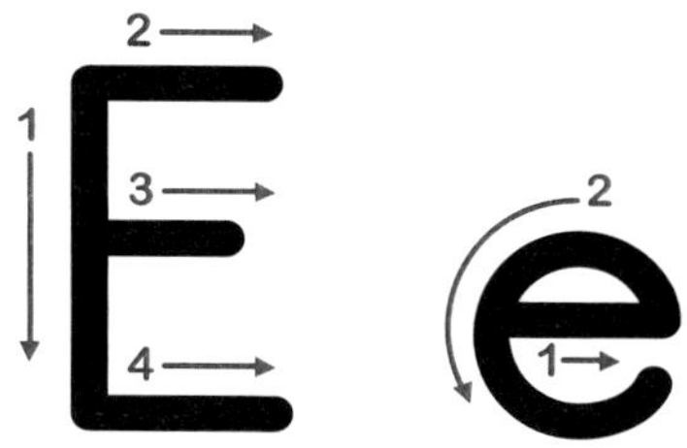

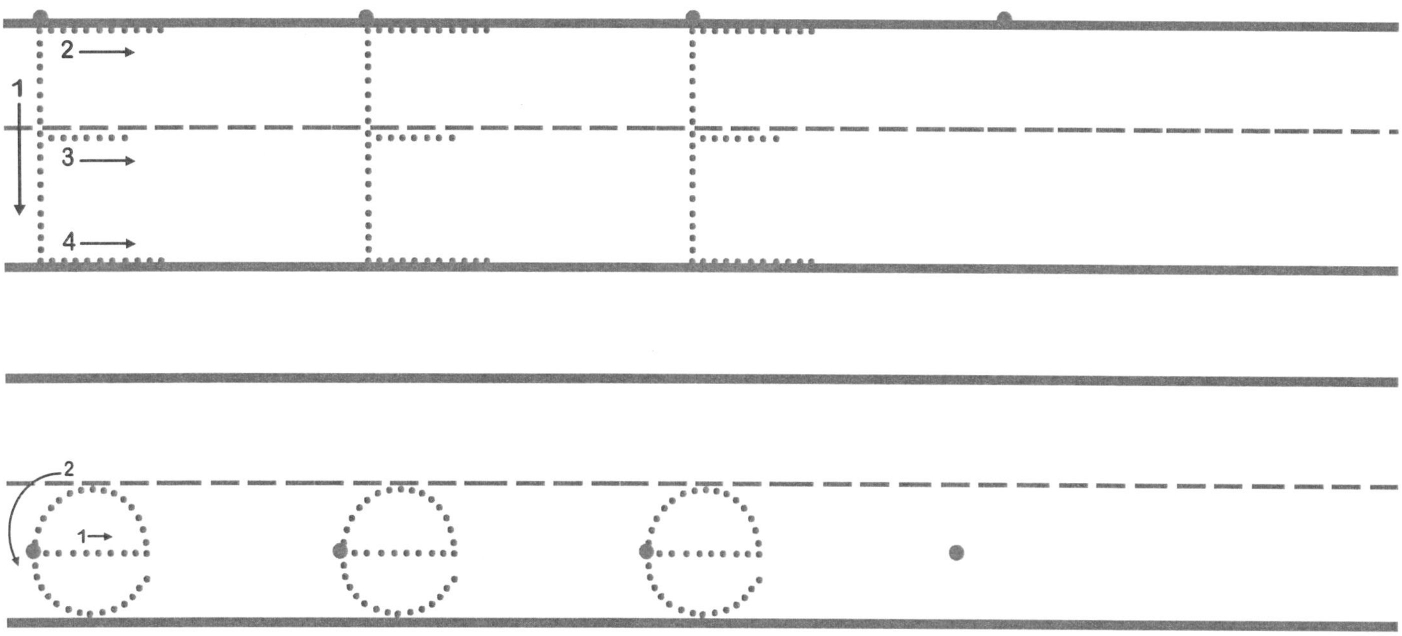

Letter Ee

Colour the egg with a capital E. 

Colour the egg with a lowercase e. 

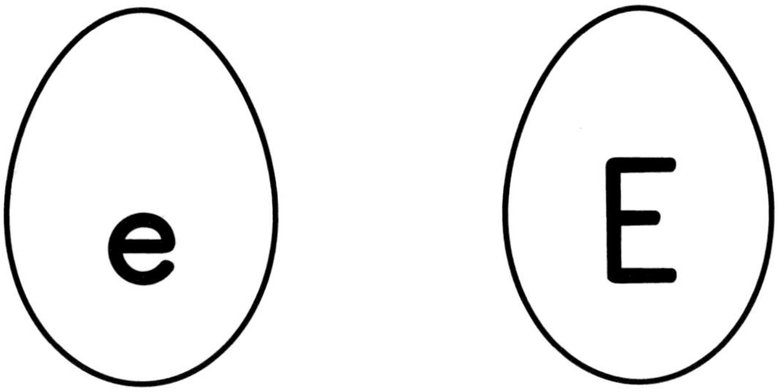

Trace and print the letters on each line.
Circle your best letter on the line.

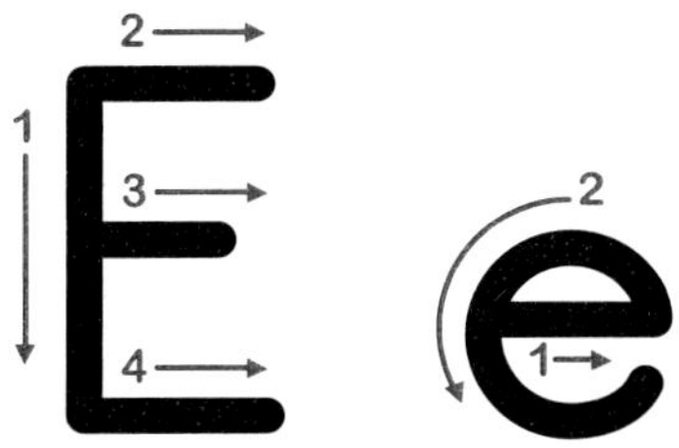

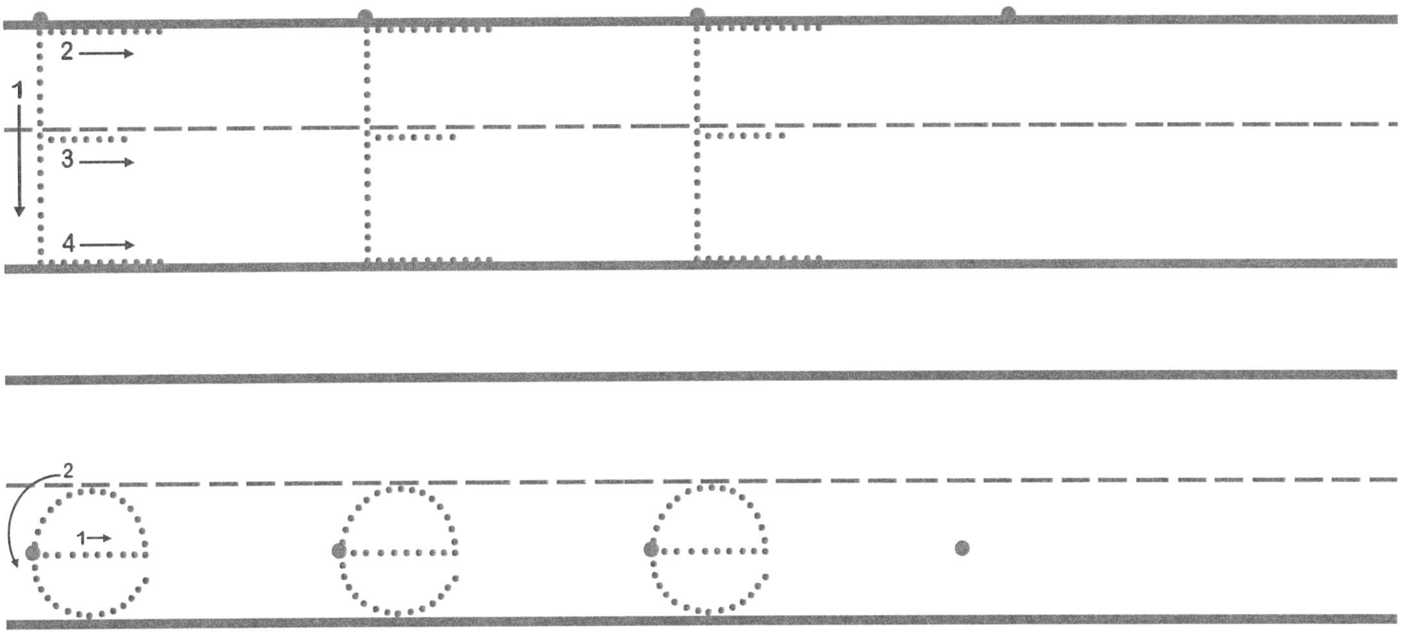

Letter Ff

F is for frog.

Trace and print the letters on each line.
Circle your best letter on the line.

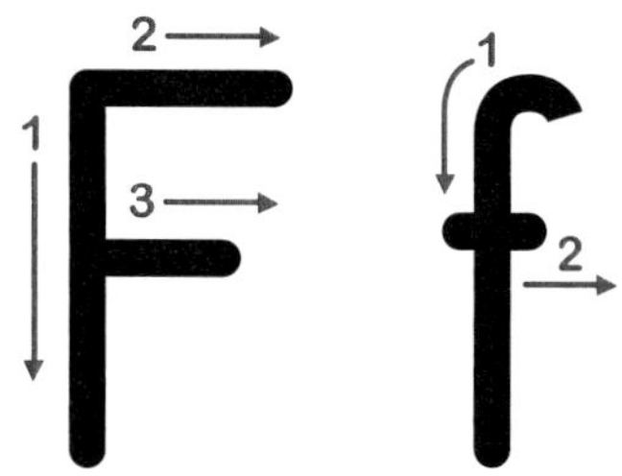

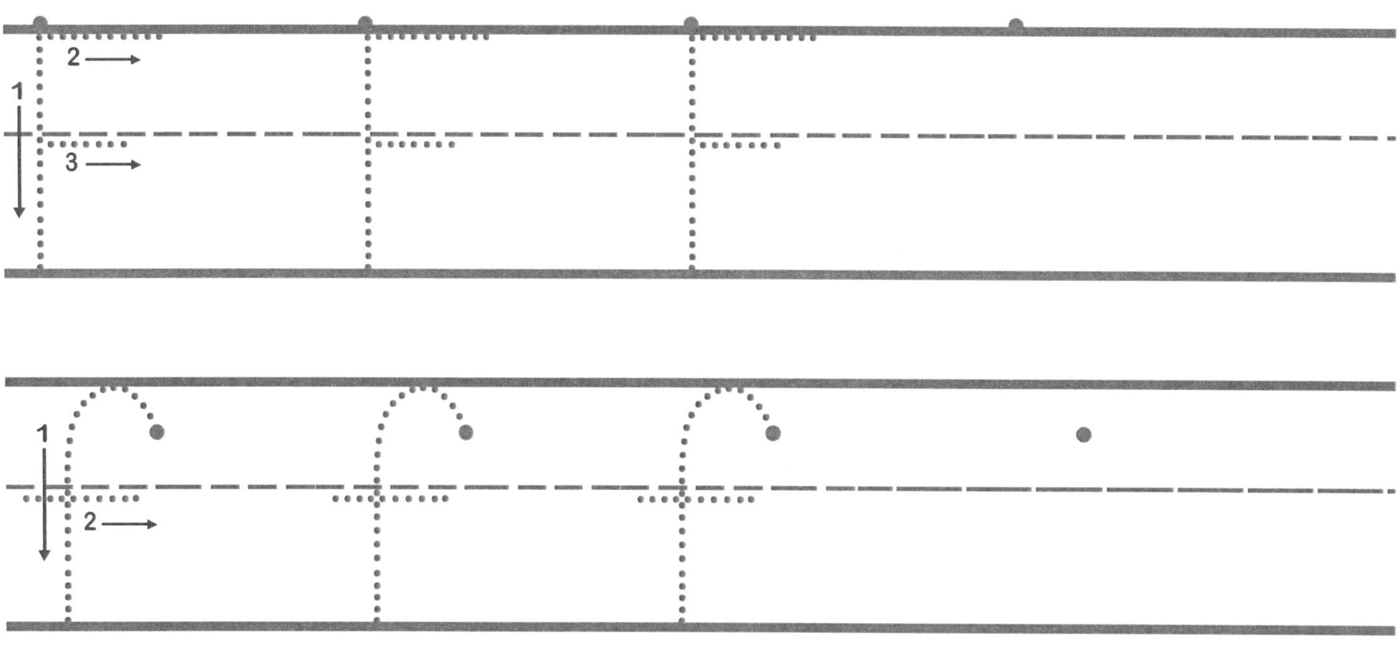

Letter Ff

Colour the fish with a capital F. orange

Colour the fish with a lowercase f. blue

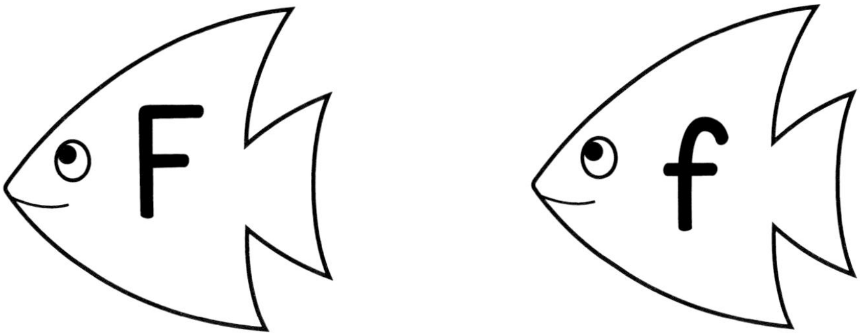

Trace and print the letters on each line.

Circle your best letter on the line.

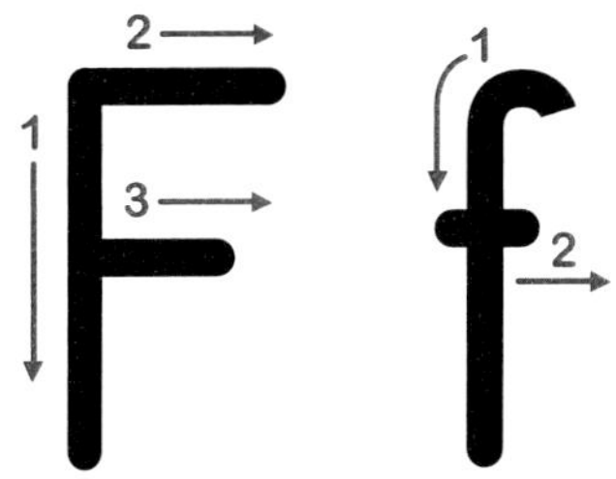

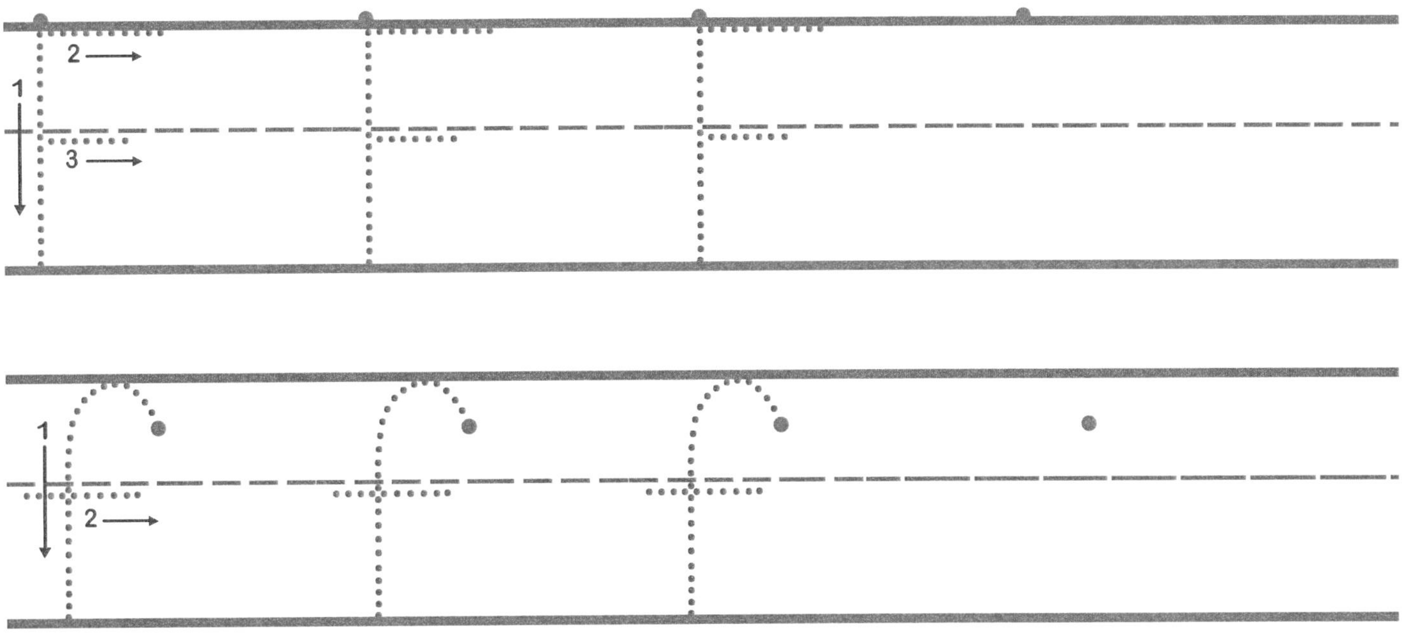

Letter Gg

G is for goat.

Trace and print the letters on each line.
Circle your best letter on the line.

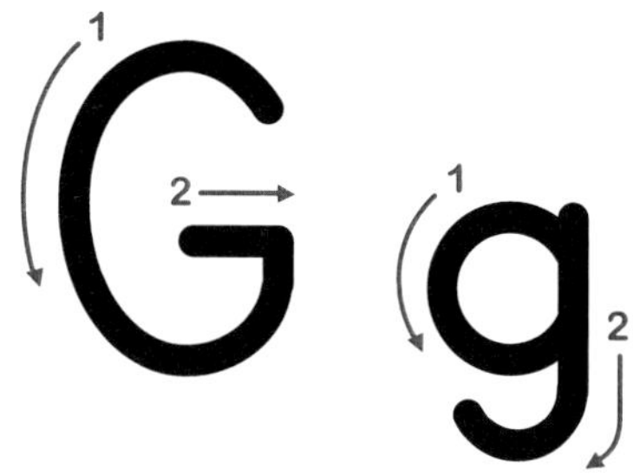

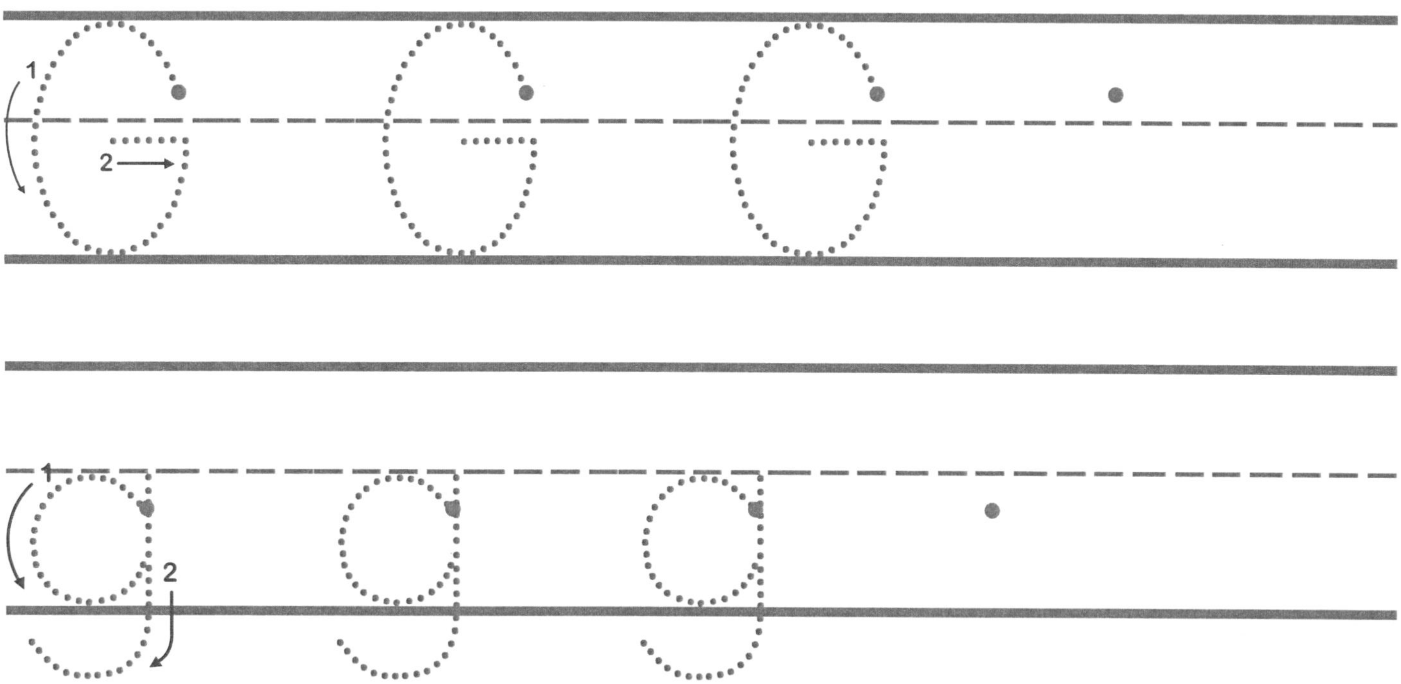

Letter Gg

Colour the glove with a capital G. 

Colour the glove with a lowercase g. 

Trace and print the letters on each line.
Circle your best letter on the line.

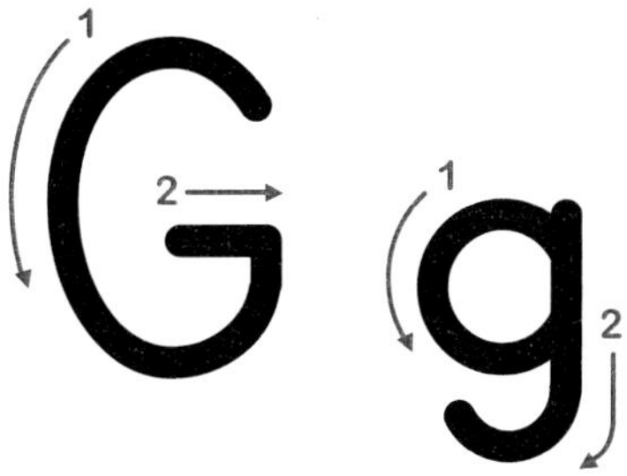

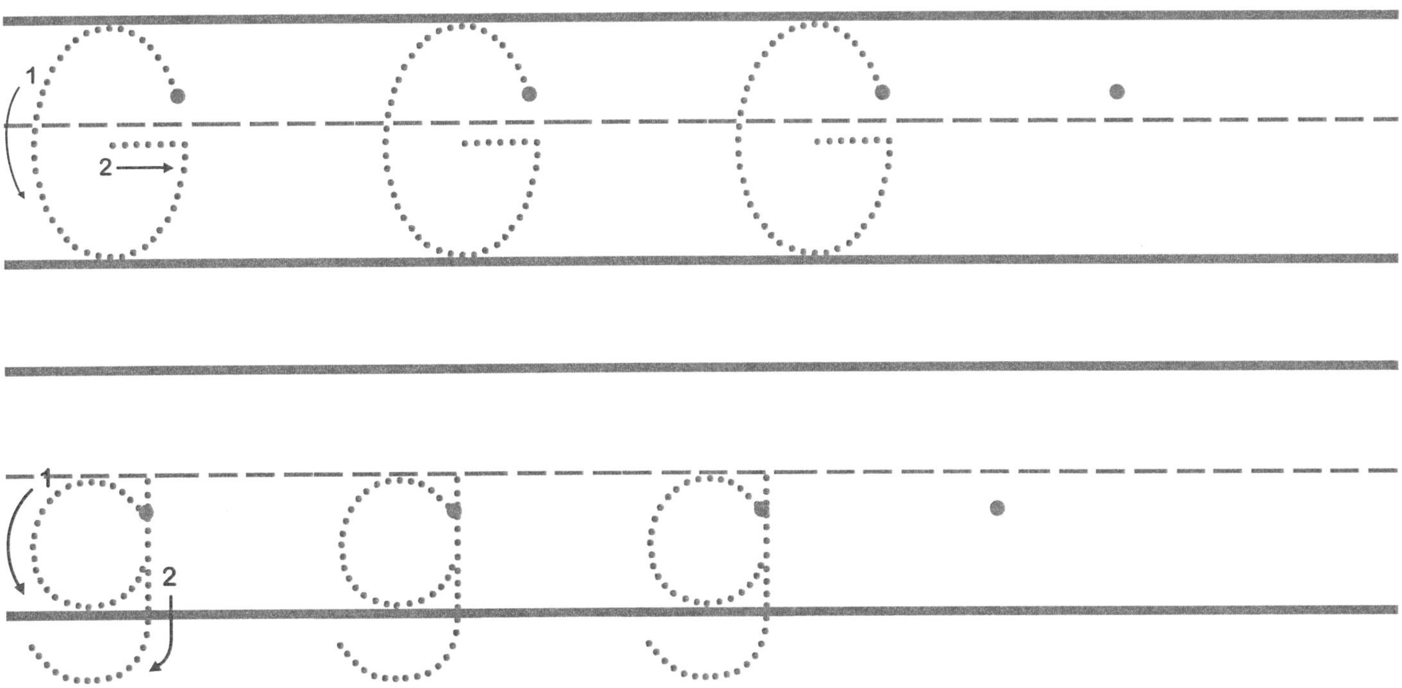

Letter Hh

H is for horse.

Trace and print the letters on each line.
Circle your best letter on the line.

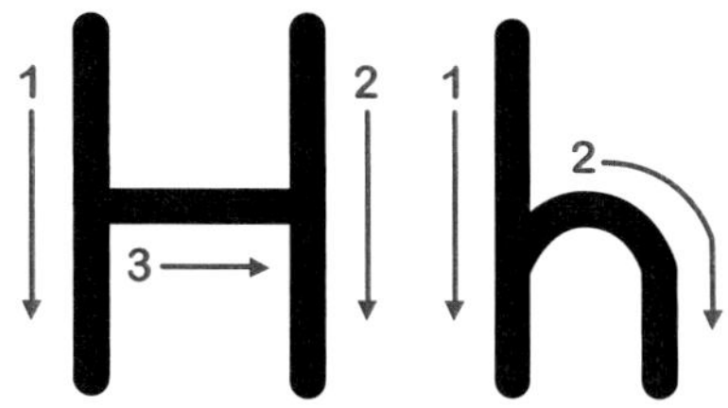

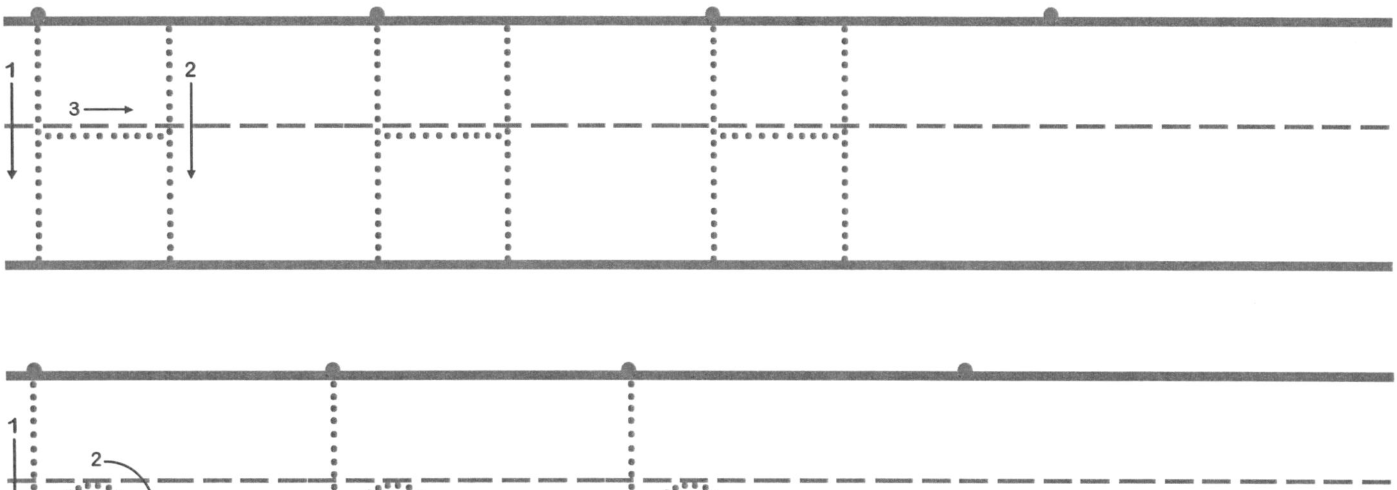

Letter Hh

Colour the house with a capital H. 

Colour the house with a lowercase h. 

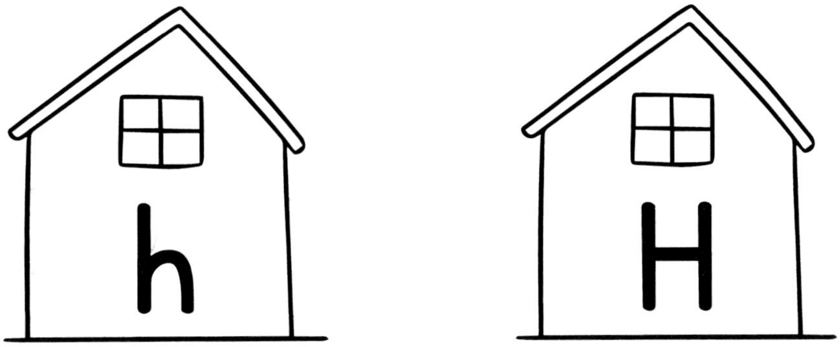

Trace and print the letters on each line.
Circle your best letter on the line.

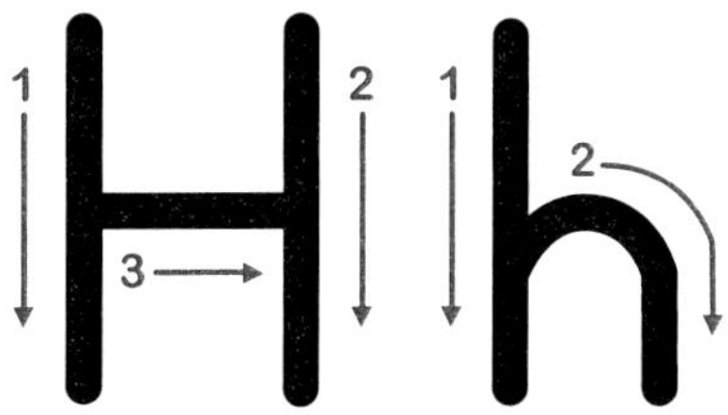

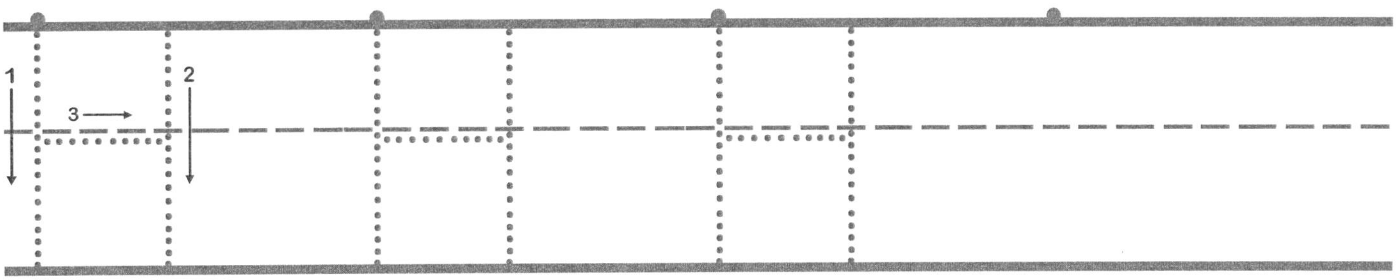

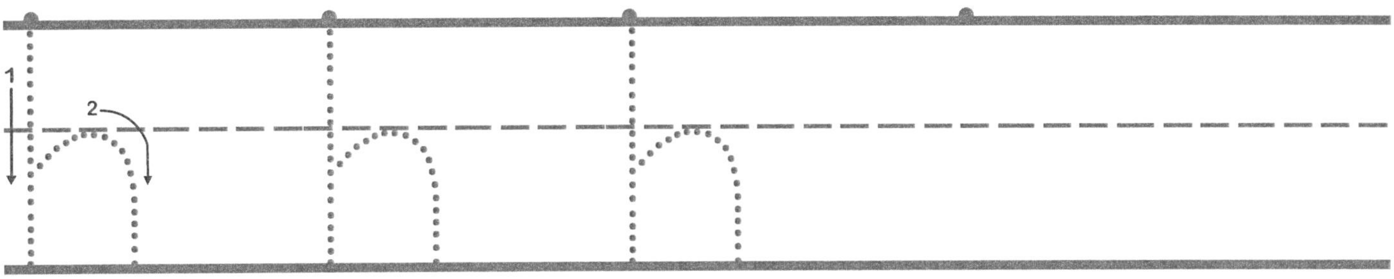

Letter Ii

I is for iguana.

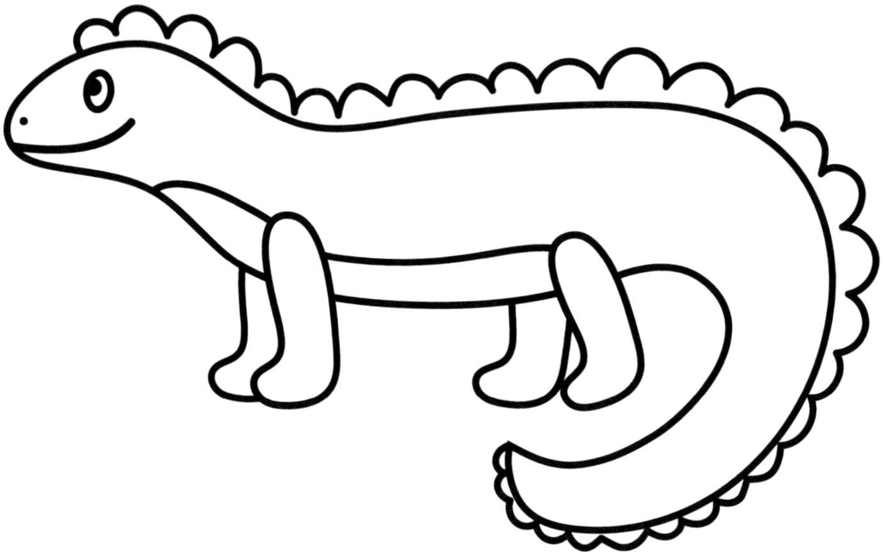

Trace and print the letters on each line.
Circle your best letter on the line.

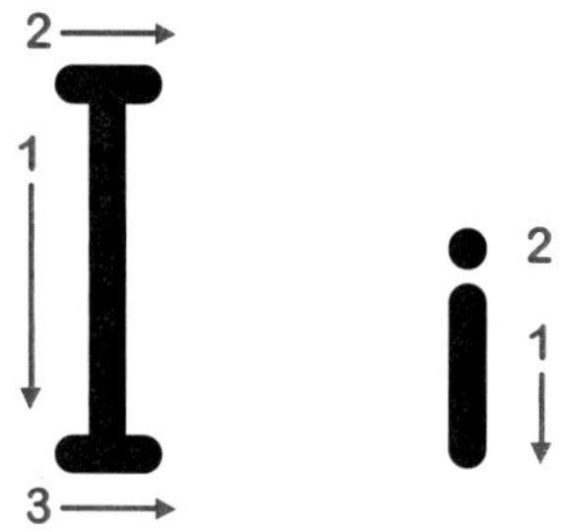

Letter Ii

Colour the igloo with a capital I. 

Colour the igloo with a lowercase i. 

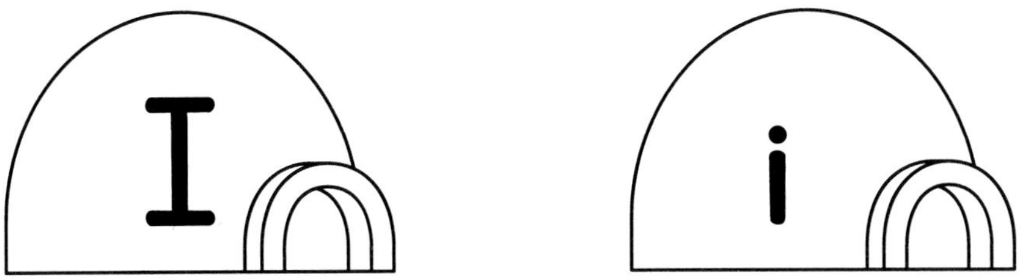

Trace and print the letters on each line.
Circle your best letter on the line.

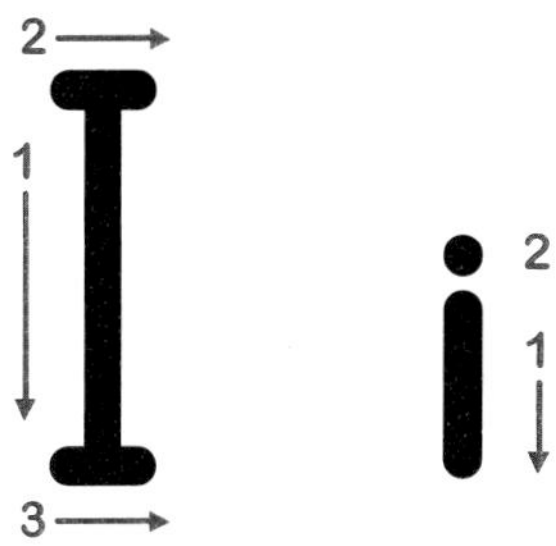

Letter Jj

J is for jellyfish.

Trace and print the letters on each line.
Circle your best letter on the line.

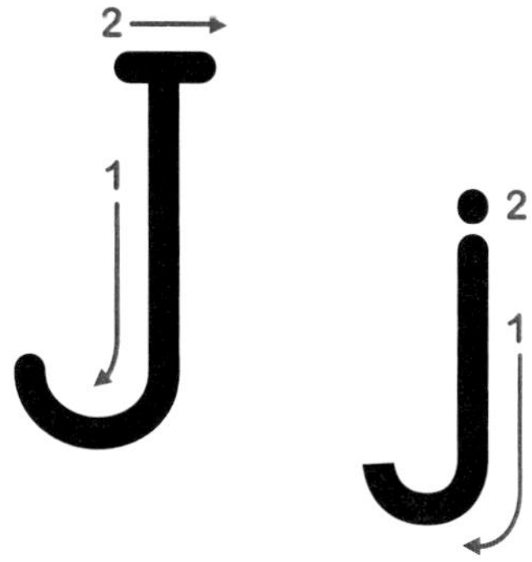

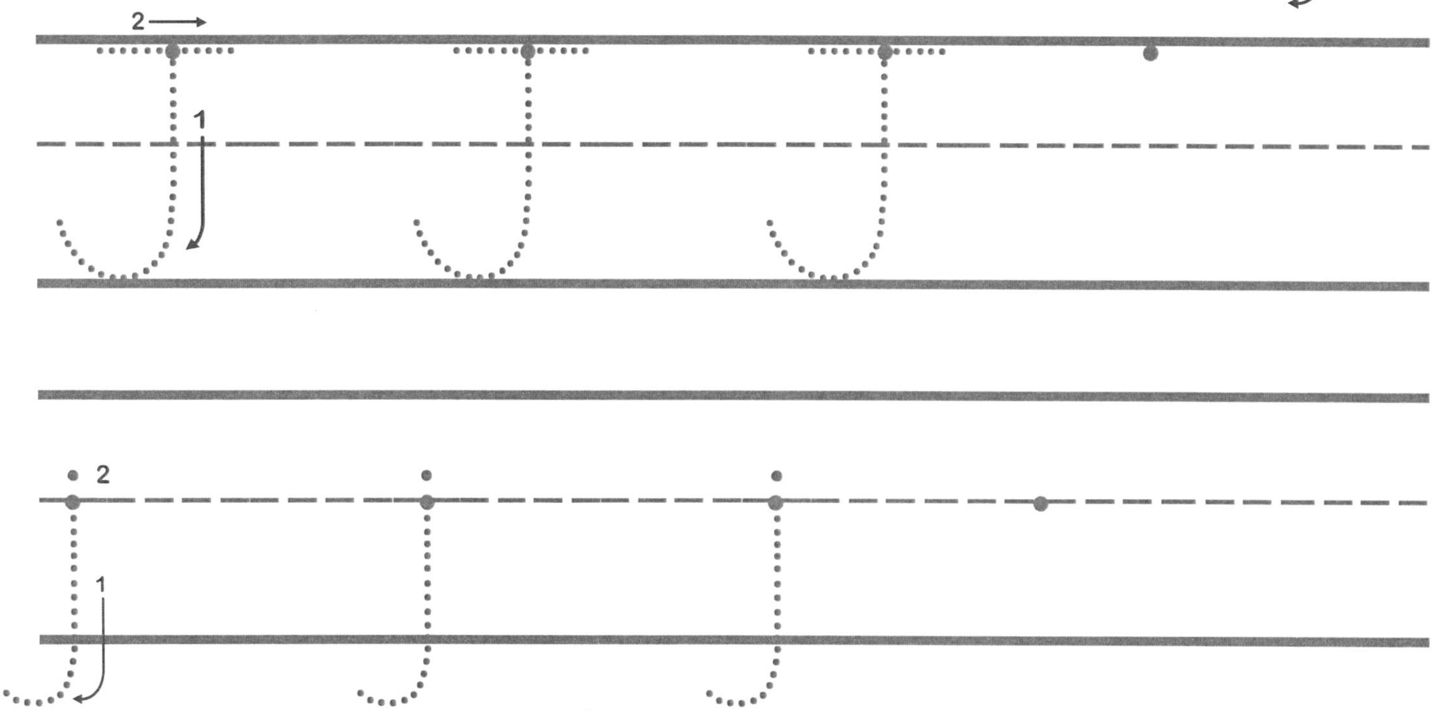

Letter Jj

Colour the jug with a capital J. yellow

Colour the jug with a lowercase j. blue

Trace and print the letters on each line.

Circle your best letter on the line.

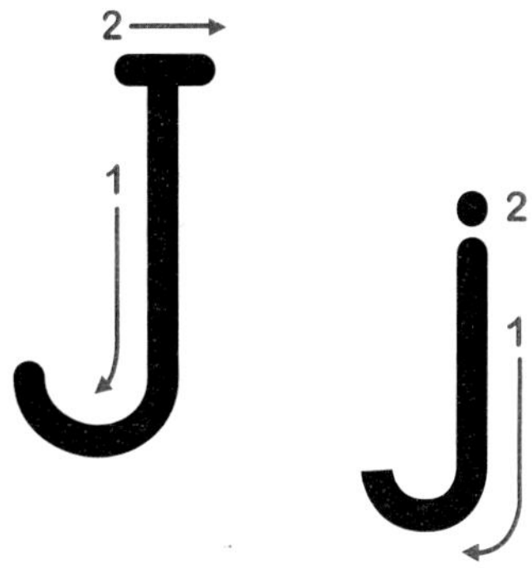

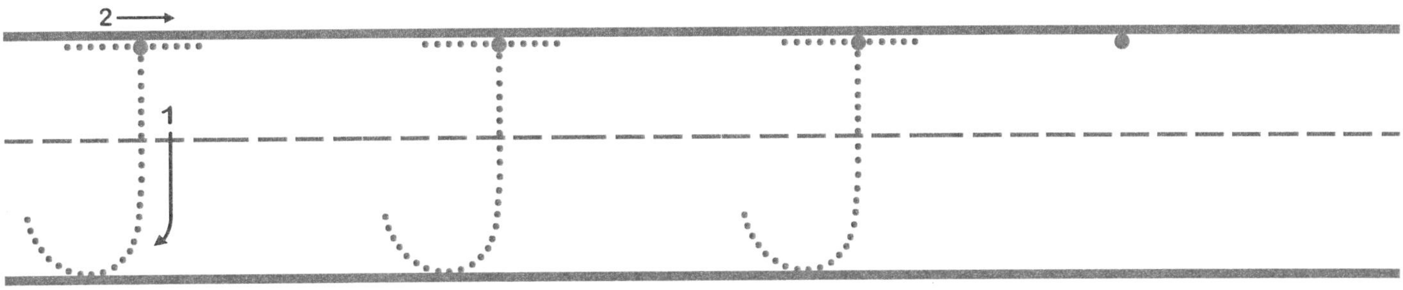

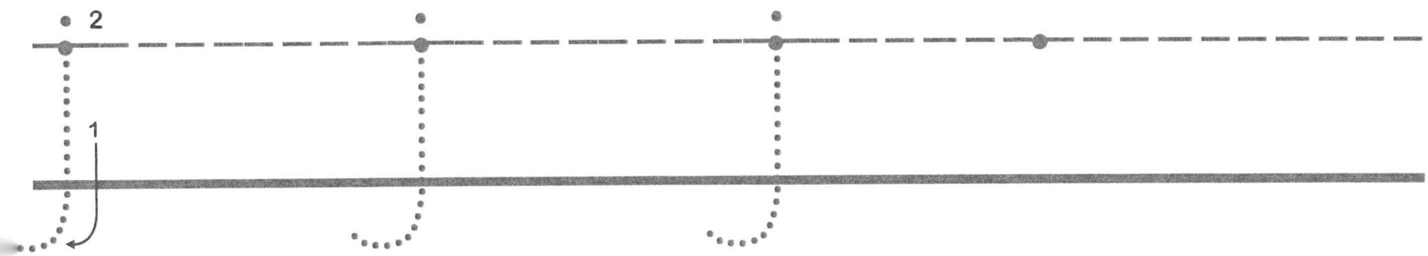

Letter Kk

K is for kangaroo.

Trace and print the letters on each line.
Circle your best letter on the line.

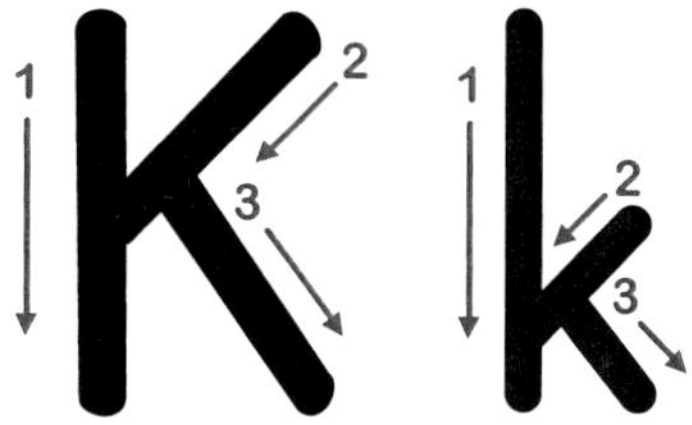

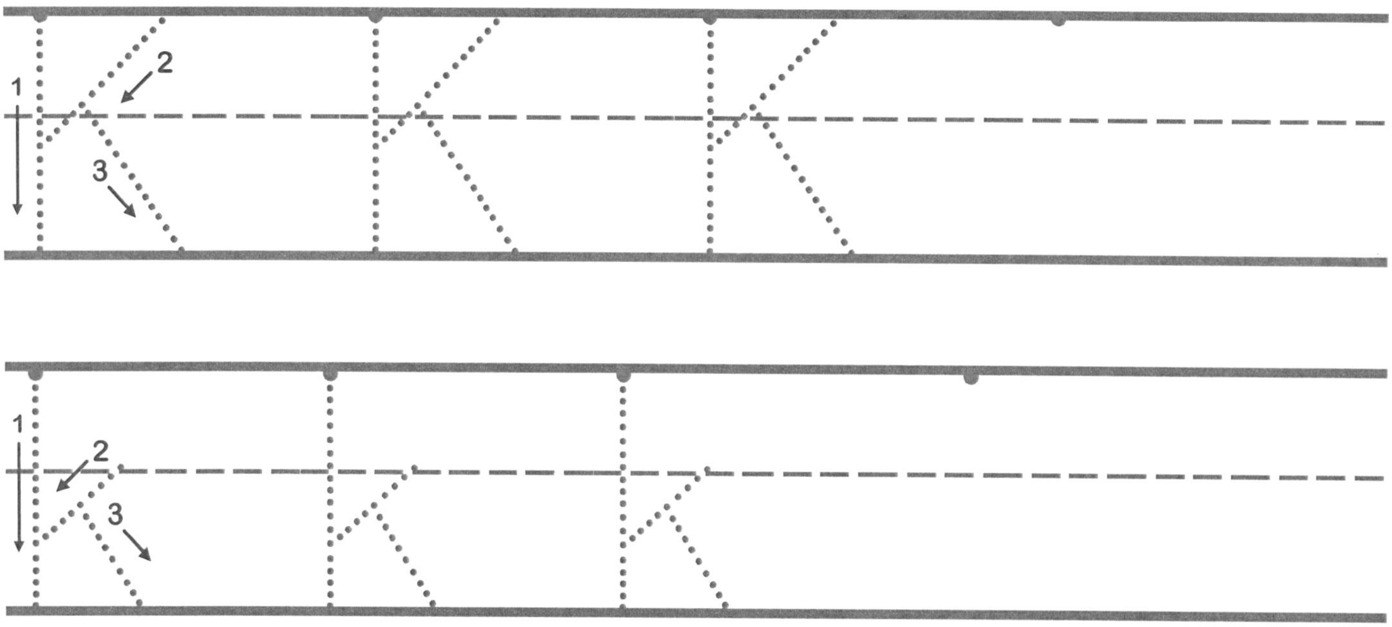

Letter Kk

Colour the kite with a capital K. green

Colour the kite with a lowercase k. blue

Trace and print the letters on each line.

Circle your best letter on the line.

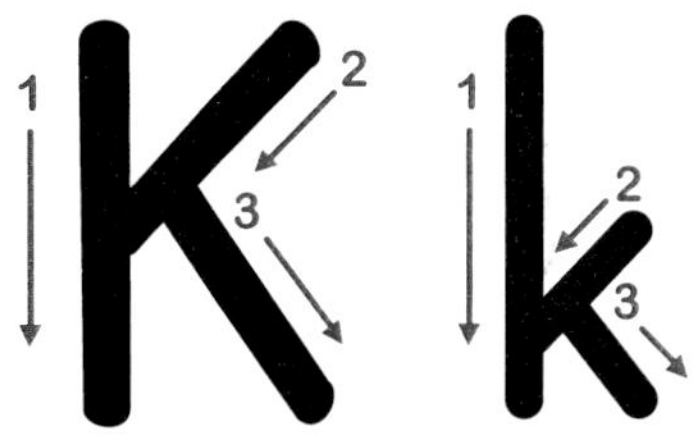

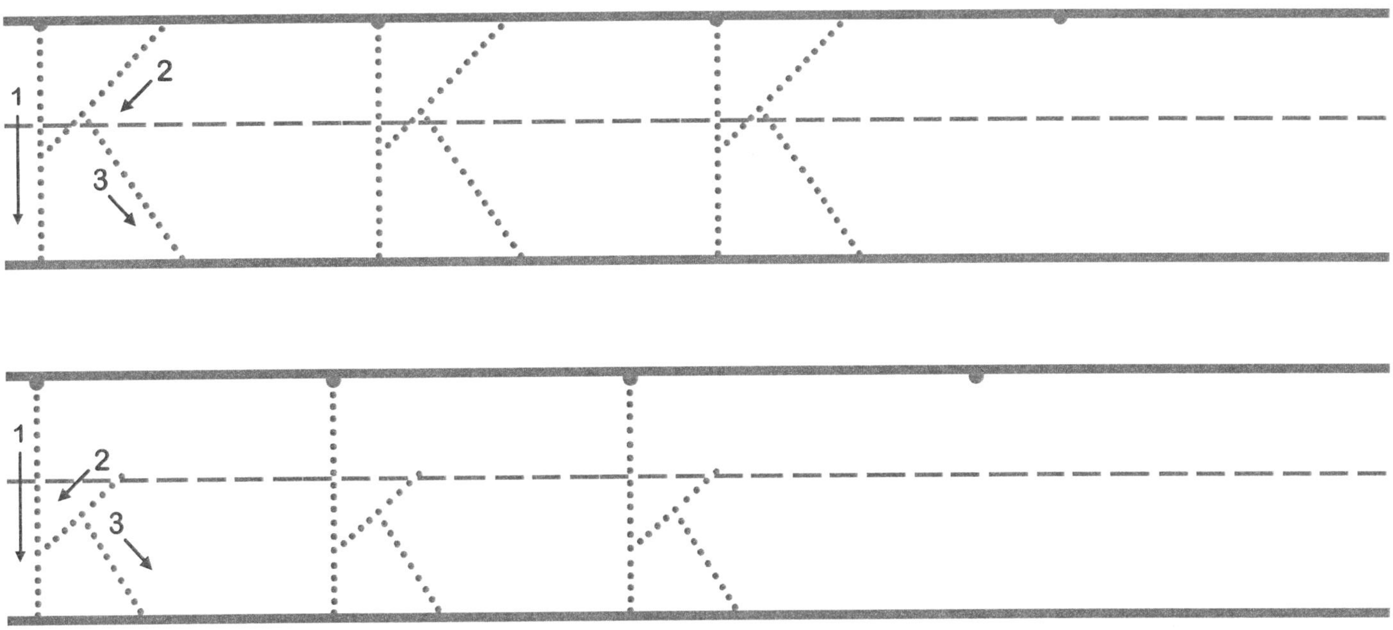

Letter Ll

L is for lizard.

Trace and print the letters on each line.
Circle your best letter on the line.

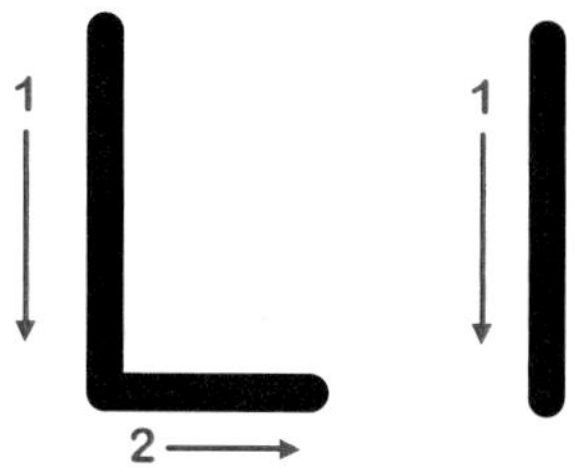

Letter Ll

Colour the lemon with a capital L. blue

Colour the lemon with a lowercase l. red

Trace and print the letters on each line.

Circle your best letter on the line.

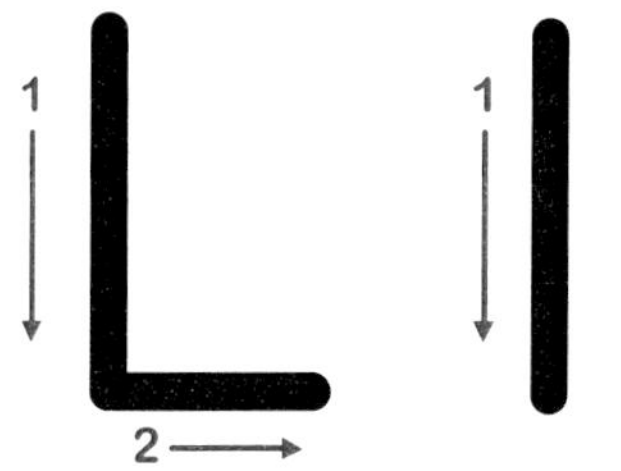

Letter Mm

M is for mouse.

Trace and print the letters on each line.
Circle your best letter on the line.

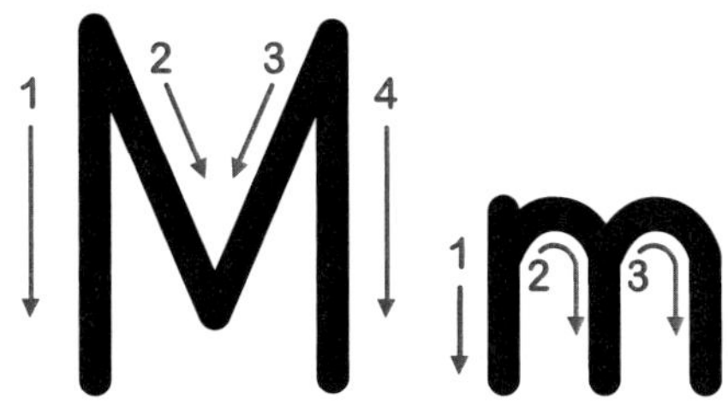

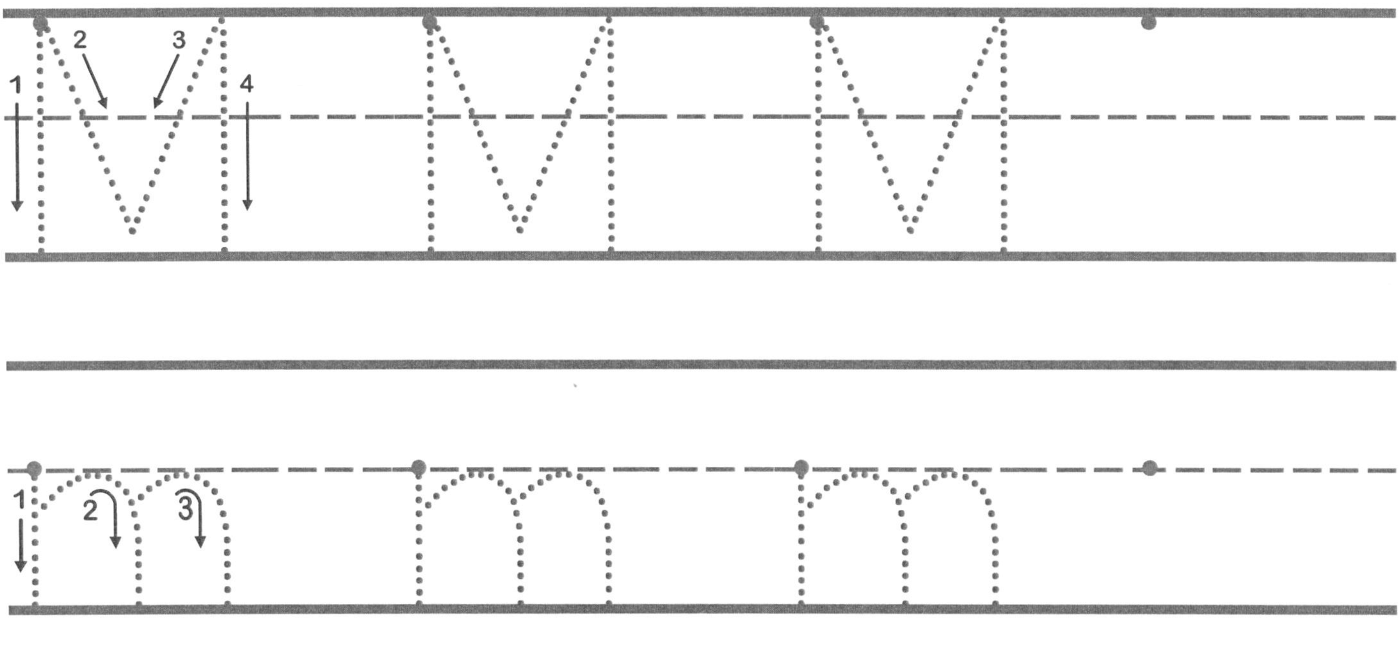

Letter Mm

Colour the map with a capital M. 

Colour the map with a lowercase m. 

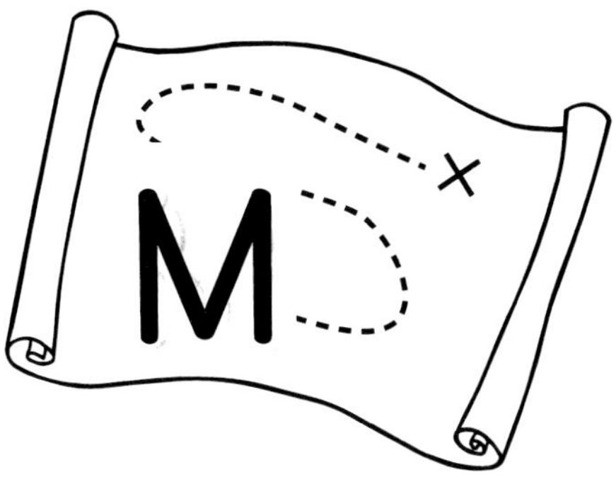

Trace and print the letters on each line.
Circle your best letter on the line.

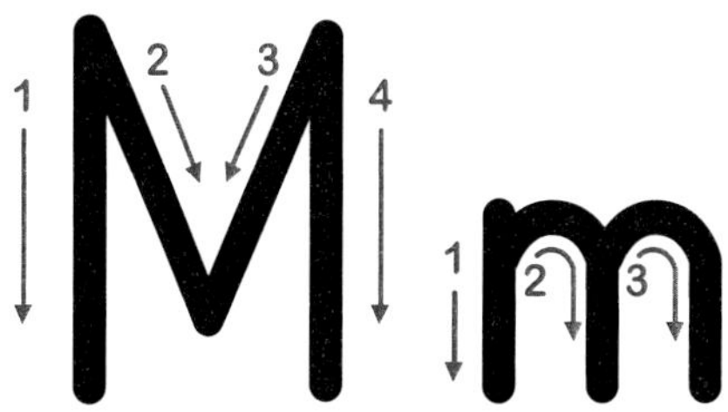

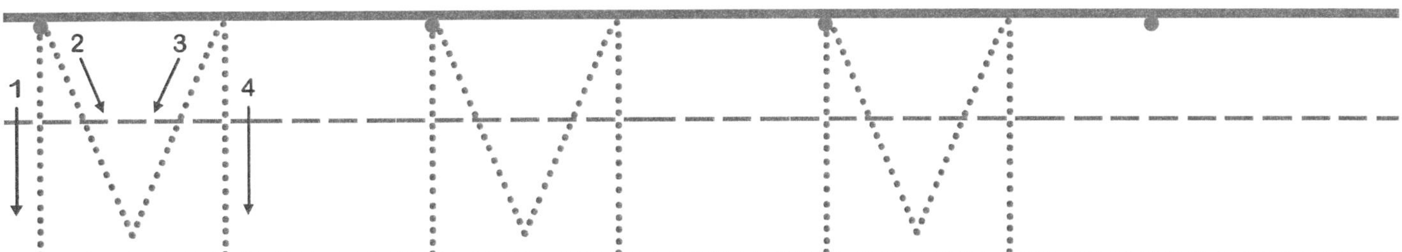

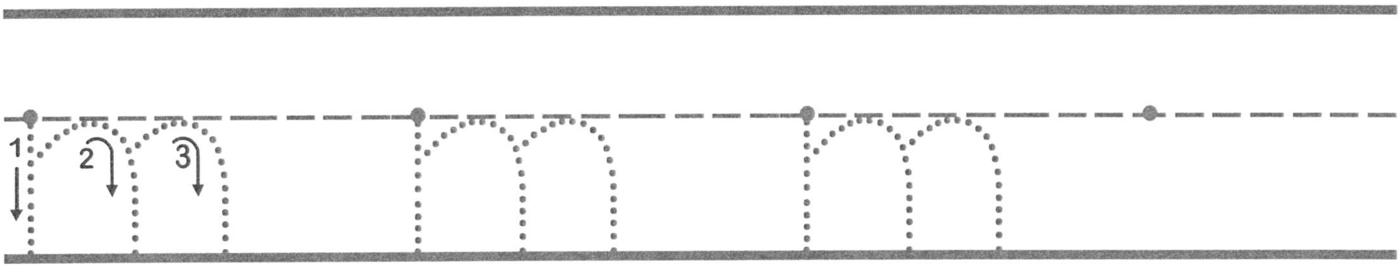

Letter Nn

N is for narwhal.

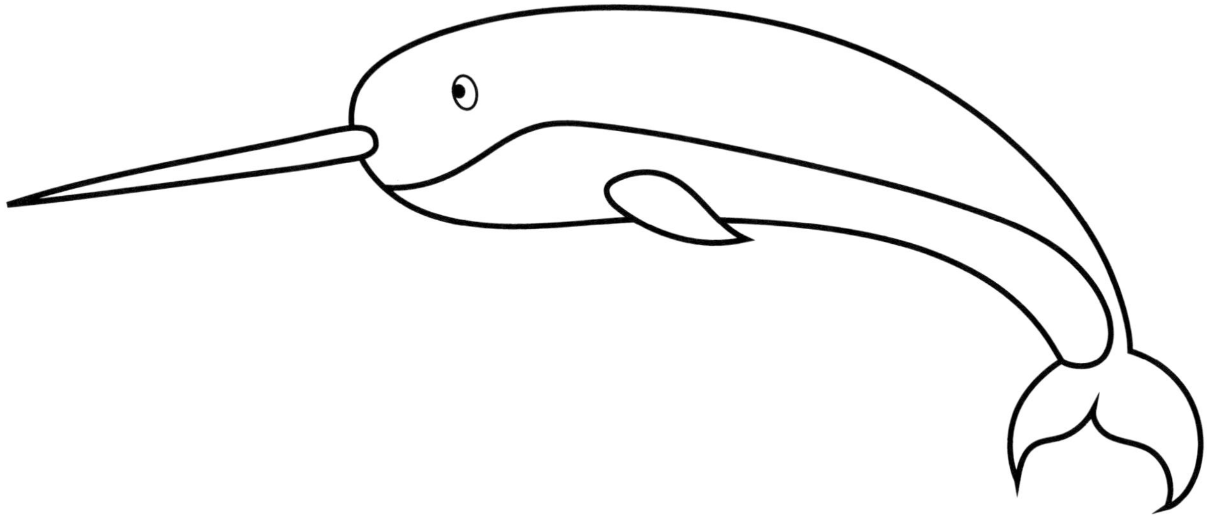

Trace and print the letters on each line.
Circle your best letter on the line.

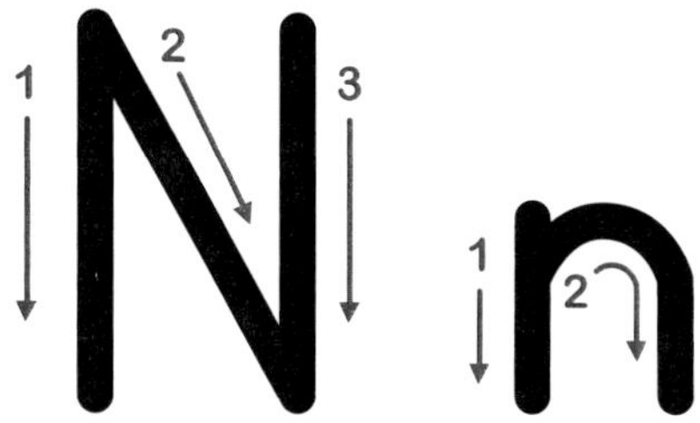

Letter Nn

Colour the net with a capital N. 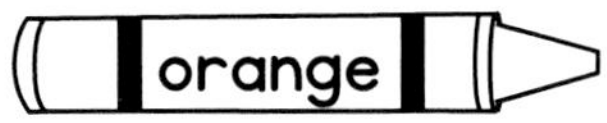

Colour the net with a lowercase n. 

Trace and print the letters on each line.
Circle your best letter on the line.

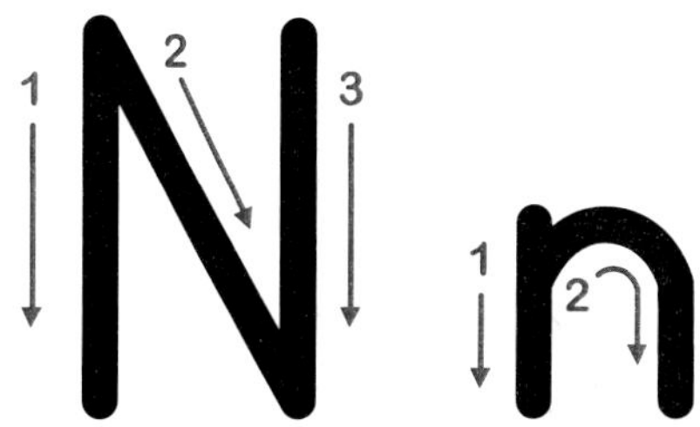

Letter Oo

O is for ostrich.

Trace and print the letters on each line.
Circle your best letter on the line.

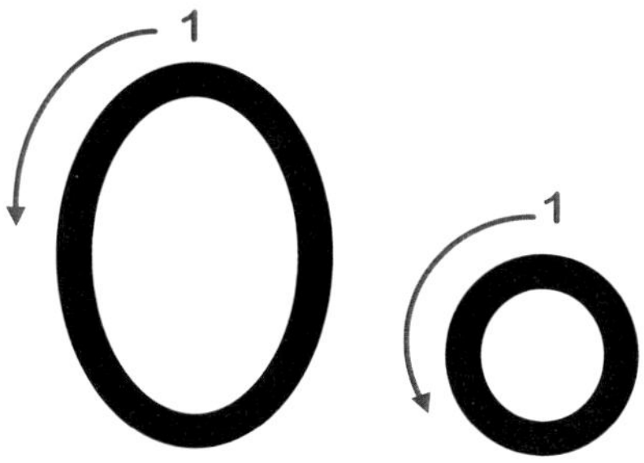

Letter Oo

Colour the orange with a capital O. 

Colour the orange with a lowercase o. 

Trace and print the letters on each line.
Circle your best letter on the line.

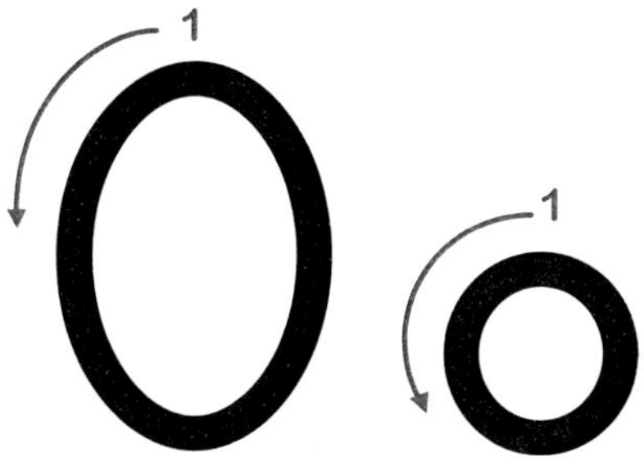

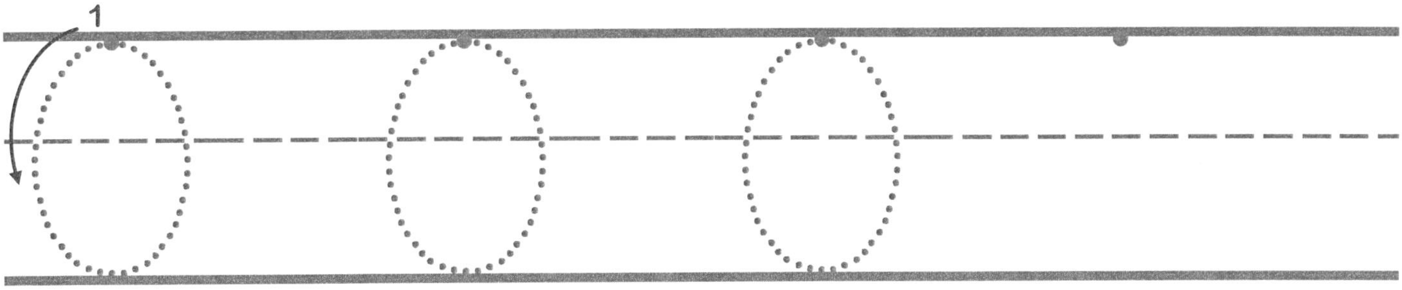

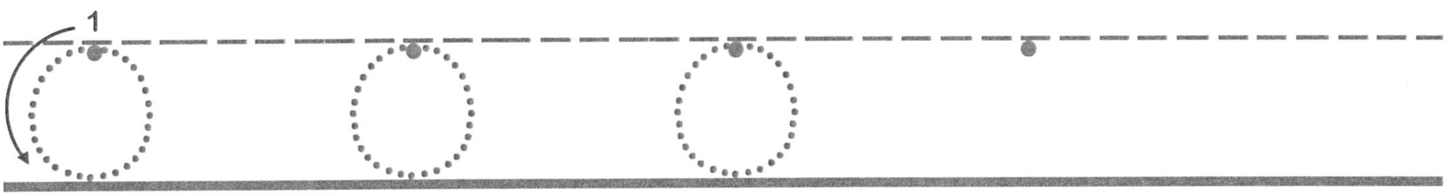

Letter Pp

P is for panda.

Trace and print the letters on each line.
Circle your best letter on the line.

P p

Letter Pp

Colour the puzzle piece with a capital P. red

Colour the puzzle piece with a lowercase p. purple

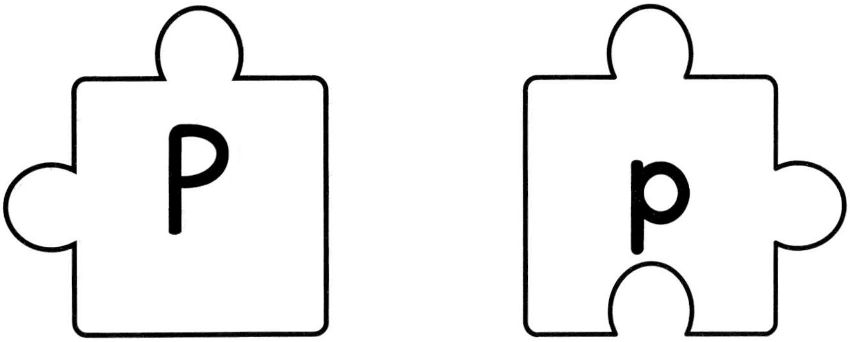

Trace and print the letters on each line.
Circle your best letter on the line.

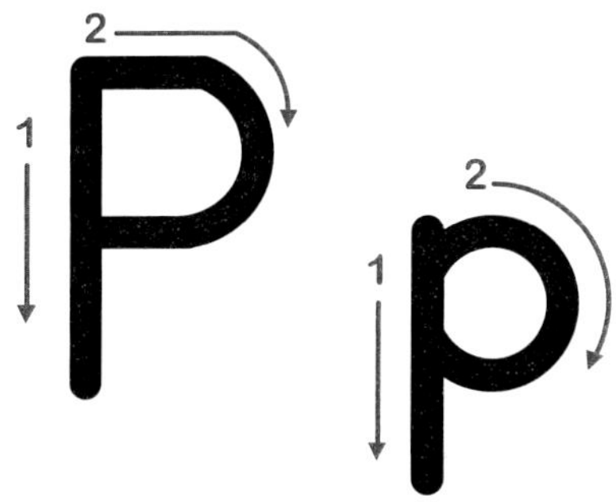

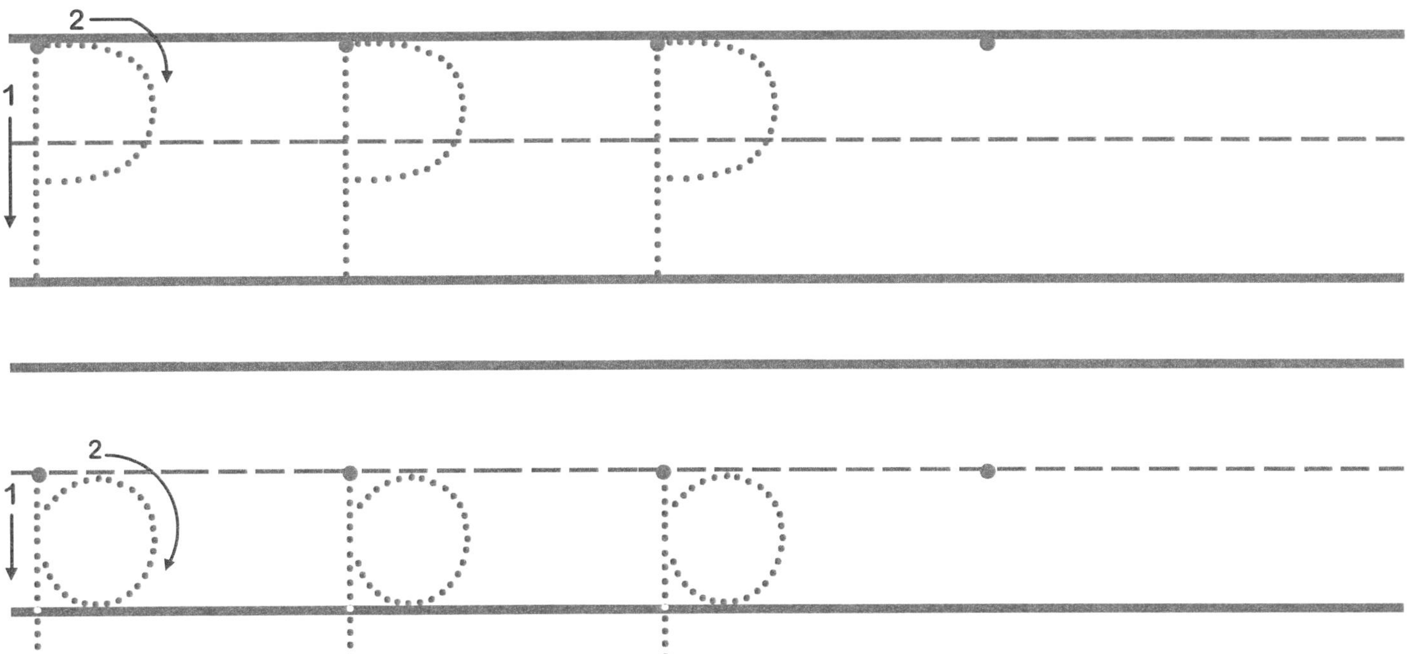

Letter Qq

Q is for quail.

Trace and print the letters on each line.
Circle your best letter on the line.

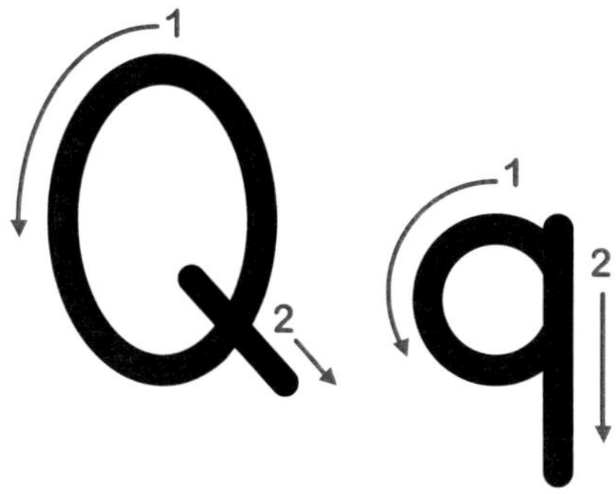

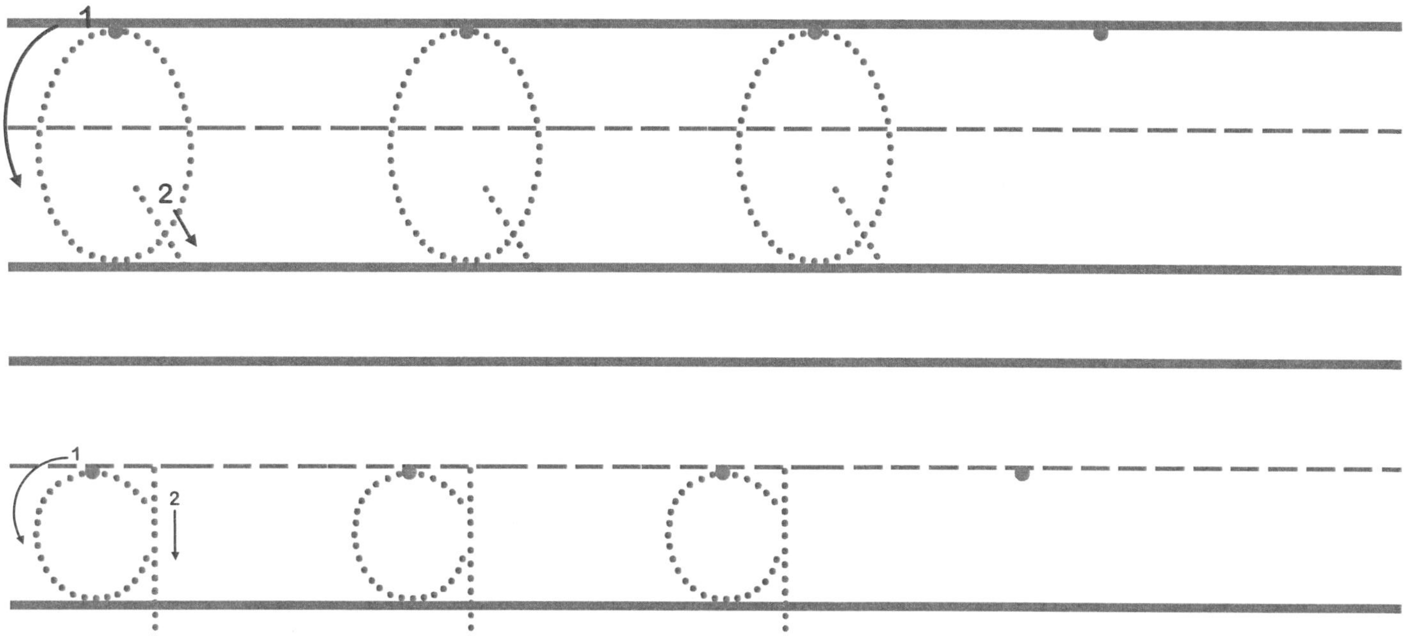

Letter Qq

Colour the quill pen with a capital Q. 

Colour the quill pen with a lowercase q. 

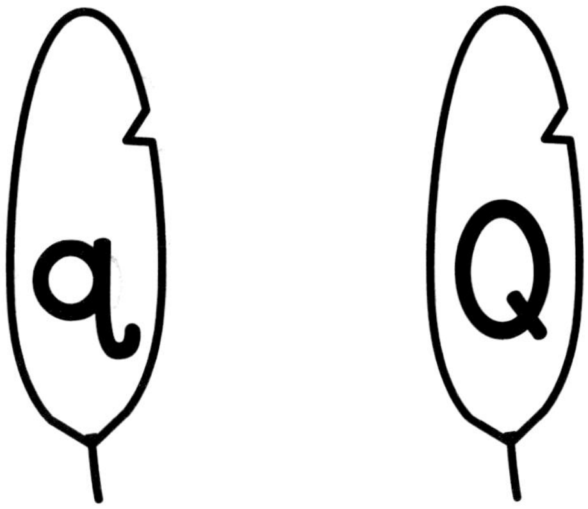

Trace and print the letters on each line.
Circle your best letter on the line.

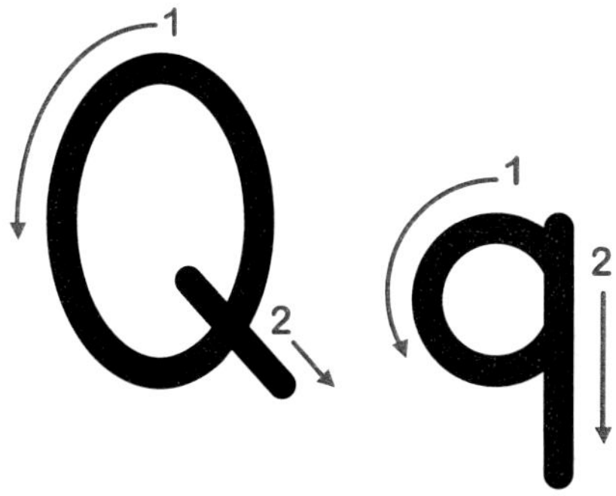

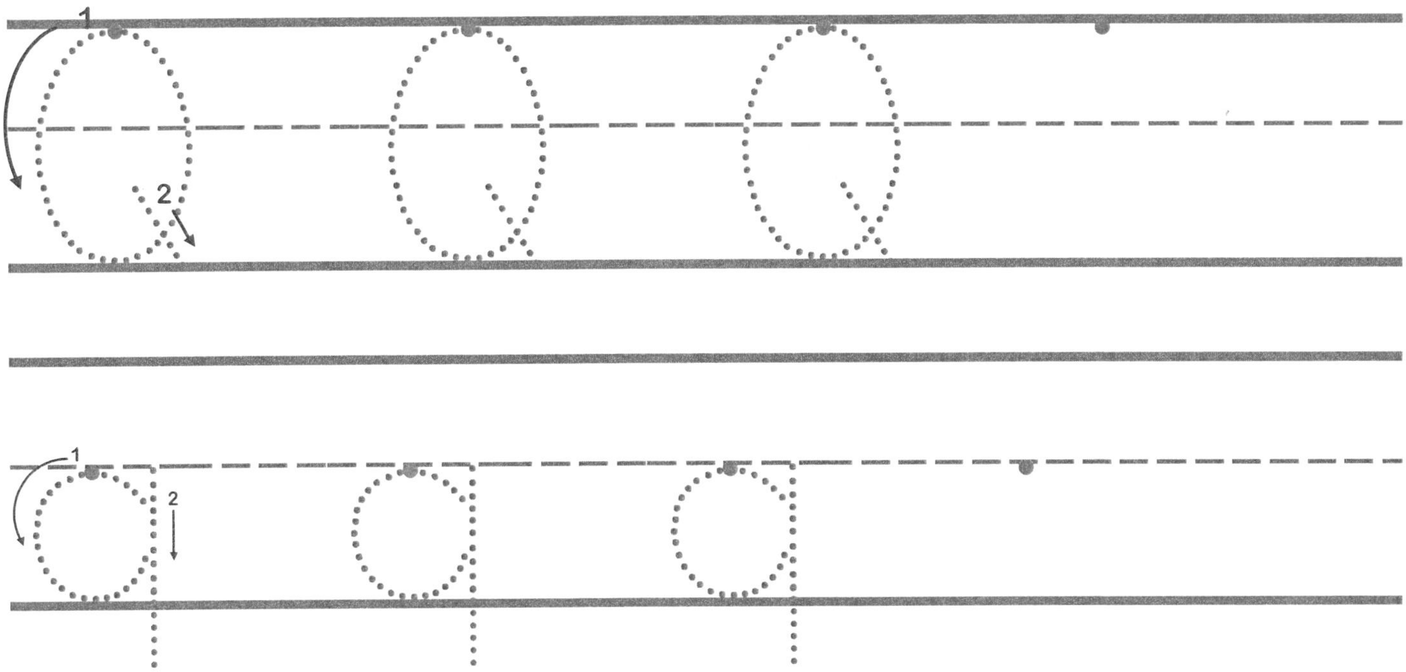

Letter Rr

R is for raccoon.

Trace and print the letters on each line.
Circle your best letter on the line.

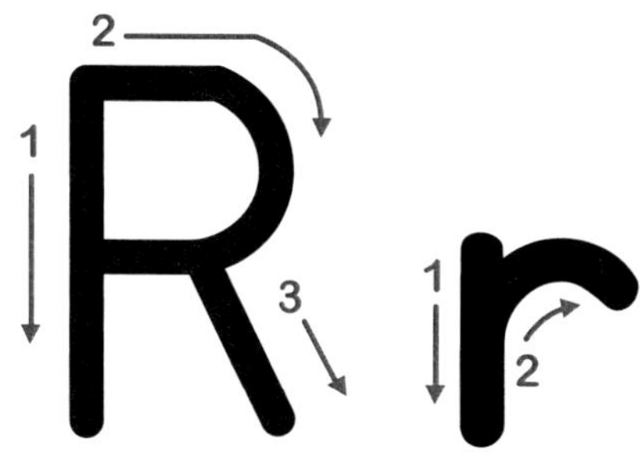

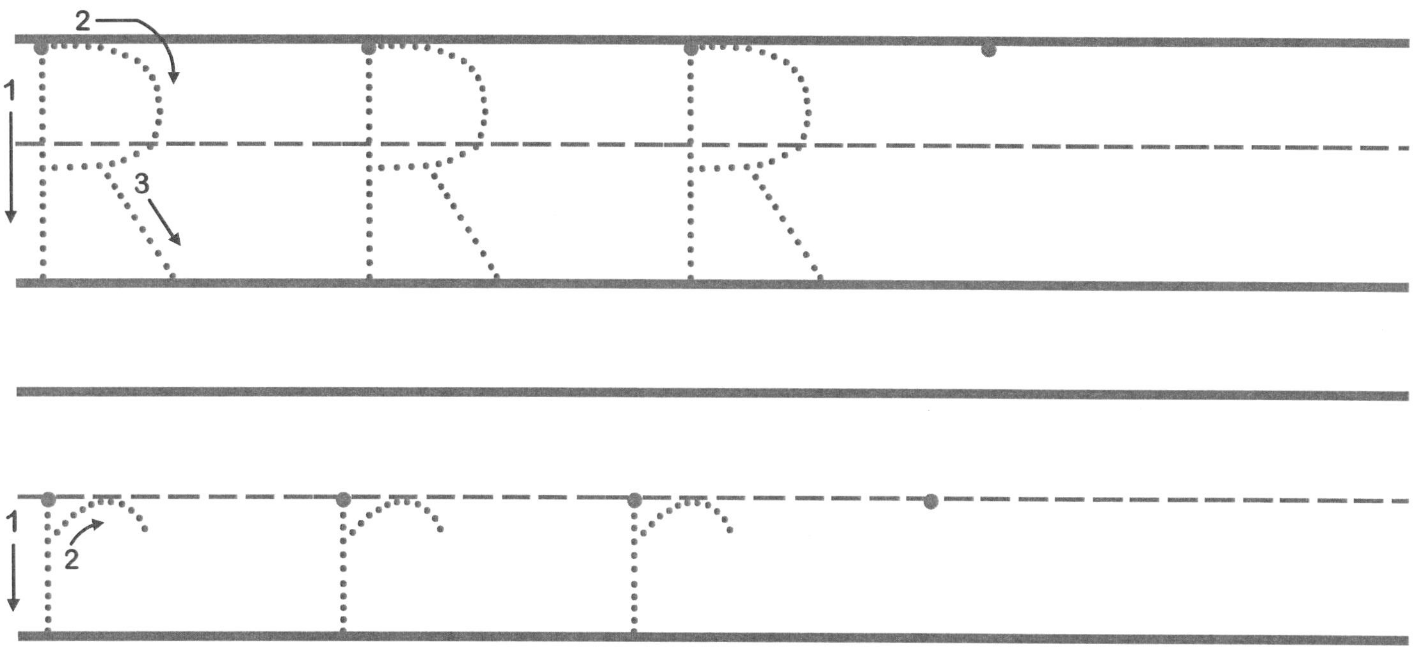

Letter Rr

Colour the rainbow with a capital R. yellow

Colour the rainbow with a lowercase r. red

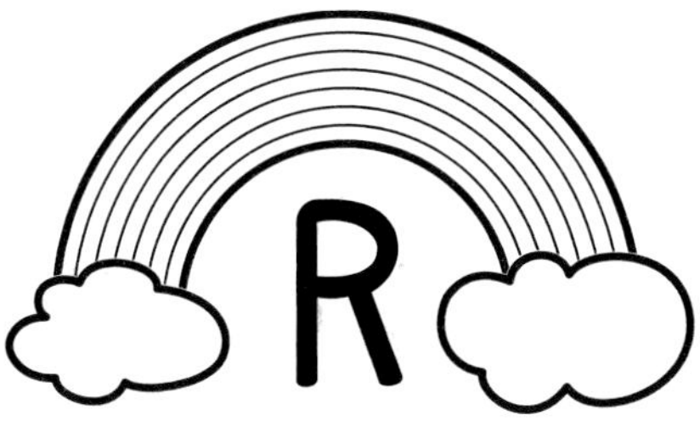

Trace and print the letters on each line.
Circle your best letter on the line.

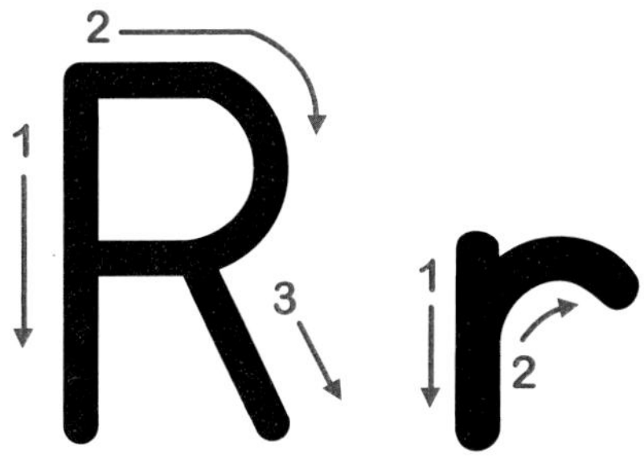

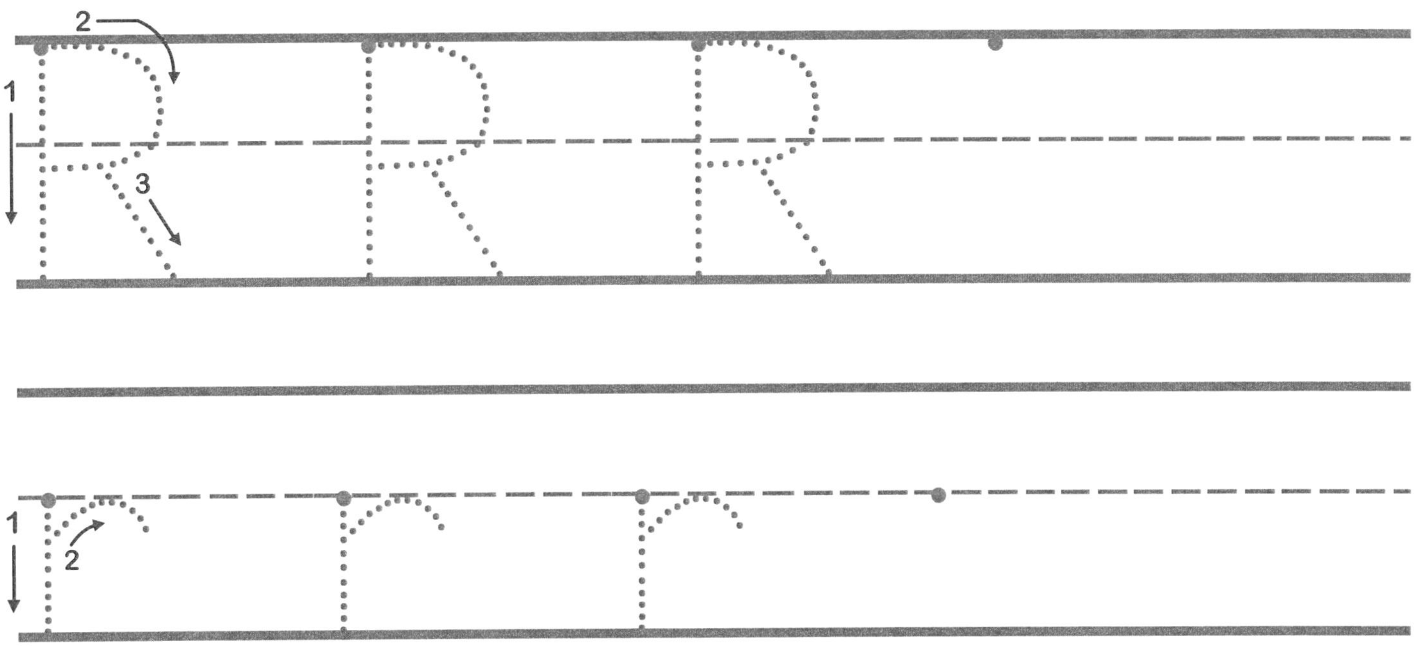

Letter Ss

S is for seagull.

Trace and print the letters on each line.
Circle your best letter on the line.

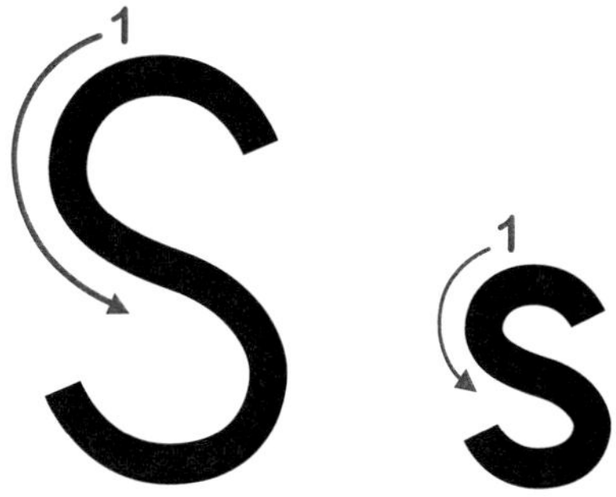

Letter Ss

Colour the star with a capital S. orange
Colour the star with a lowercase s. yellow

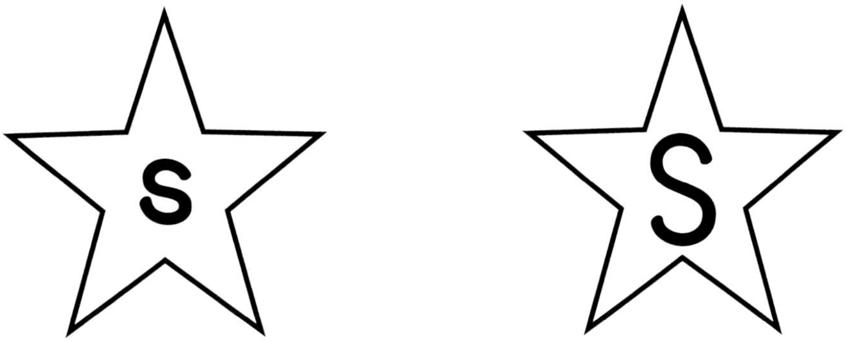

Trace and print the letters on each line.
Circle your best letter on the line.

S s

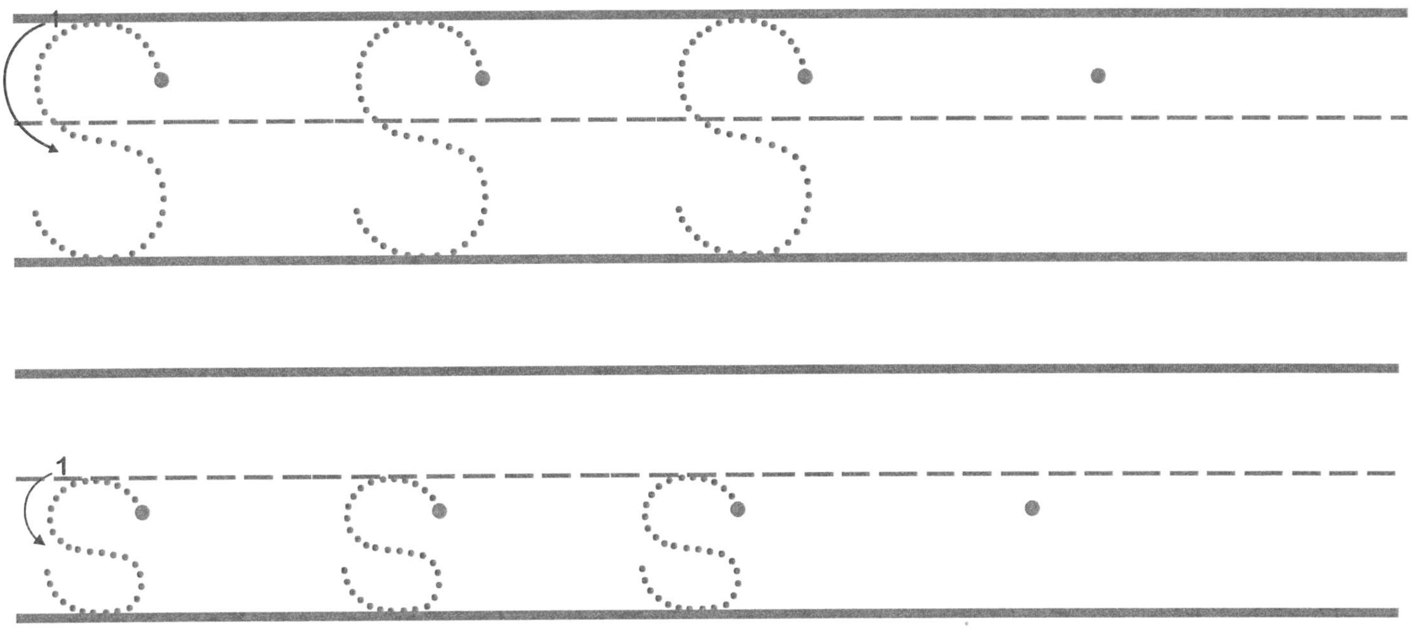

Letter Tt

T is for turtle.

Trace and print the letters on each line.
Circle your best letter on the line.

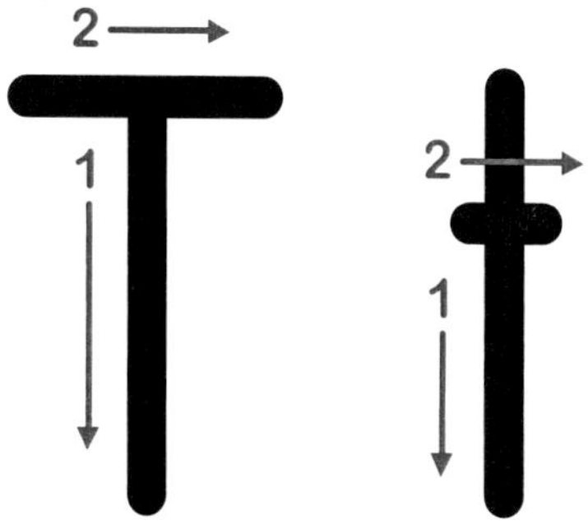

Letter Tt

Colour the tiger with a capital T. green

Colour the tiger with a lowercase t. blue

Trace and print the letters on each line.
Circle your best letter on the line.

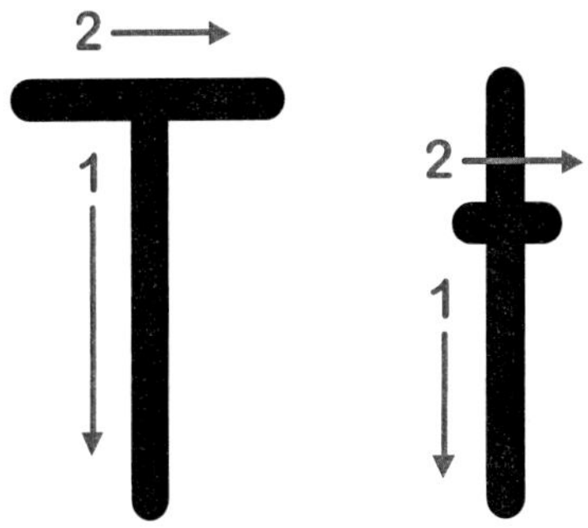

Letter Uu

U is for unicorn.

Trace and print the letters on each line.
Circle your best letter on the line.

U u

Letter Uu

Colour the umbrella with a capital U. red

Colour the umbrella with a lowercase u. green

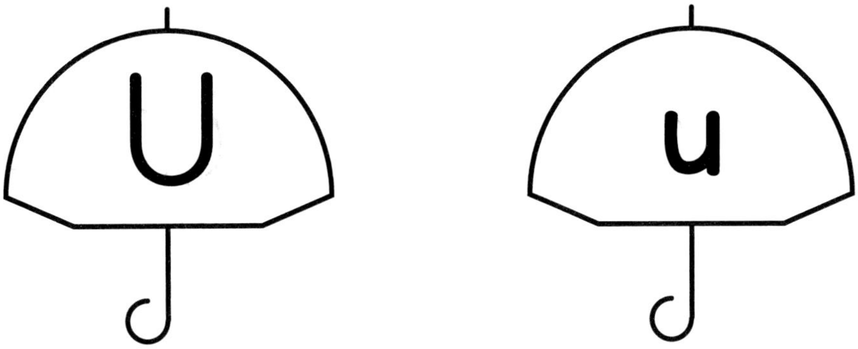

Trace and print the letters on each line.
Circle your best letter on the line.

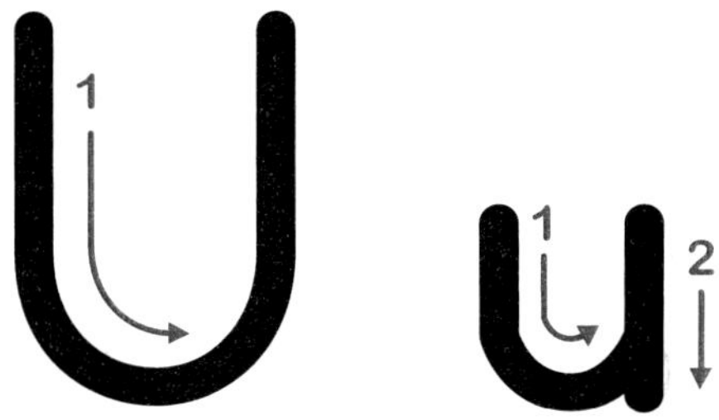

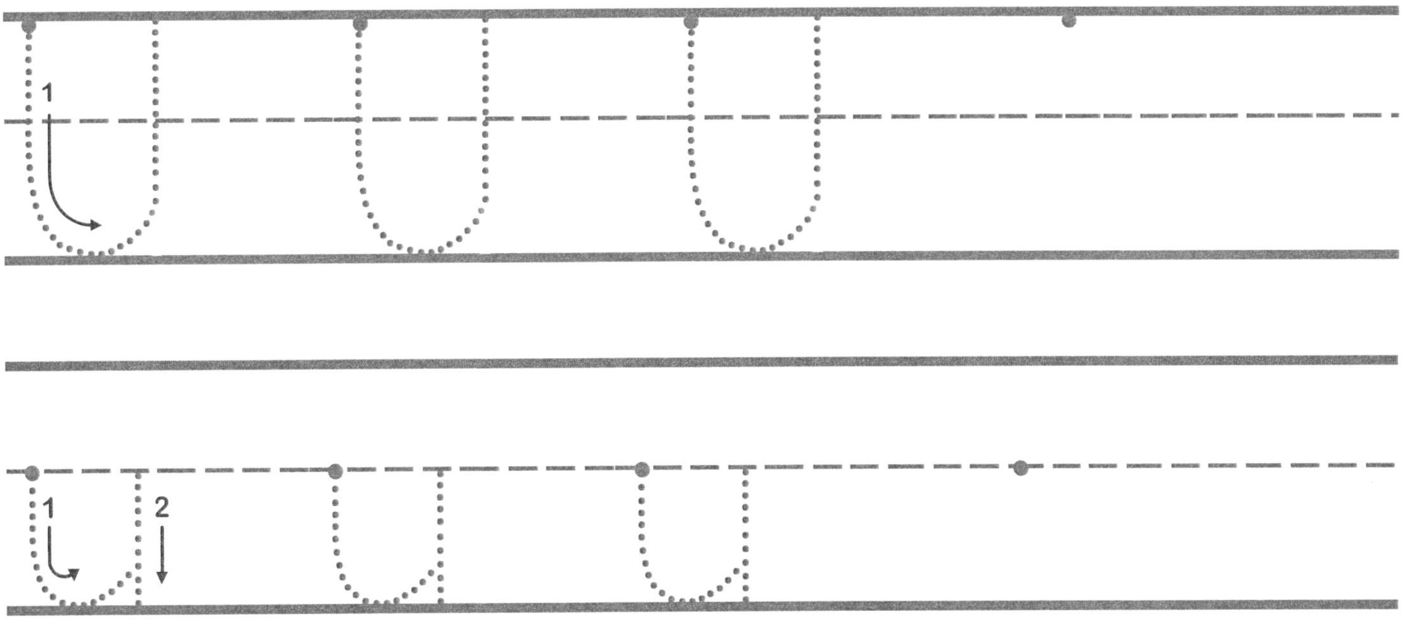

Letter Vv

V is for vulture.

Trace and print the letters on each line.
Circle your best letter on the line.

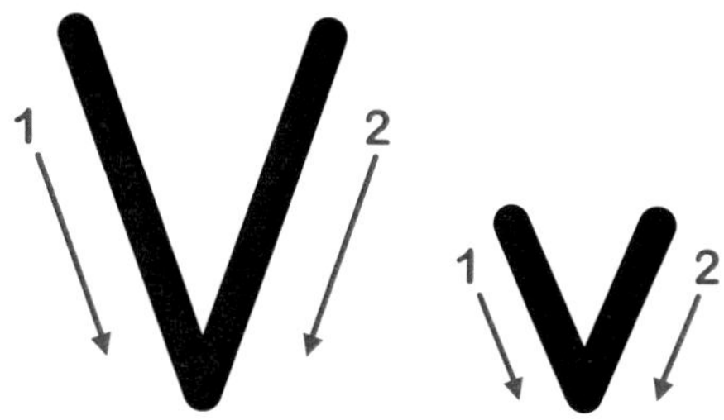

Letter Vv

Colour the vase with a capital V. green

Colour the vase with a lowercase v. blue

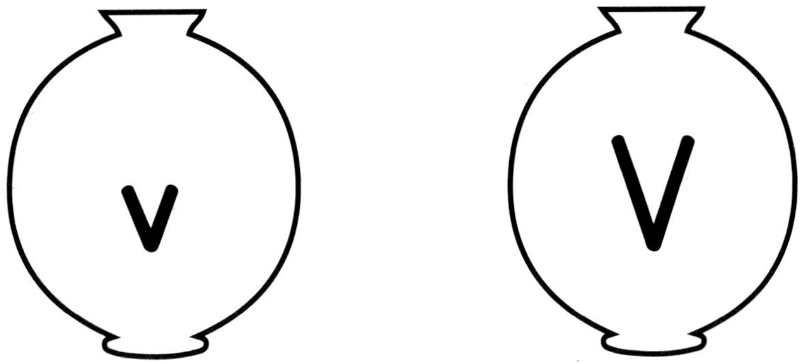

Trace and print the letters on each line.
Circle your best letter on the line.

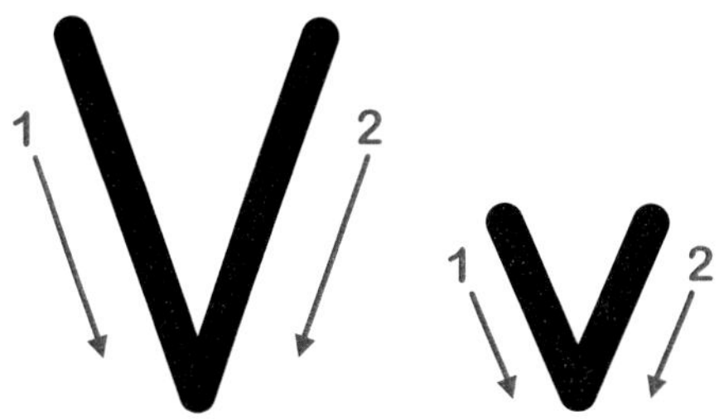

Letter Ww

W is for wolf.

Trace and print the letters on each line.
Circle your best letter on the line.

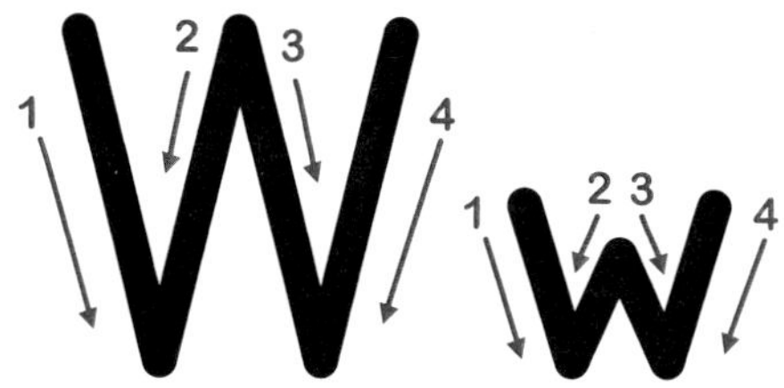

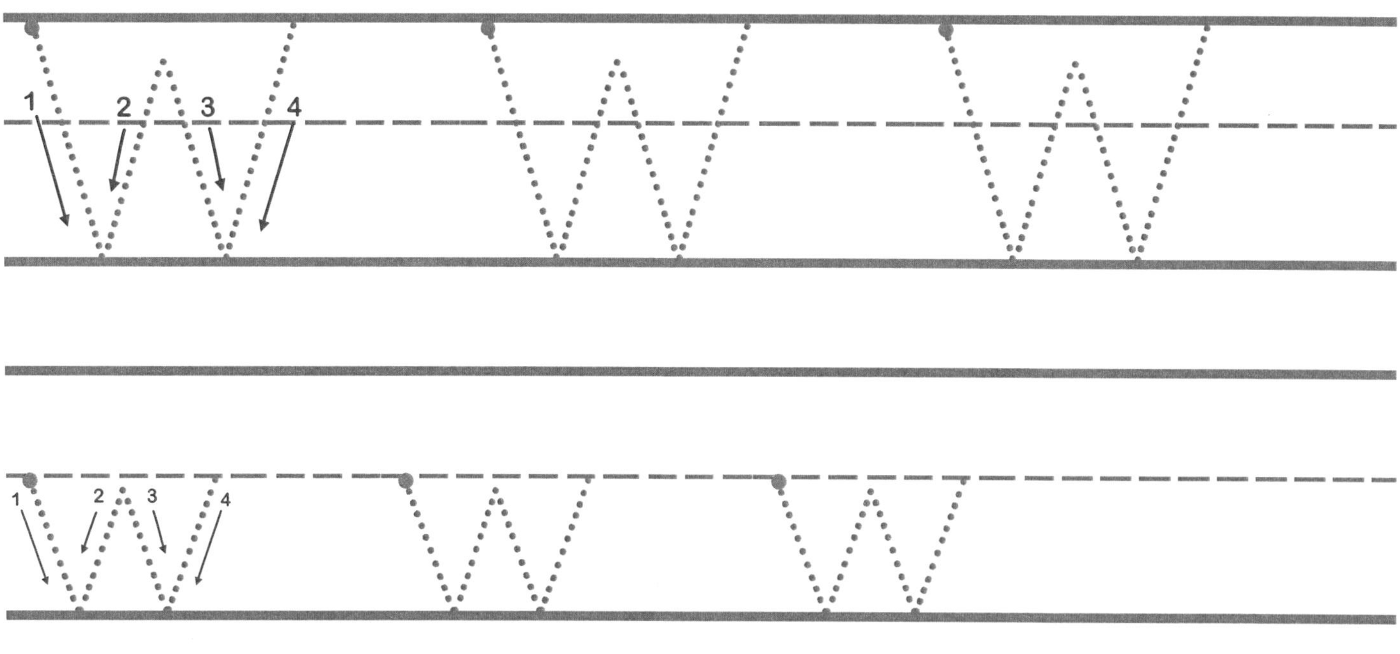

Letter Ww

Colour the wedge with a capital W. purple

Colour the wedge with a lowercase w. red

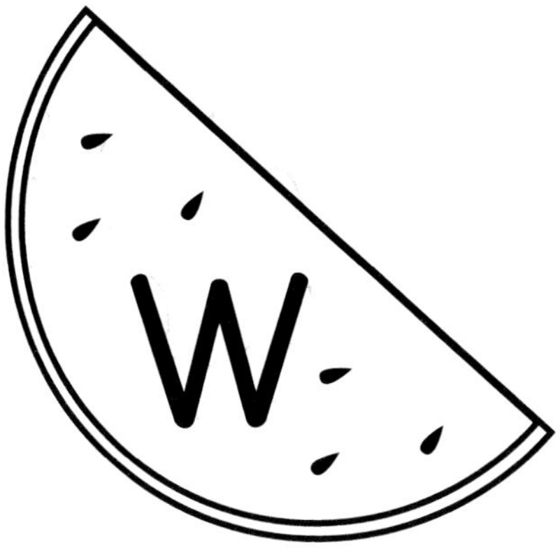

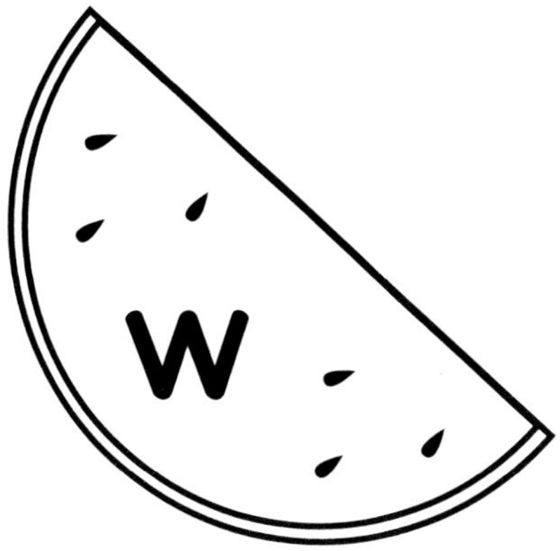

Trace and print the letters on each line.
Circle your best letter on the line.

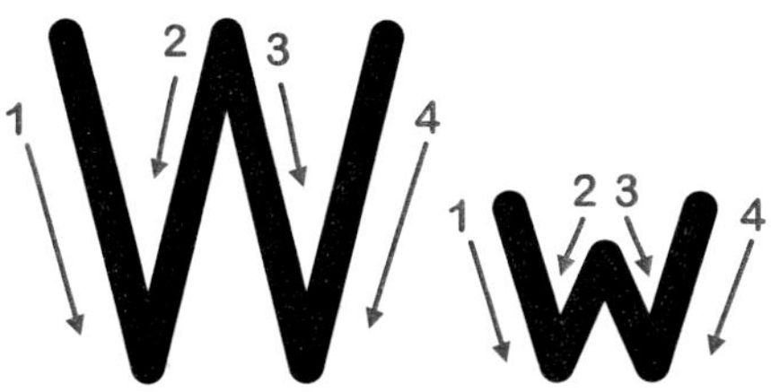

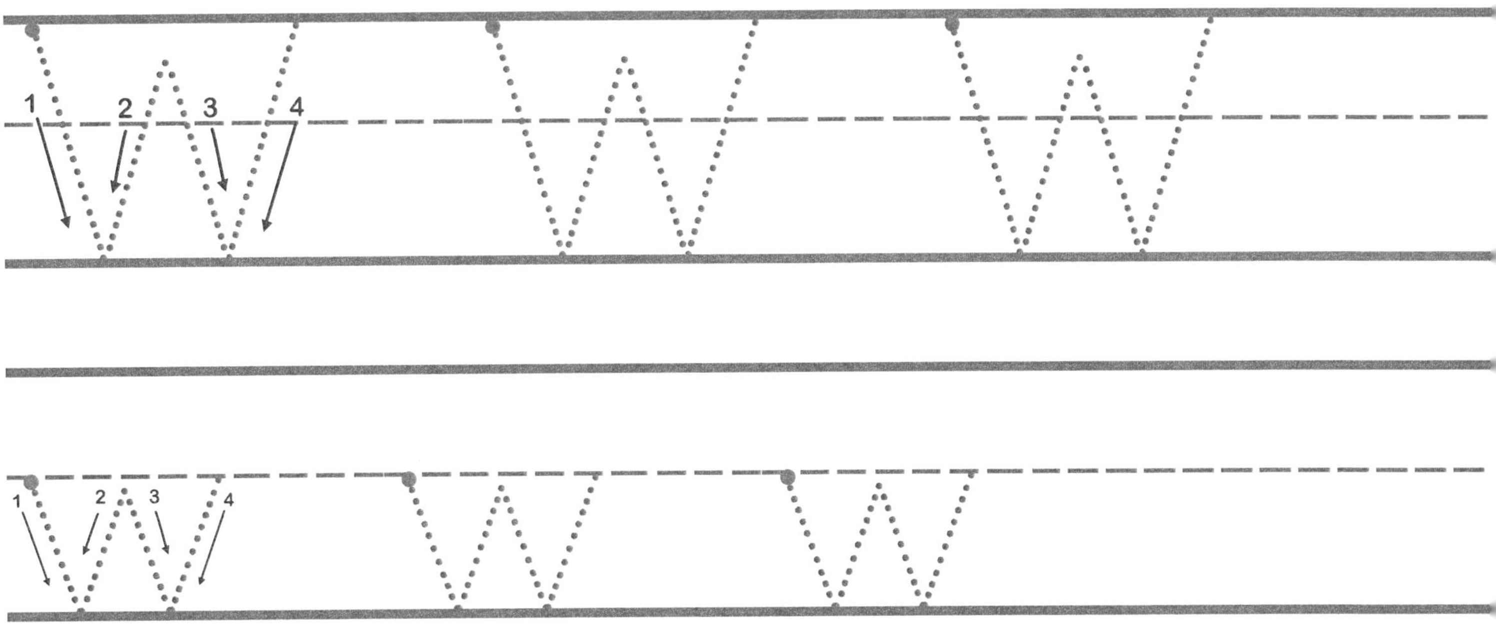

Letter Xx

X is for x-ray fish.

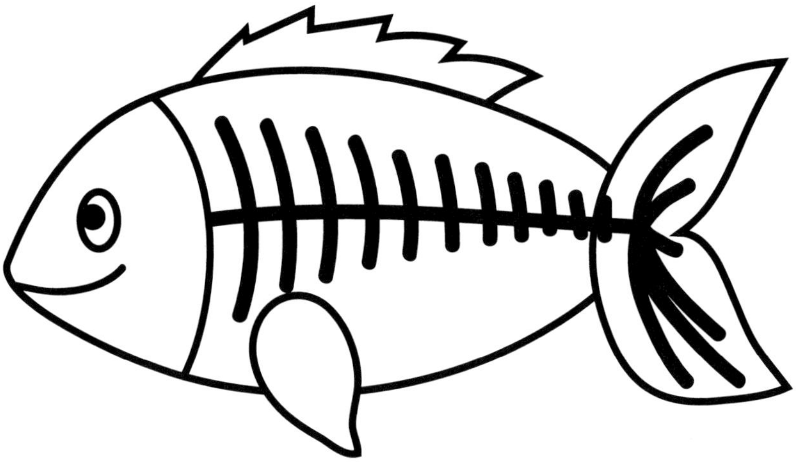

Trace and print the letters on each line.
Circle your best letter on the line.

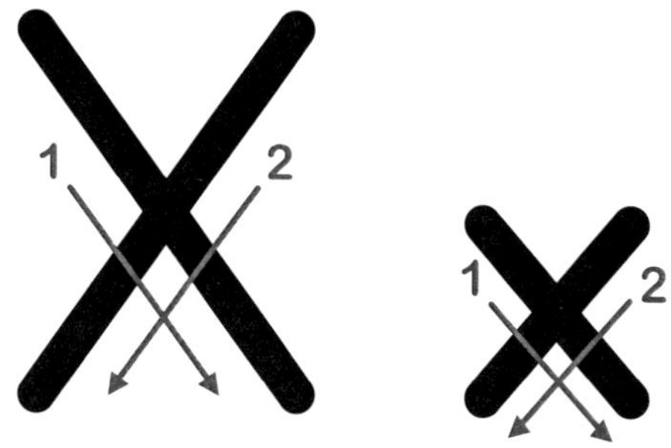

Letter Xx

Colour the xylophone with a capital X. 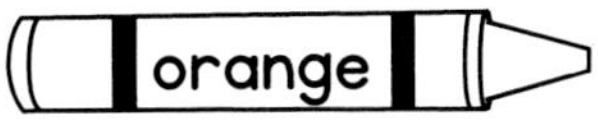

Colour the xylophone with a lowercase x. 

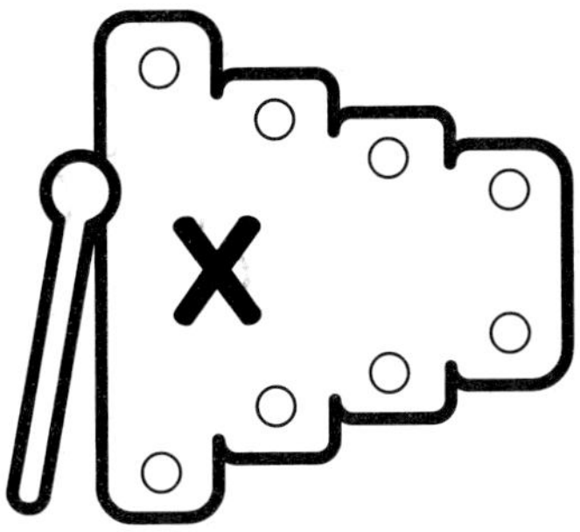

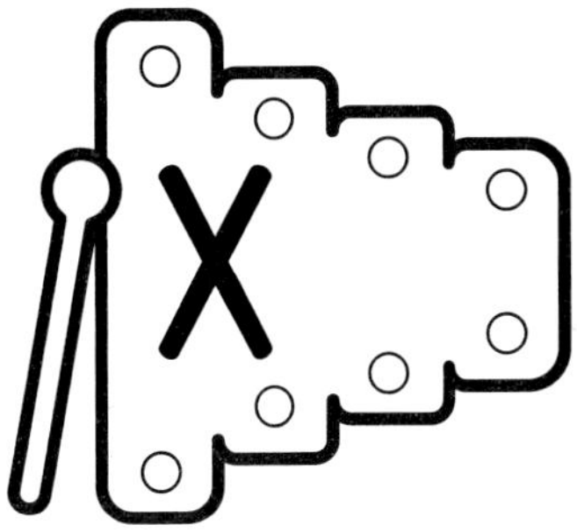

Trace and print the letters on each line.
Circle your best letter on the line.

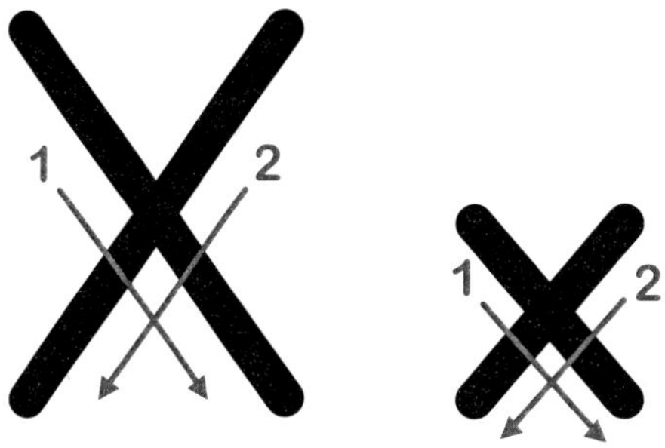

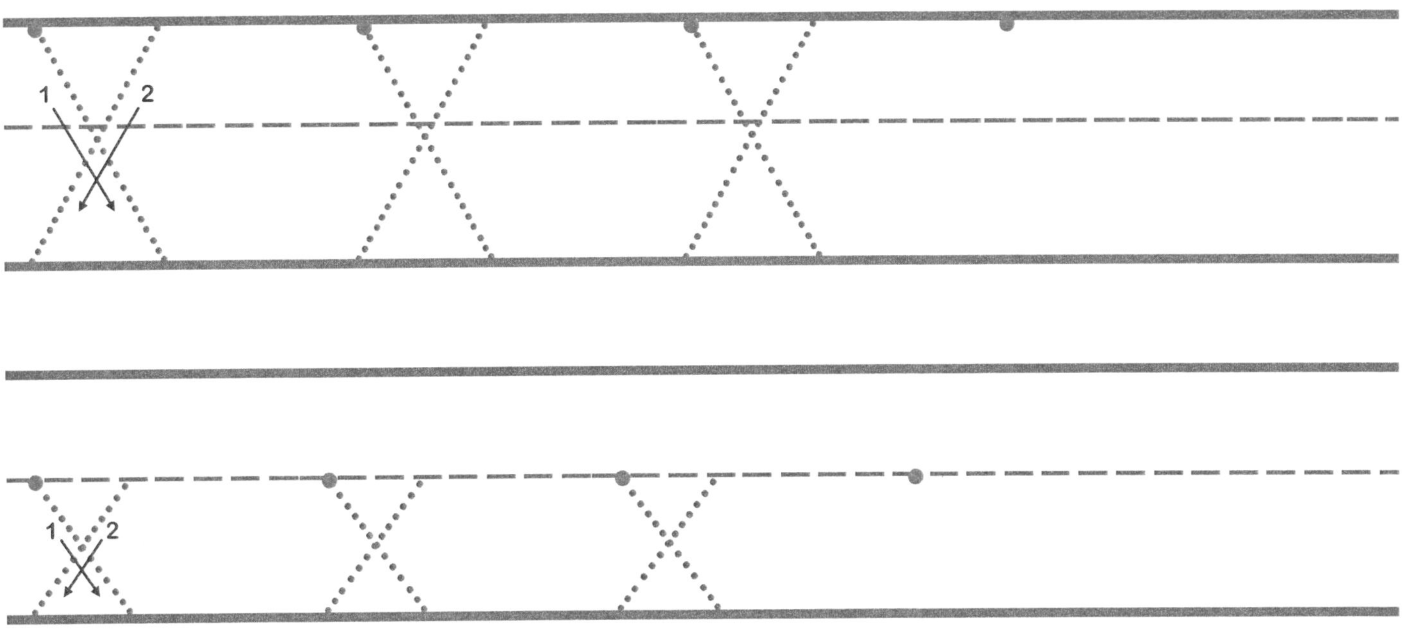

Letter Yy

Y is for yak.

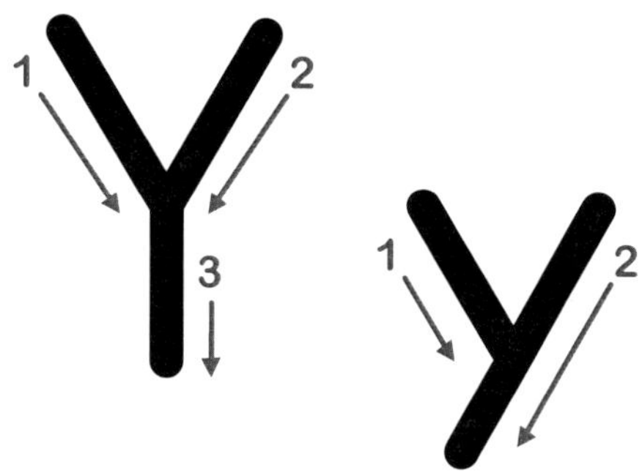

Trace and print the letters on each line.
Circle your best letter on the line.

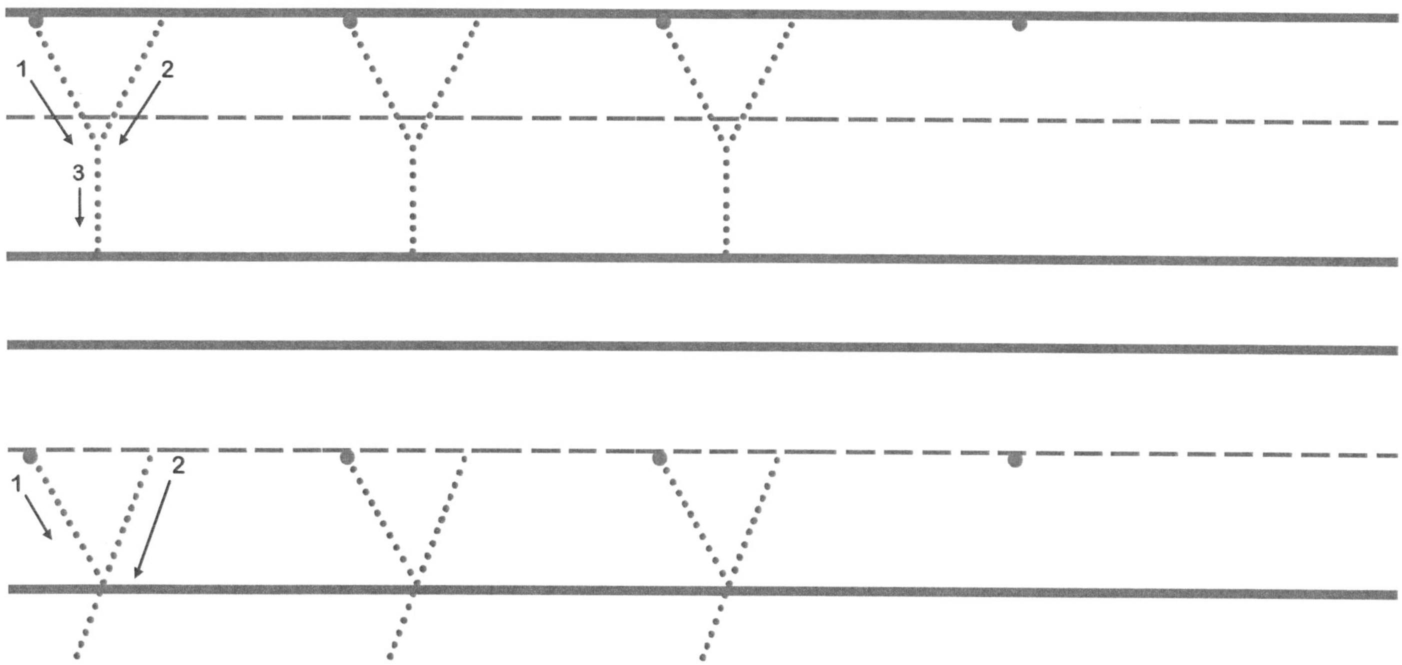

Letter Yy

Colour the yo-yo with a capital Y. 

Colour the yo-yo with a lowercase y. 

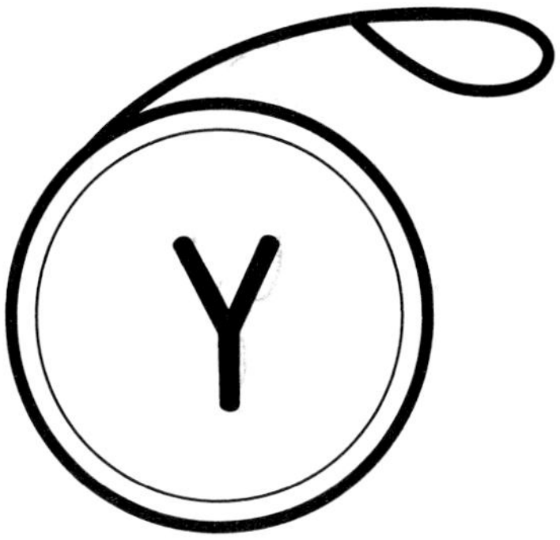

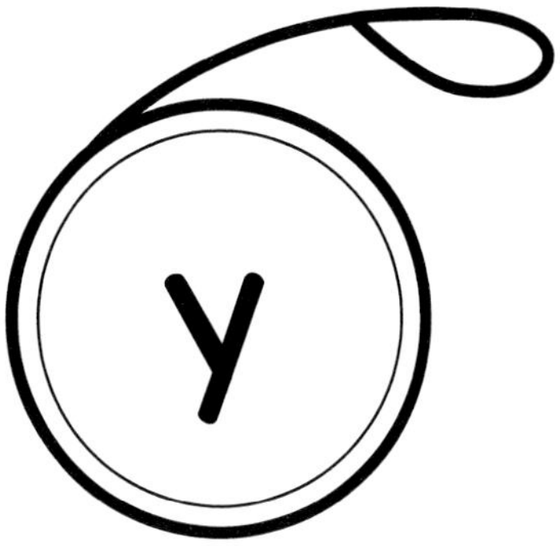

Trace and print the letters on each line.
Circle your best letter on the line.

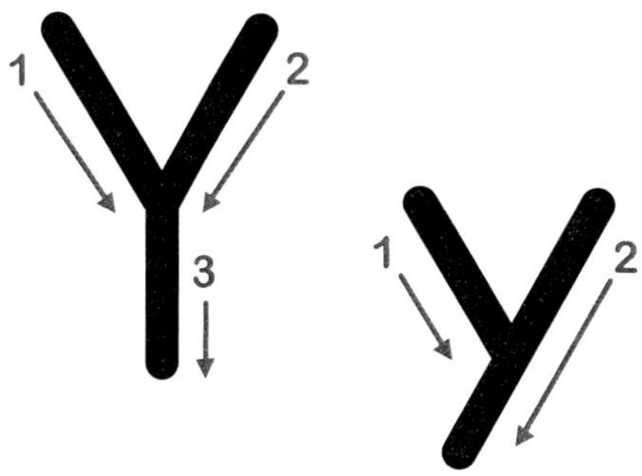

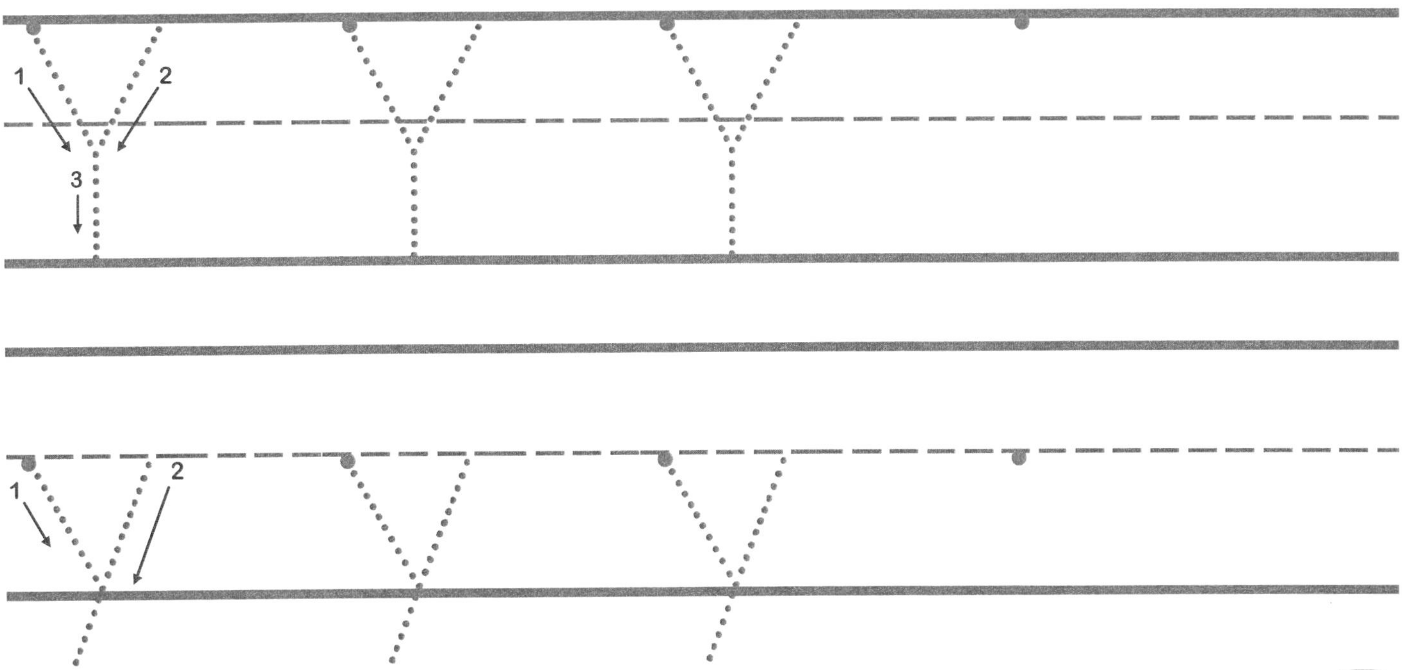

Letter Zz

Z is for zebra.

Trace and print the letters on each line.
Circle your best letter on the line.

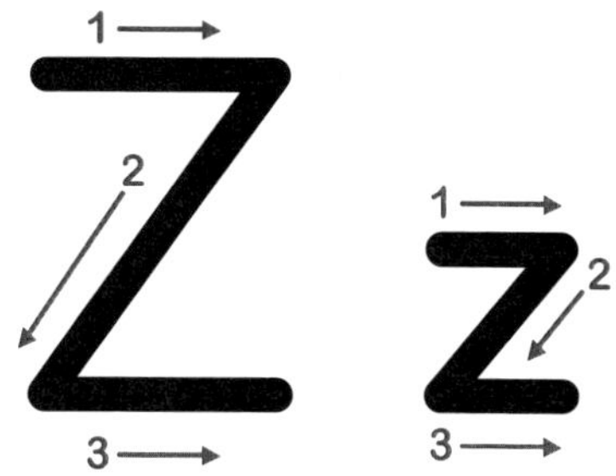

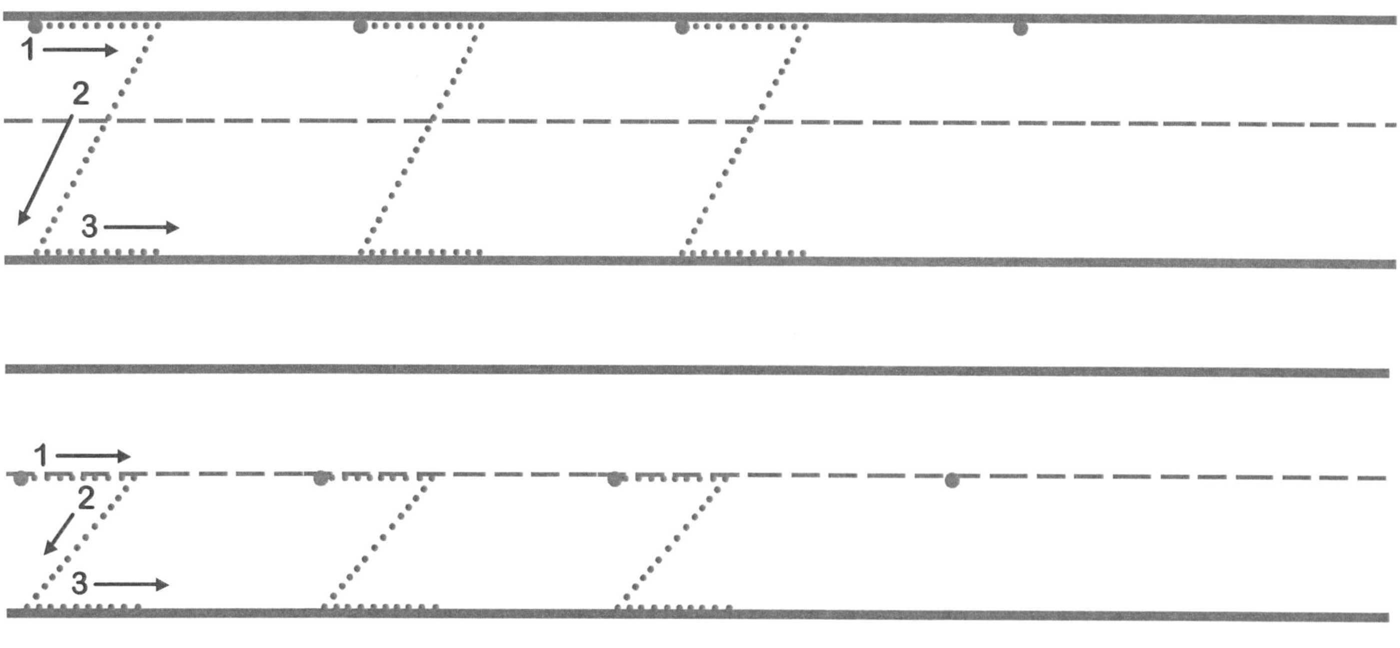

Letter Zz

Colour the zigzag with a capital Z. 

Colour the zigzag with a lowercase z. 

Trace and print the letters on each line.
Circle your best letter on the line.

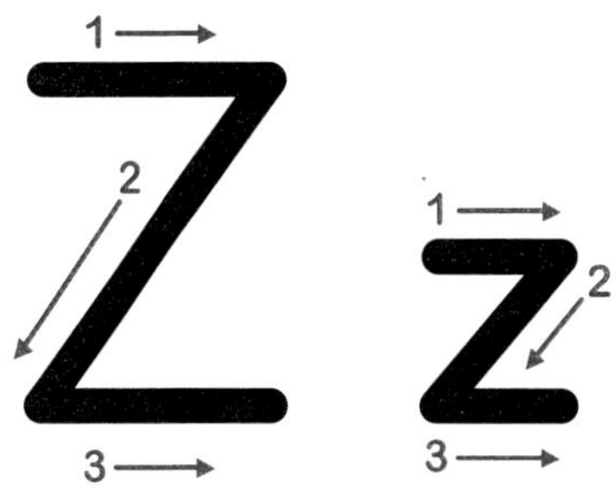

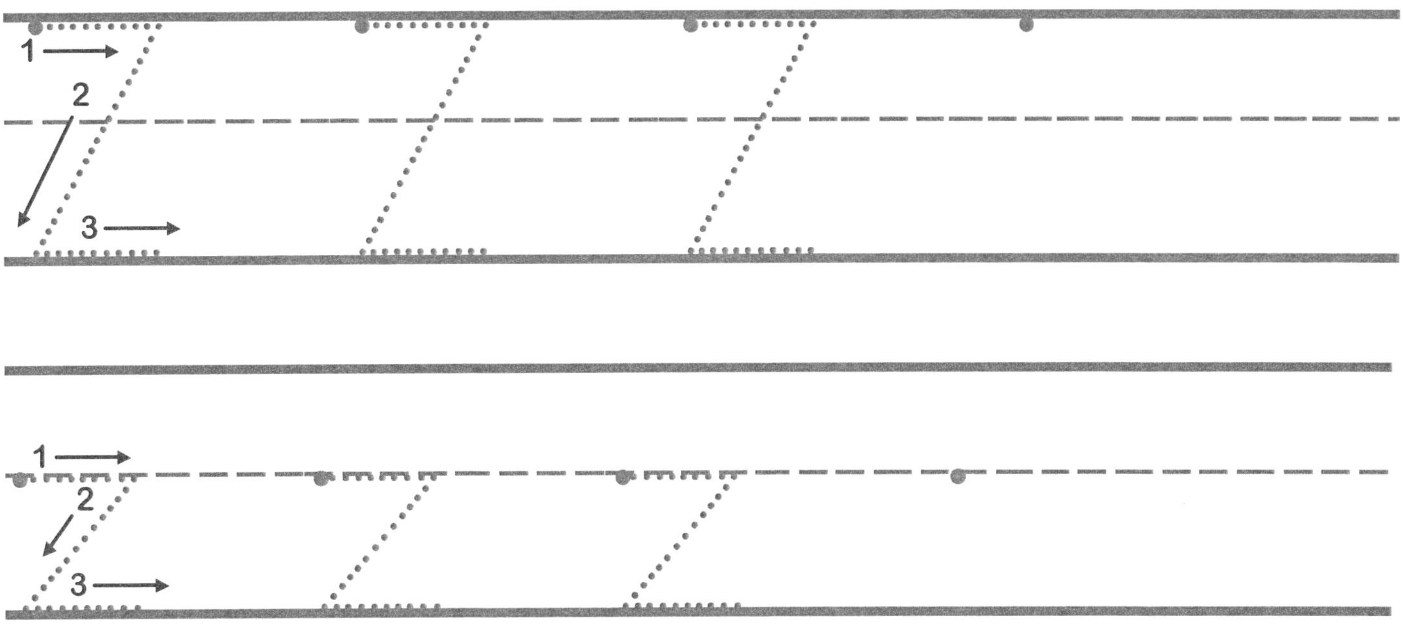

Alphabet Train Fun

Fill in the missing uppercase letters of the alphabet.
Colour the train.

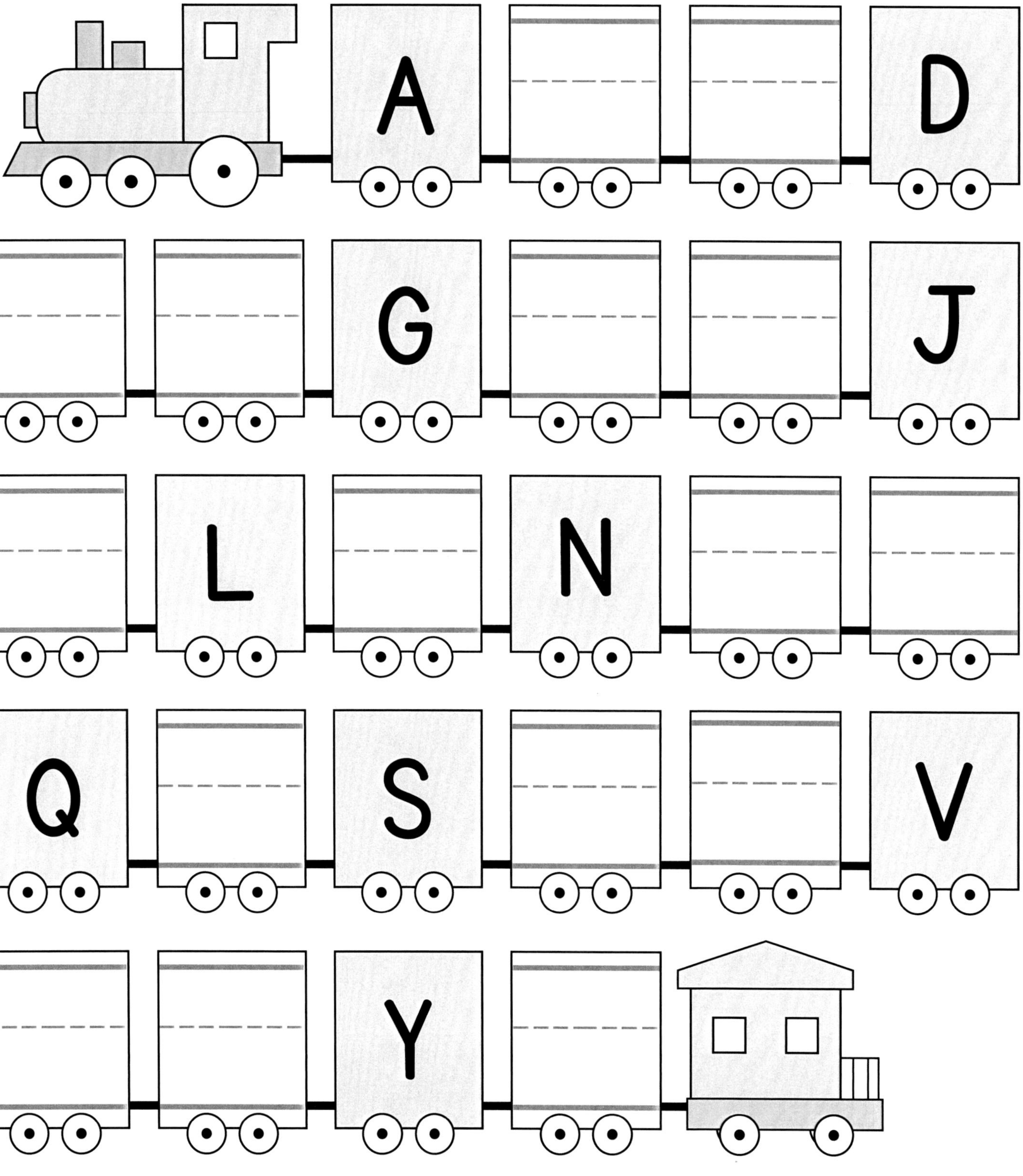

Reading Readiness

Beginning Letter Sounds

Colour the pictures that have the beginning sound of the letter in the box.

A

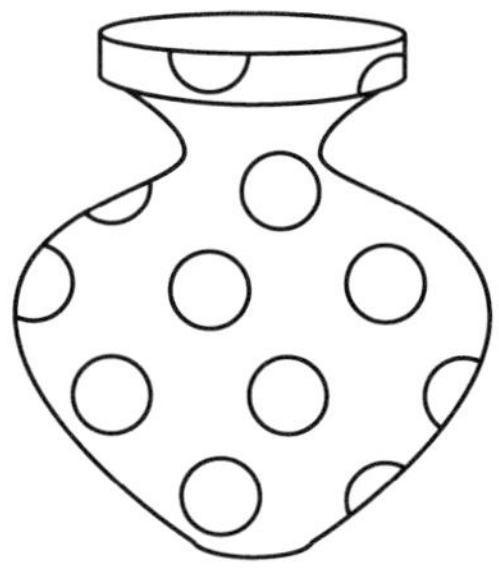

Beginning Letter Sounds

Colour the pictures that have the beginning sound of the letter in the box.

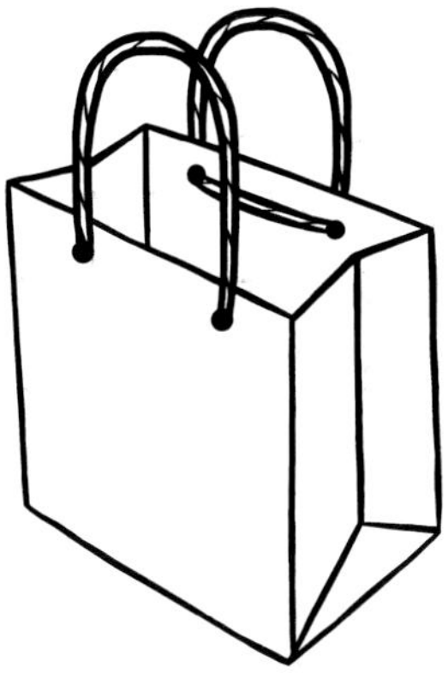

B

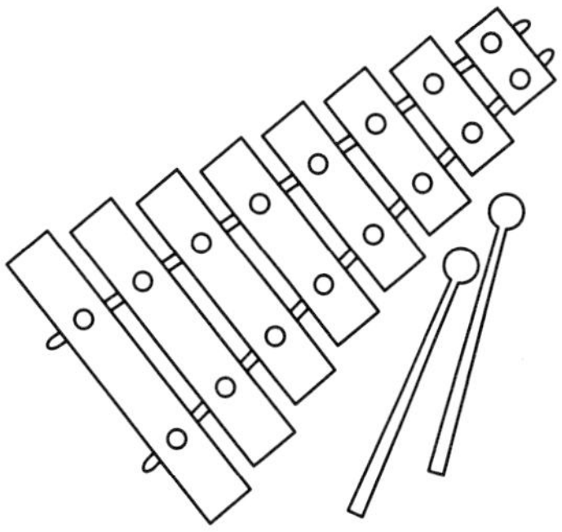

Beginning Letter Sounds

Colour the pictures that have the beginning sound of the letter in the box.

C

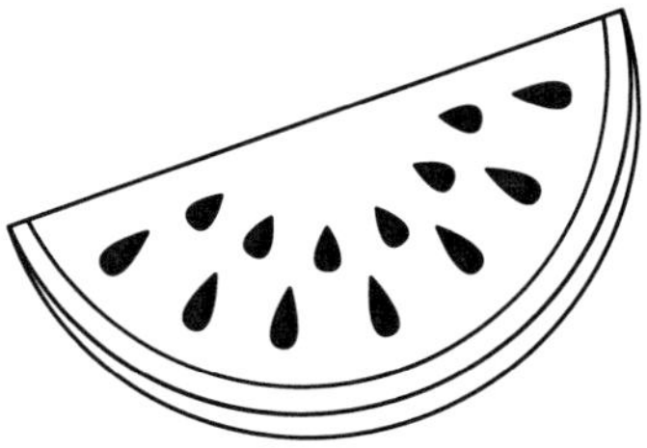

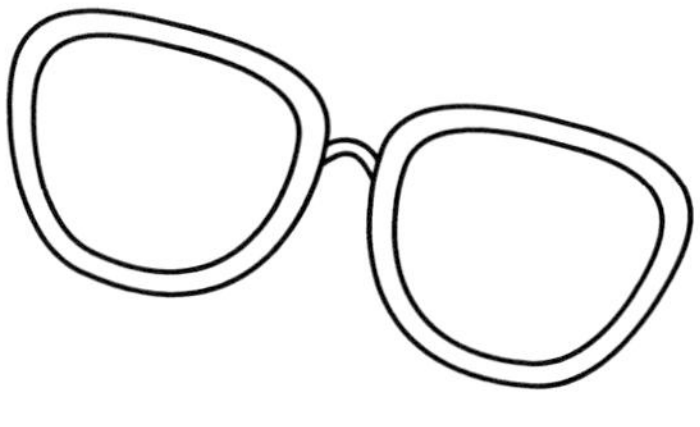

Beginning Letter Sounds

Colour the pictures that have the beginning sound of the letter in the box.

D

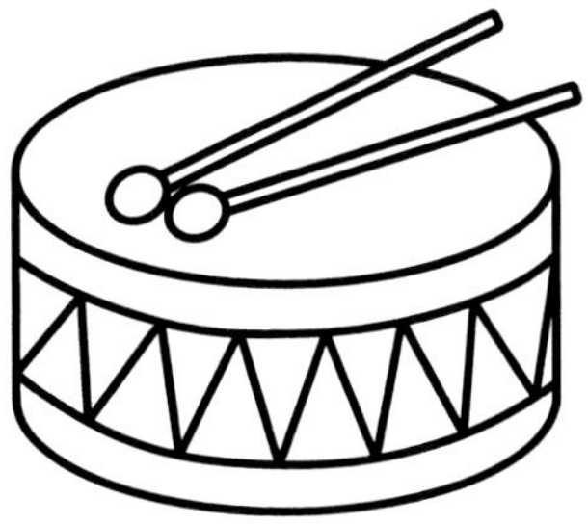

Beginning Letter Sounds

Colour the pictures that have the beginning sound of the letter in the box.

E

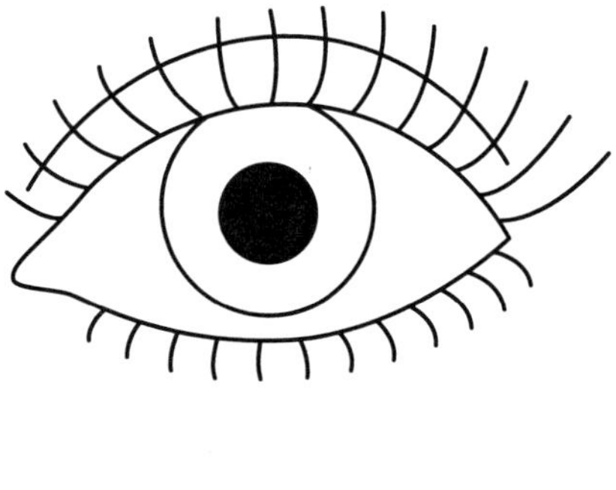

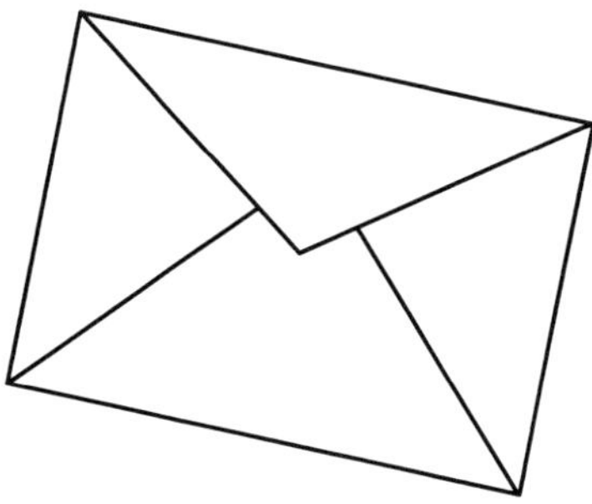

Beginning Letter Sounds

Colour the pictures that have the beginning sound of the letter in the box.

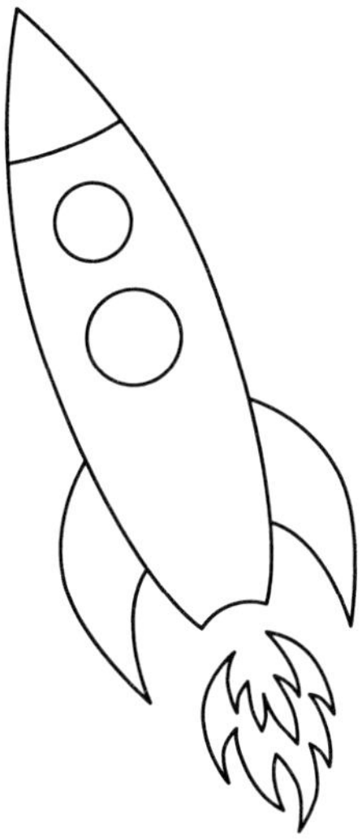

F

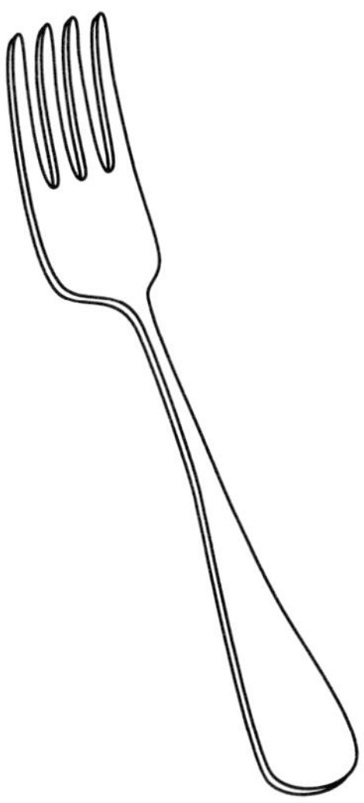

Beginning Letter Sounds

Colour the pictures that have the beginning sound of the letter in the box.

Beginning Letter Sounds

Colour the pictures that have the beginning sound of the letter in the box.

Beginning Letter Sounds

Colour the pictures that have the beginning sound of the letter in the box.

Beginning Letter Sounds

Colour the pictures that have the beginning sound of the letter in the box.

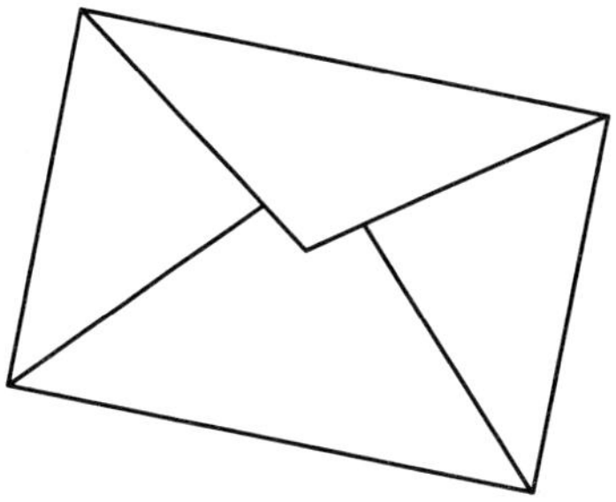

J

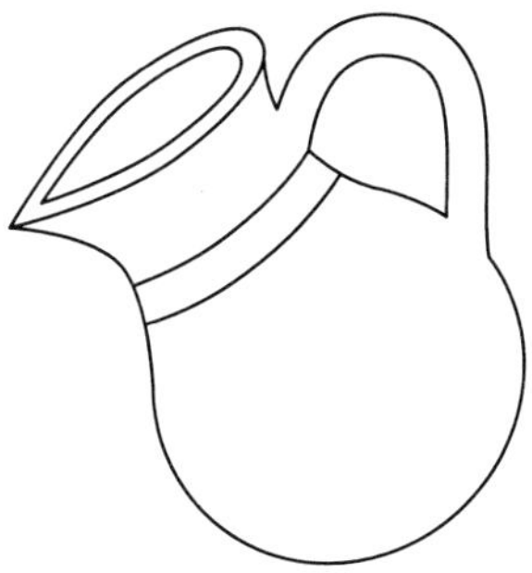

Beginning Letter Sounds

Colour the pictures that have the beginning sound of the letter in the box.

Beginning Letter Sounds

Colour the pictures that have the beginning sound of the letter in the box.

Beginning Letter Sounds

Colour the pictures that have the beginning sound of the letter in the box.

Beginning Letter Sounds

Colour the pictures that have the beginning sound of the letter in the box.

N

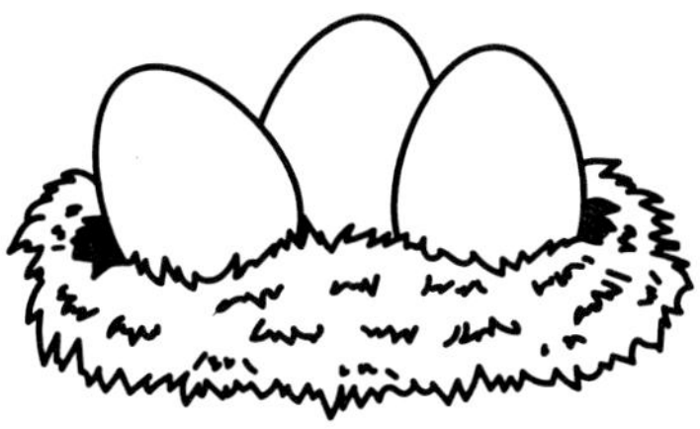

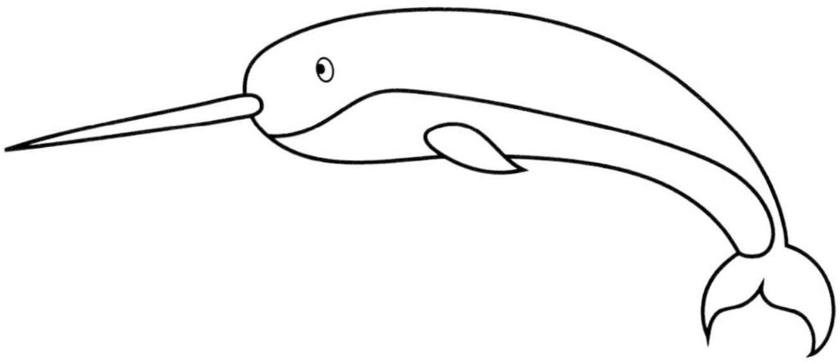

Beginning Letter Sounds

Colour the pictures that have the beginning sound of the letter in the box.

Beginning Letter Sounds

Colour the pictures that have the beginning sound of the letter in the box.

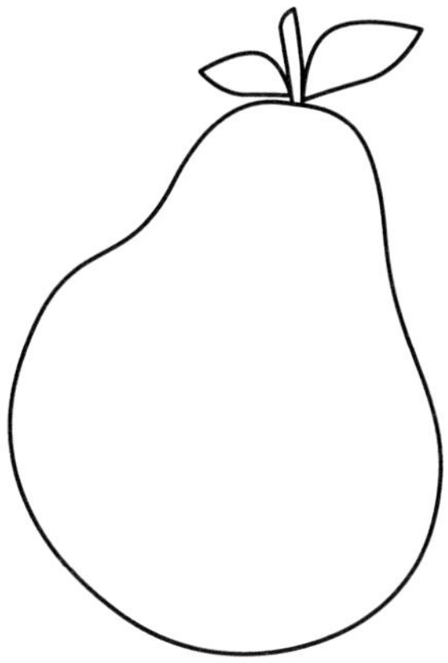

P

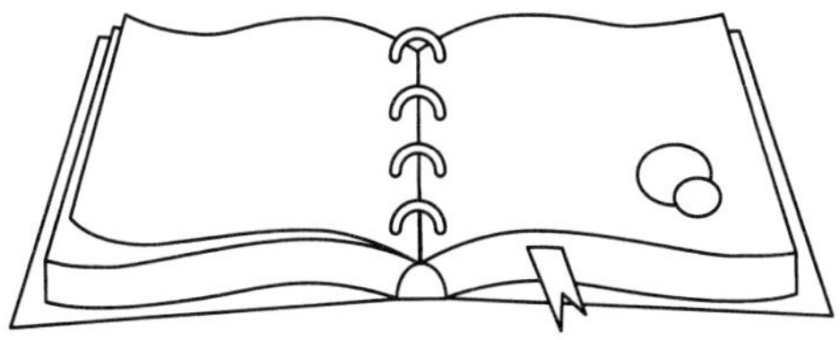

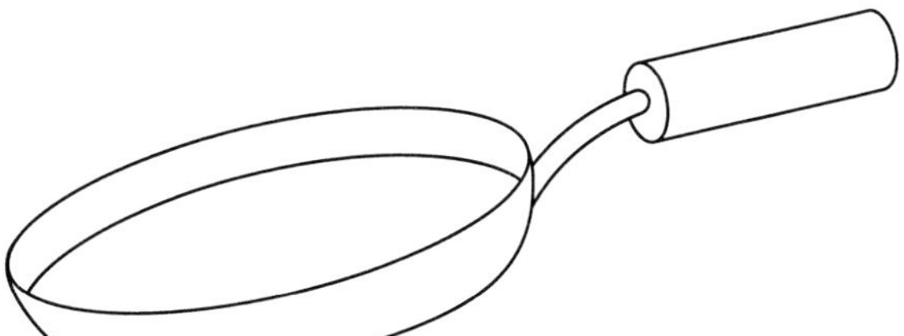

Beginning Letter Sounds

Colour the pictures that have the beginning sound of the letter in the box.

Beginning Letter Sounds

Colour the pictures that have the beginning sound of the letter in the box.

Beginning Letter Sounds

Colour the pictures that have the beginning sound of the letter in the box.

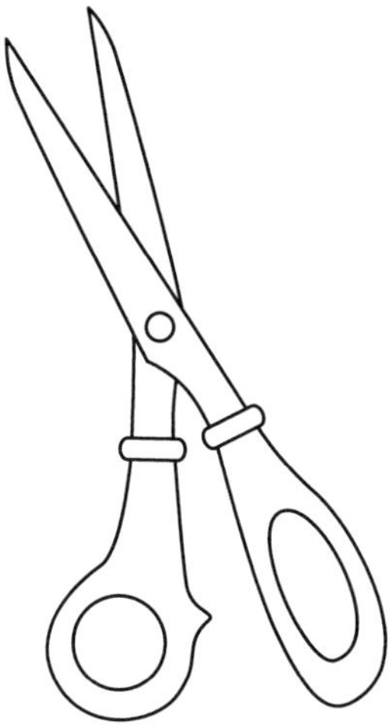

S

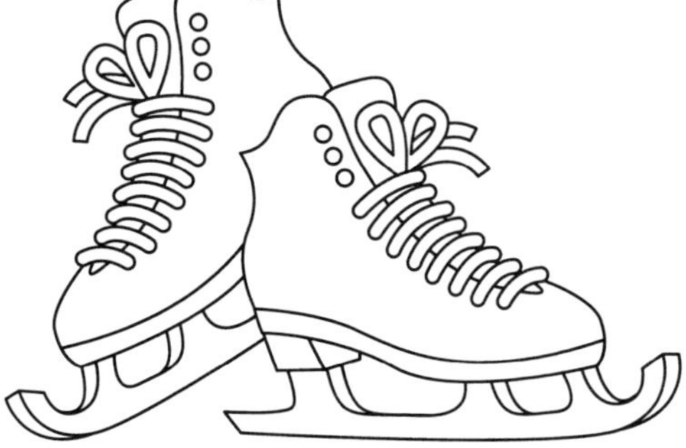

Beginning Letter Sounds

Colour the pictures that have the beginning sound of the letter in the box.

Beginning Letter Sounds

Colour the pictures that have the beginning sound of the letter in the box.

U

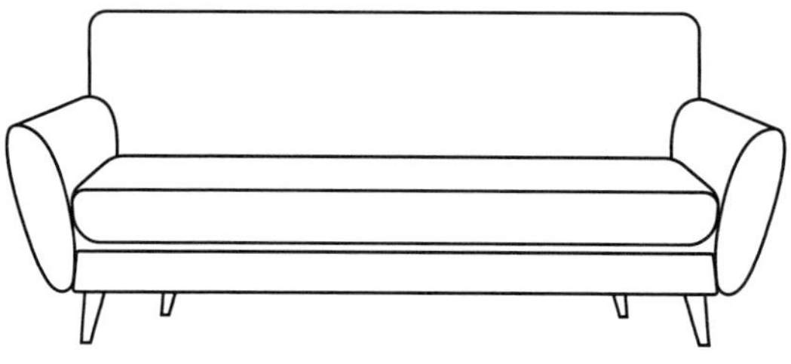

Beginning Letter Sounds

Colour the pictures that have the beginning sound of the letter in the box.

V

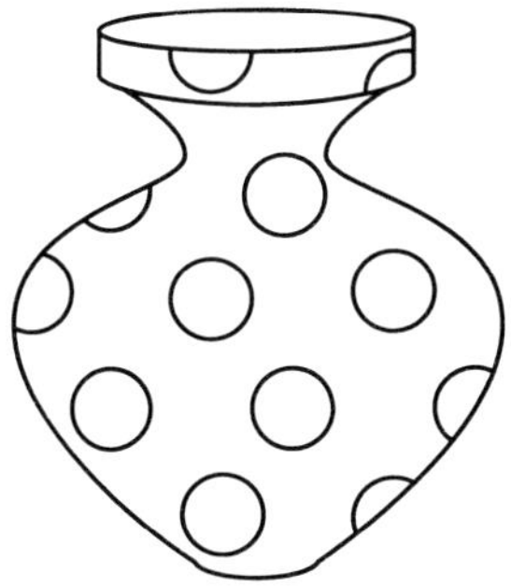

Beginning Letter Sounds

Colour the pictures that have the beginning sound of the letter in the box.

W

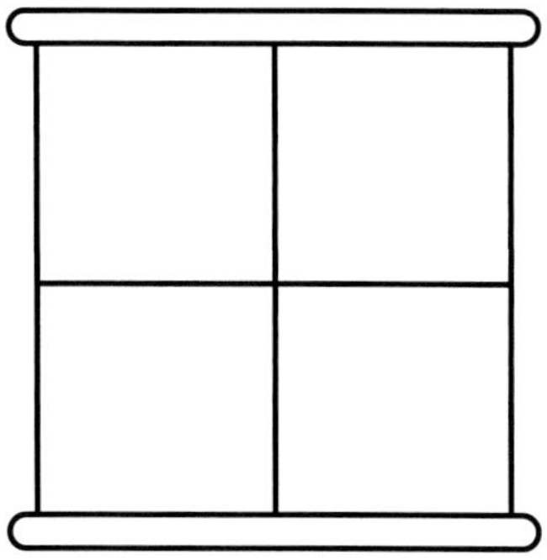

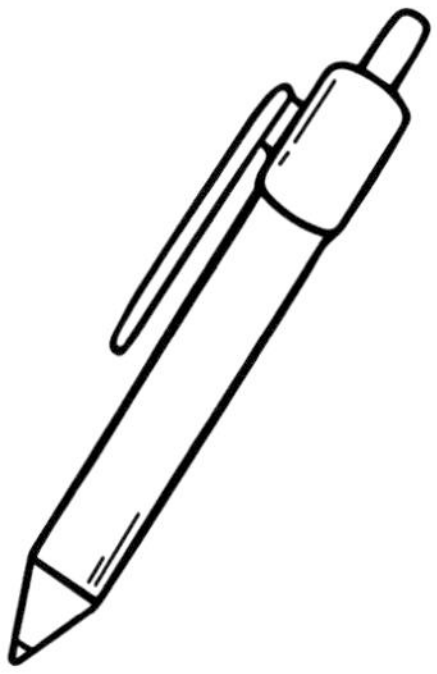

Beginning Letter Sounds

Colour the pictures that have the beginning sound of the letter in the box.

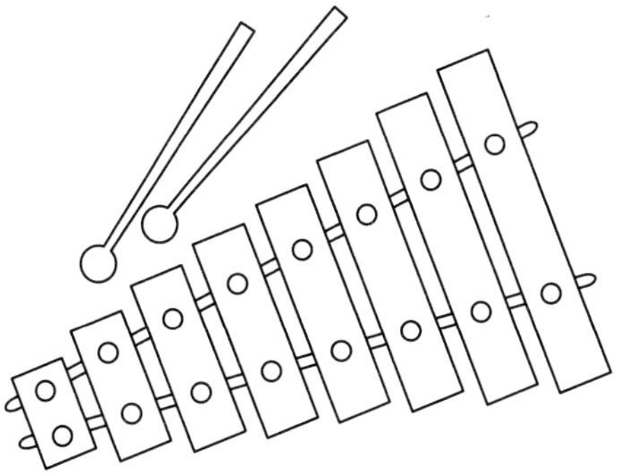

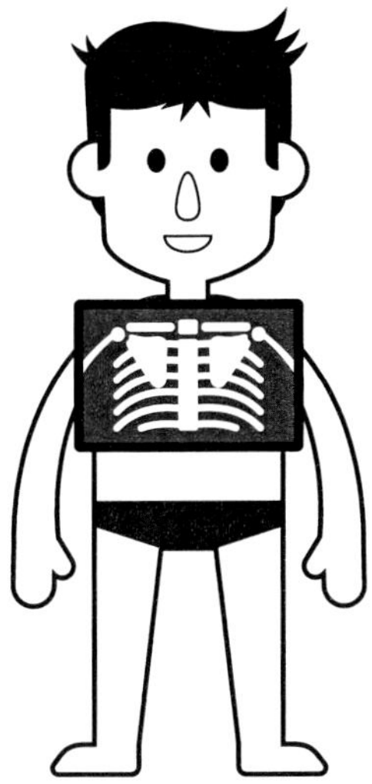

X

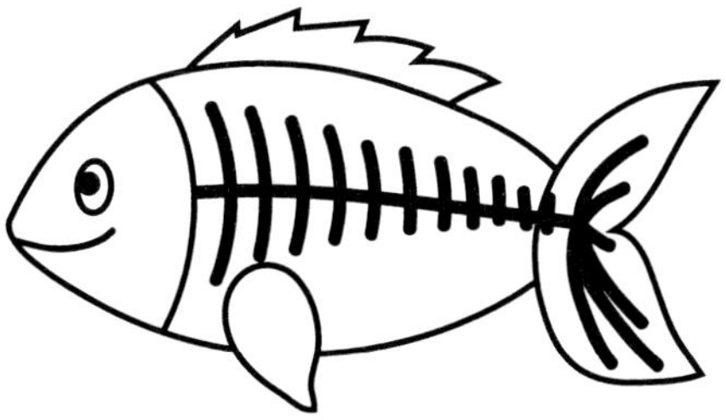

Beginning Letter Sounds

Colour the pictures that have the beginning sound of the letter in the box.

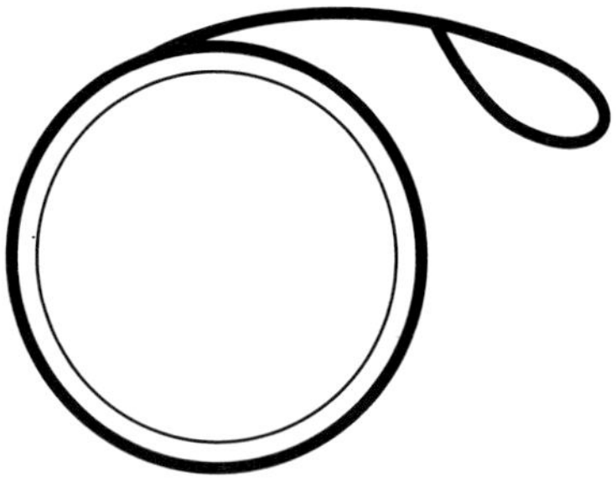

y

Beginning Letter Sounds

Colour the pictures that have the beginning sound of the letter in the box.

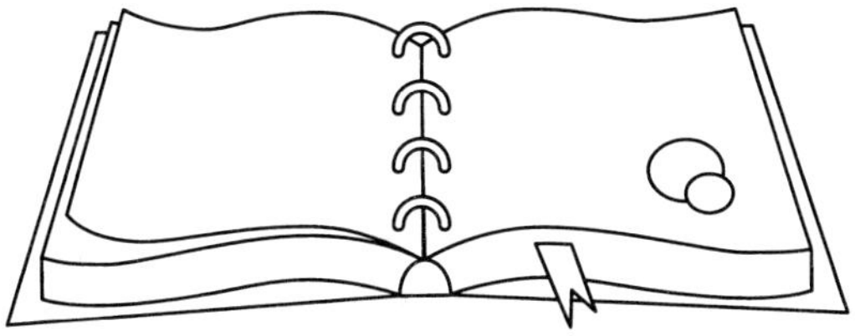

Z

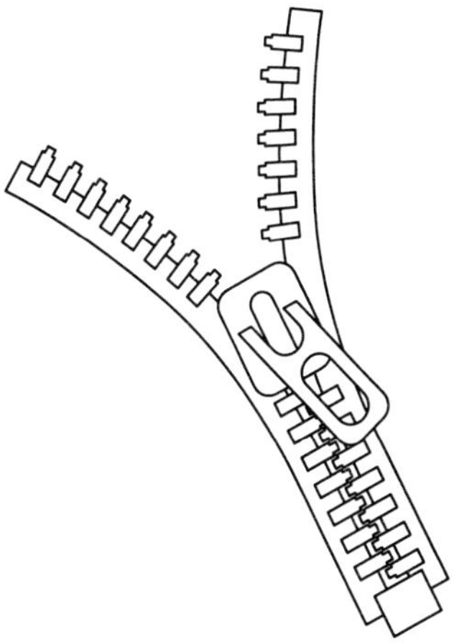

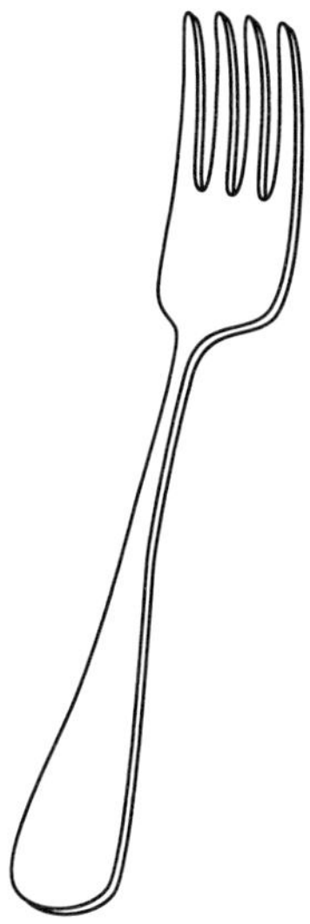

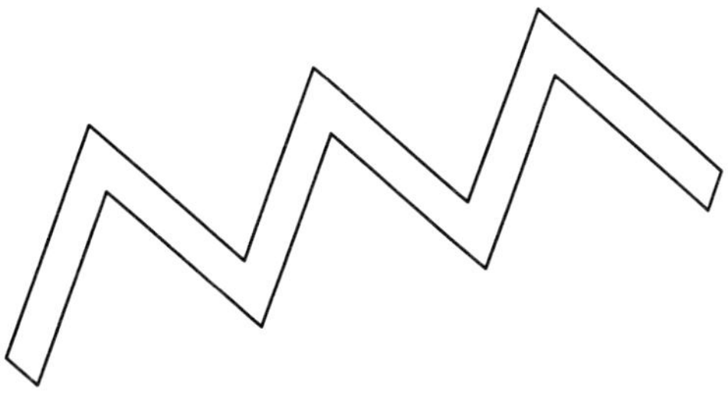

Beginning Letter Sounds

Say the name of the animal out loud. Print the beginning letter sound.

Colour the zebra. red

Colour the frog. green

Colour the unicorn. purple

Colour the narwhal. blue

Beginning Letter Sounds

Say the name of the animal out loud. Print the beginning letter sound.

Colour the kangaroo. purple Colour the dog. orange

Colour the seagull. yellow Colour the lizard. green

Beginning Letter Sounds

Say the name of the animal out loud. Print the beginning letter sound.

Colour the wolf. blue

Colour the panda. red

Colour the quail. green

Colour the bee. yellow

Beginning Letter Sounds

Say the name of the animal out loud. Print the beginning letter sound.

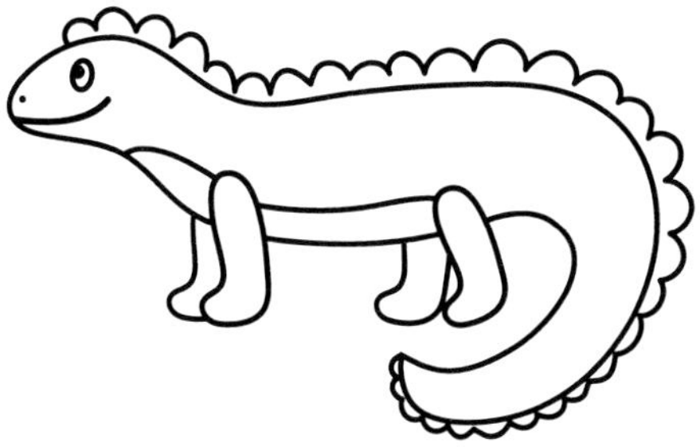

Colour the eagle. orange

Colour the turtle. green

Colour the ostrich. purple

Colour the iguana. blue

Beginning Letter Sounds

Say the name of the animal out loud. Print the beginning letter sound.

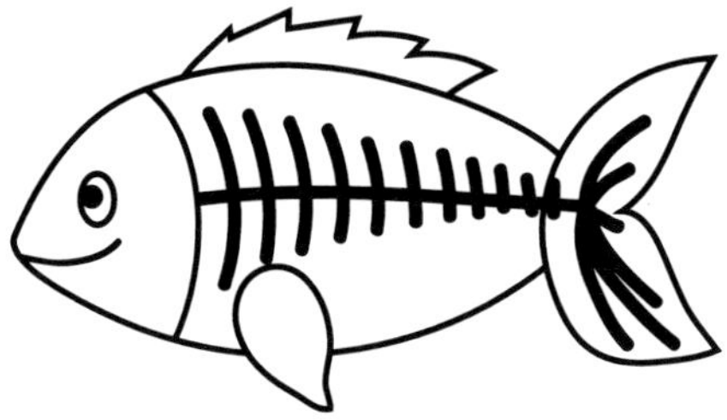

Colour the goat. red

Colour the x-ray fish. green

Colour the ant. yellow

Colour the horse. blue

Beginning Letter Sounds

Say the name of the animal out loud. Print the beginning letter sound.

Colour the cow. red

Colour the jellyfish. blue

Colour the yak. green

Colour the vulture. black

Beginning Letter Sounds

Say the name of the animal out loud. Print the beginning letter sound.

Colour the mouse.	orange	Colour the raccoon.	purple
Colour the octopus.	red	Colour the snail.	blue

Beginning Letter Sounds

Draw a picture of your favourite animal.

Print the beginning letter sound of the animal.

Beginning Letter Sound Match

Say the name of the object out loud. Draw a line from the object to the correct beginning letter sound. Colour the pictures.

n

e

Beginning Letter Sound Match

Say the name of the object out loud. Draw a line from the object to the correct beginning letter sound. Colour the pictures.

p

a

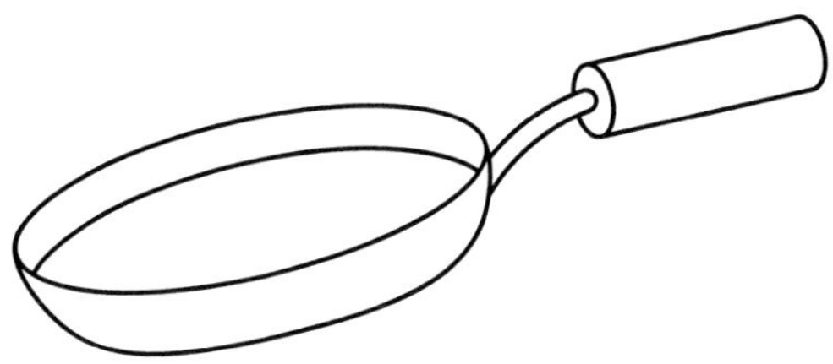

Beginning Letter Sound Match

Say the name of the object out loud. Draw a line from the object to the correct beginning letter sound. Colour the pictures.

t

o

Beginning Letter Sound Match

Say the name of the object out loud. Draw a line from the object to the correct beginning letter sound. Colour the pictures.

b

l

Beginning Letter Sound Match

Say the name of the object out loud. Draw a line from the object to the correct beginning letter sound. Colour the pictures.

s

c

Beginning Letter Sound Match

Say the name of the object out loud. Draw a line from the object to the correct beginning letter sound. Colour the pictures.

m

d

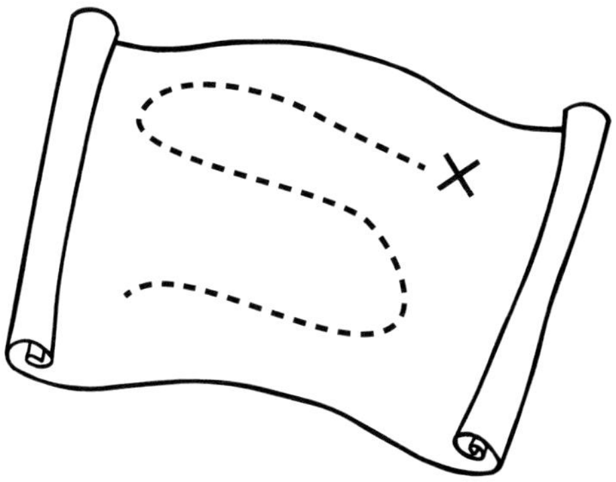

Connect the Dots: Alphabet

Think About It!

What do turtles do on their birthdays?
They shell-ebrate!

Numbers and Counting Skills

Number 0

0

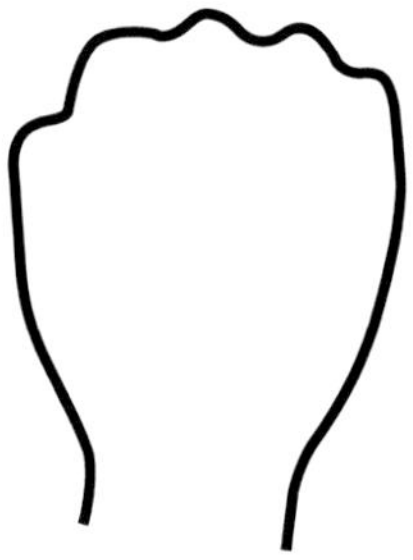

Trace and print the number.
Circle your best 0 on the line.

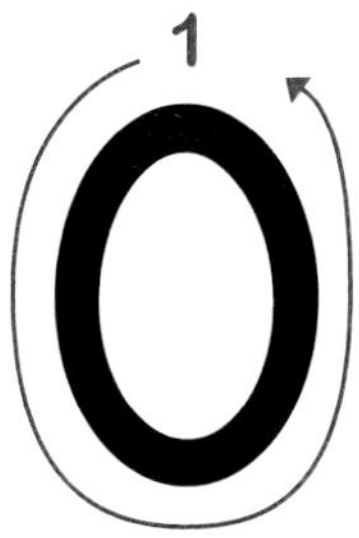

Number 0

Count the gumballs in the machine.
Circle the correct number.

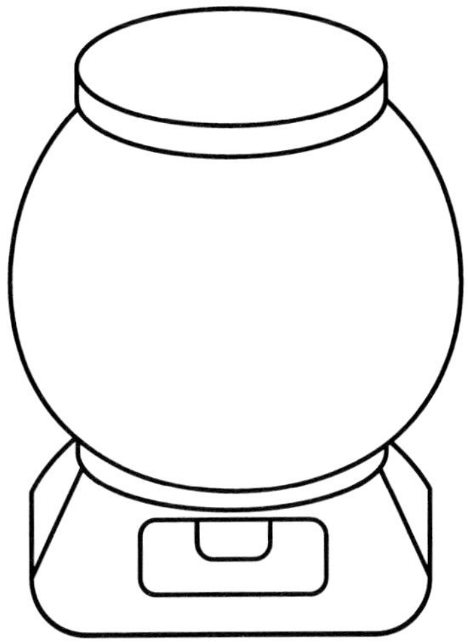

0 1 2

Draw ●s to show the number 0.

Number 1

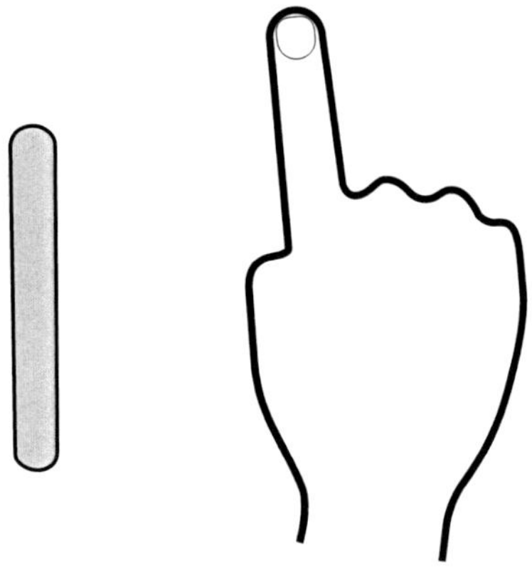

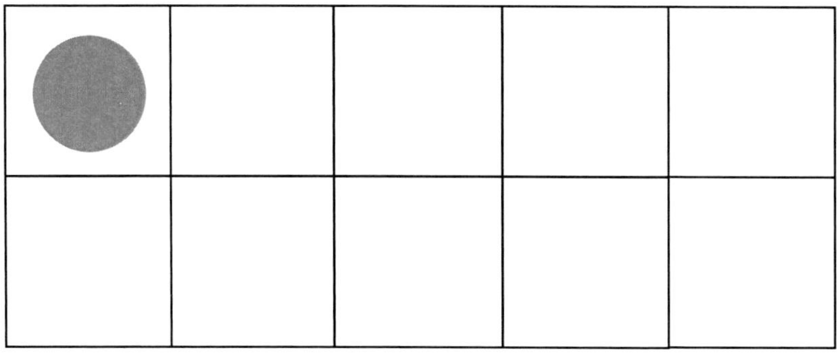

Trace and print the number.
Circle your best 1 on the line.

Number 1

Count the narwhal.
Circle the correct number.

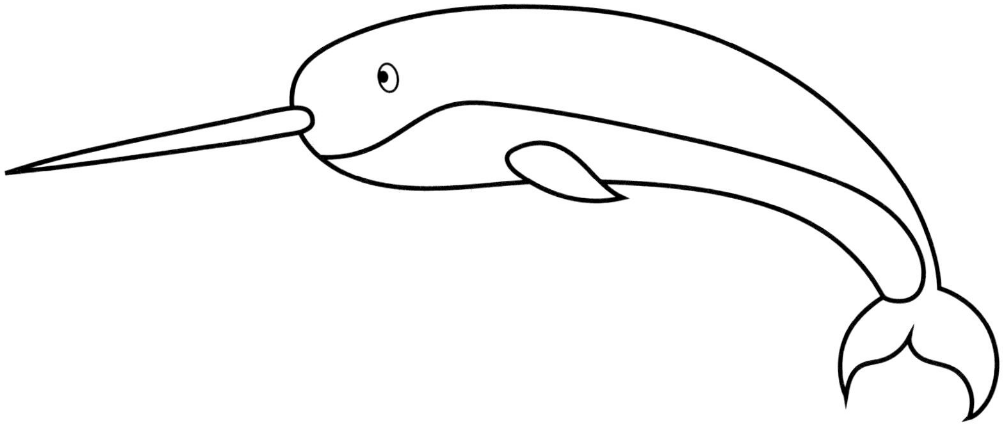

0 1 2

Draw ●s to show the number 1.

Number 2

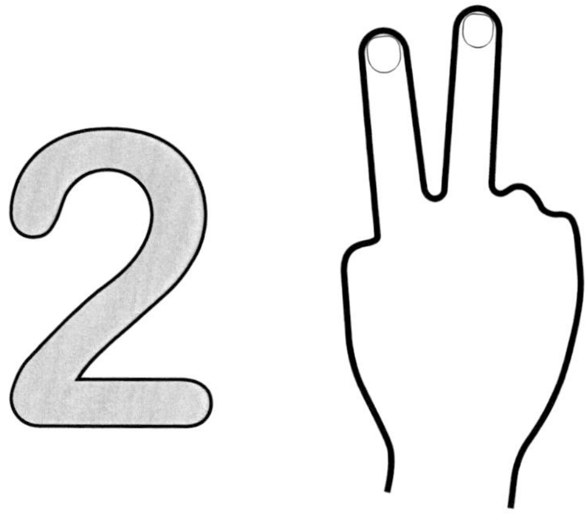

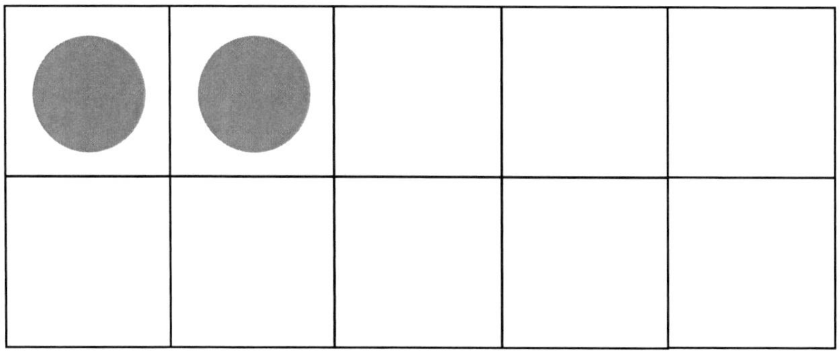

Trace and print the number.
Circle your best 2 on the line.

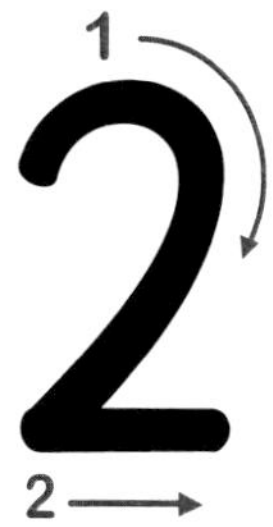

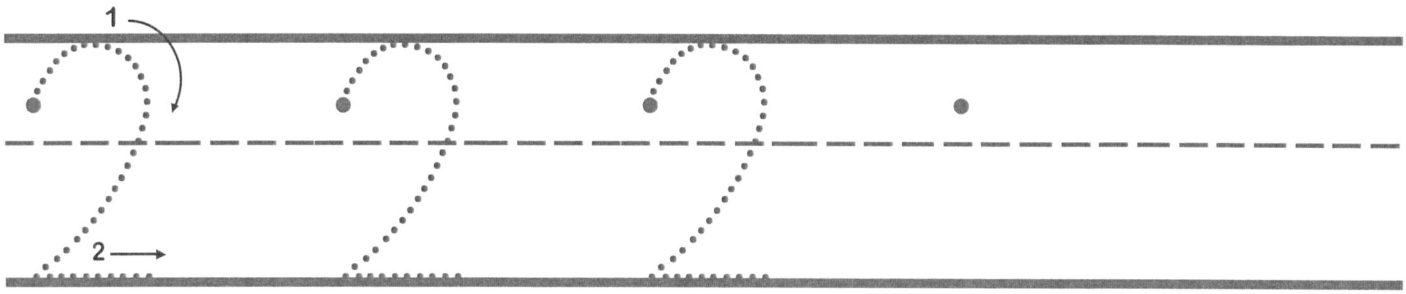

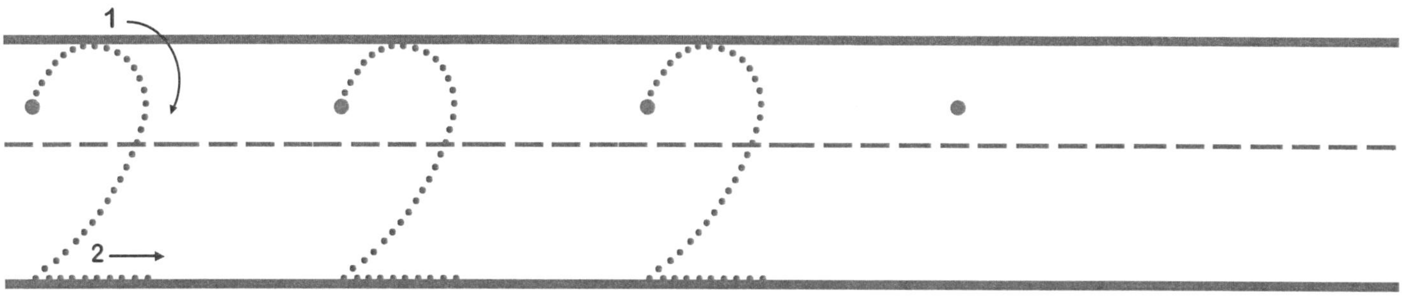

Number 2

Count the frogs.
Circle the correct number.

0 1 2

Draw ●s to show the number 2.

Number 3

3

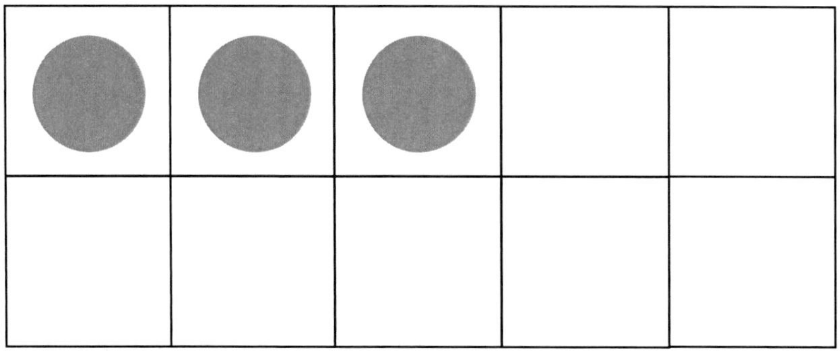

Trace and print the number.
Circle your best 3 on the line.

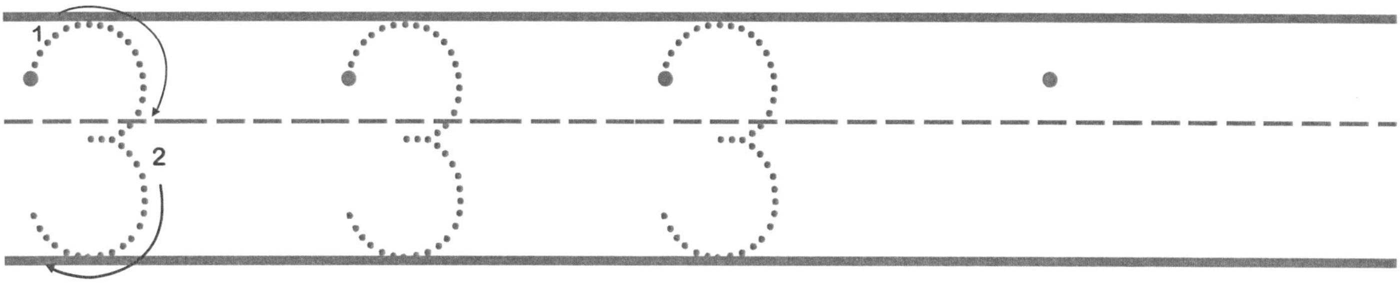

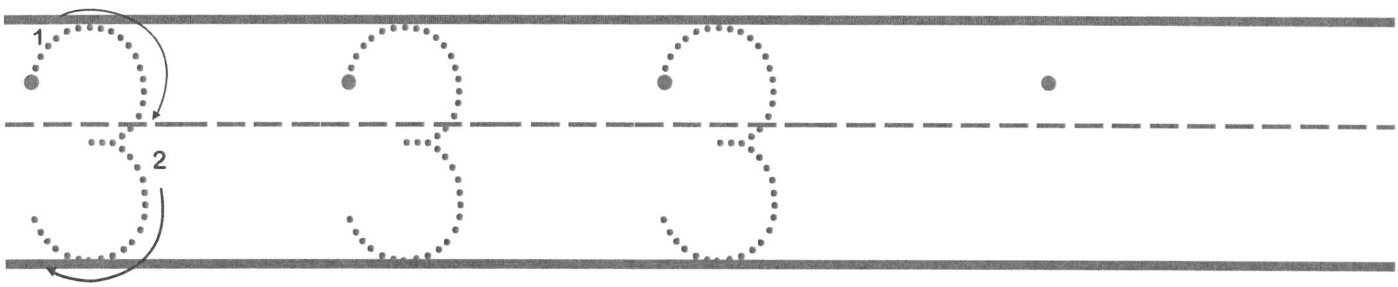

Number 3

Count the lizards.
Circle the correct number.

3 4 5

Draw ●s to show the number 3.

Number 4

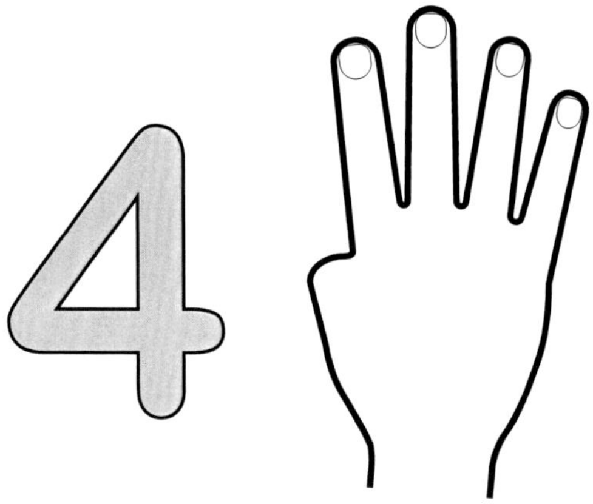

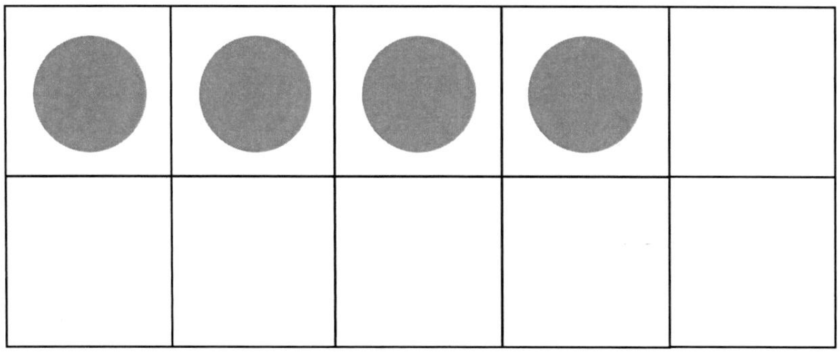

Trace and print the number.
Circle your best 4 on the line.

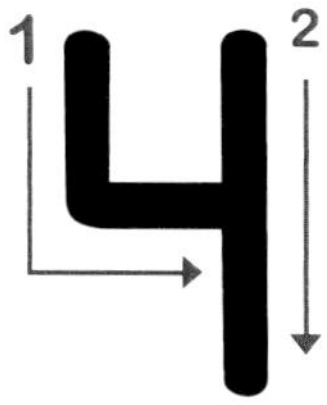

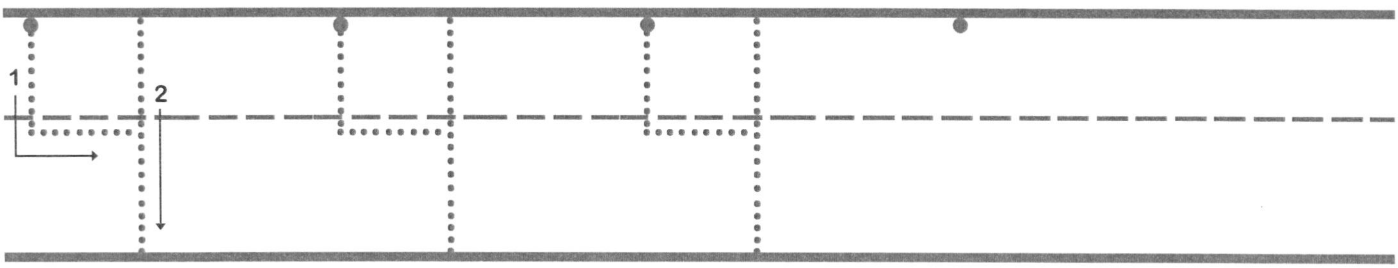

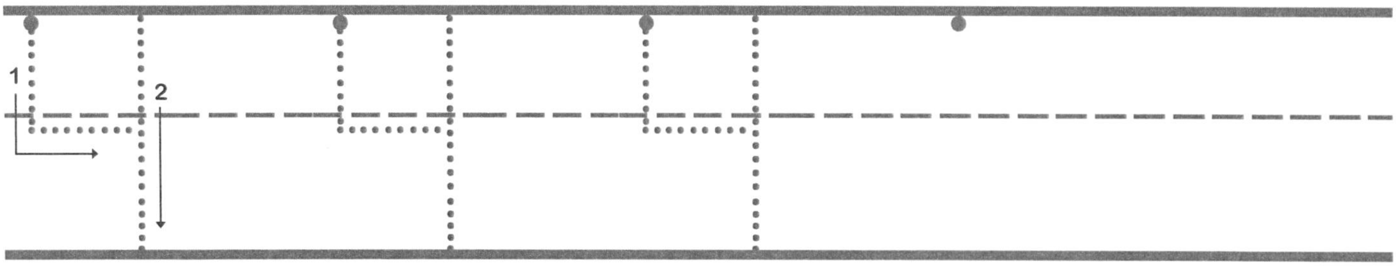

Number 4

Count the dogs.
Circle the correct number.

3 4 5

Draw ●s to show the number 4.

Number 5

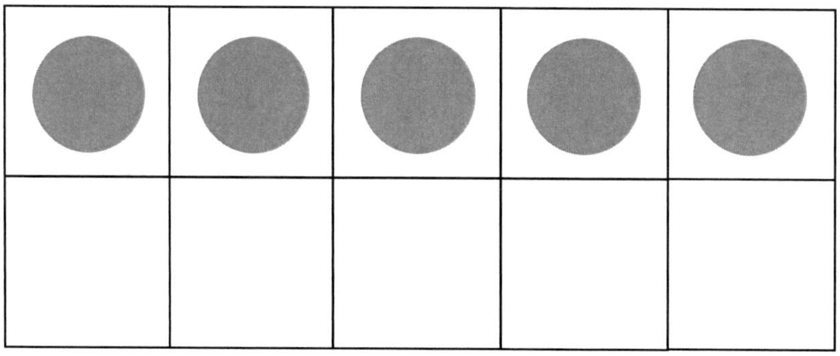

Trace and print the number.
Circle your best 5 on the line.

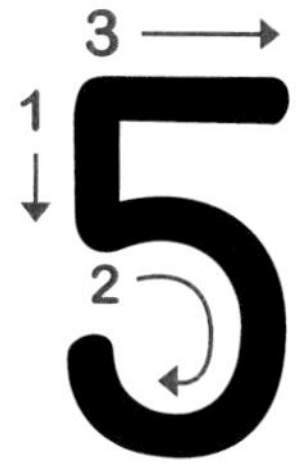

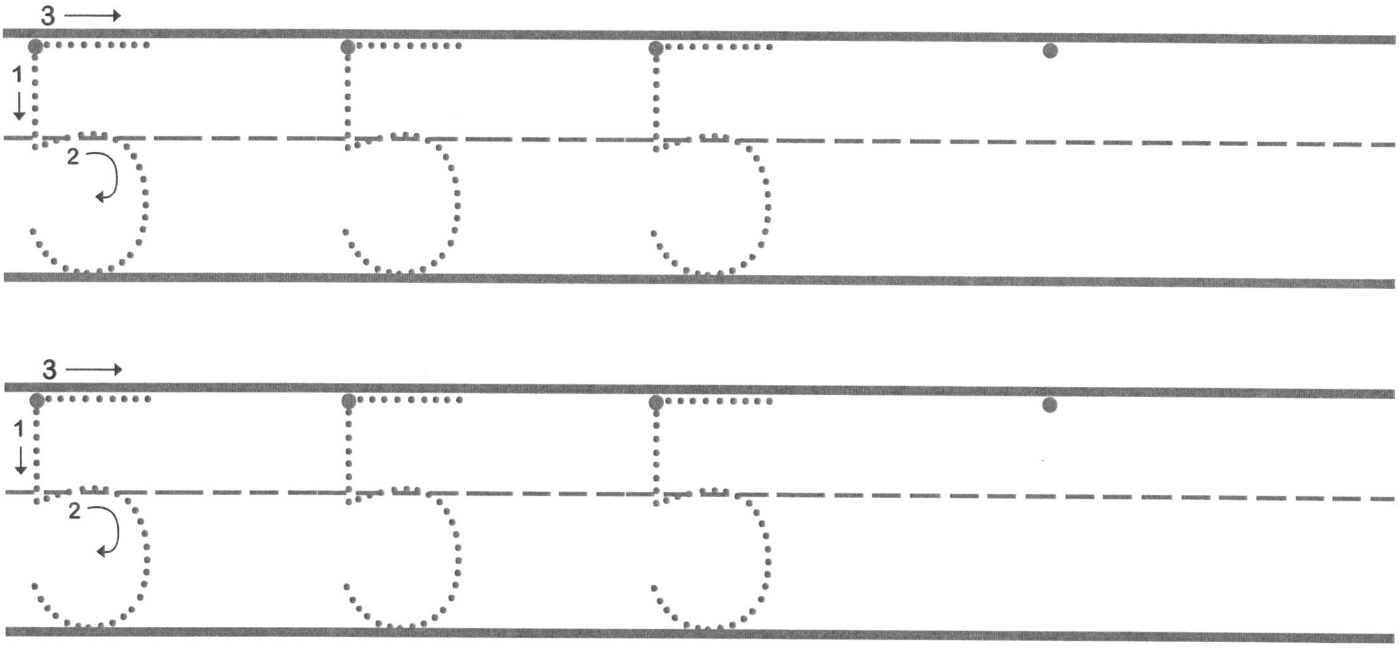

Number 5

Count the seagulls.
Circle the correct number.

3 4 5

Draw ●s to show the number 5.

Number 6

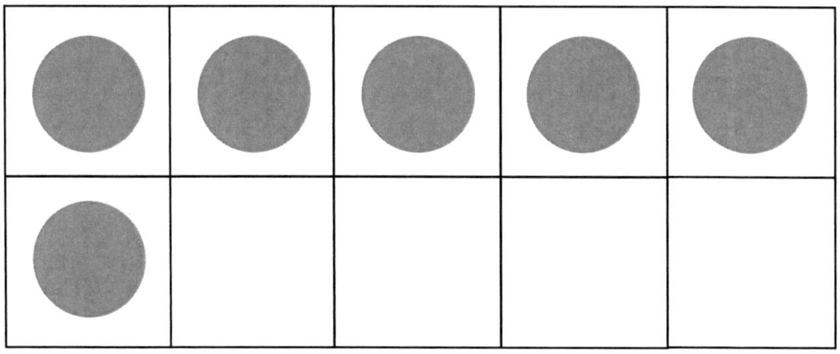

Trace and print the number.
Circle your best 6 on the line.

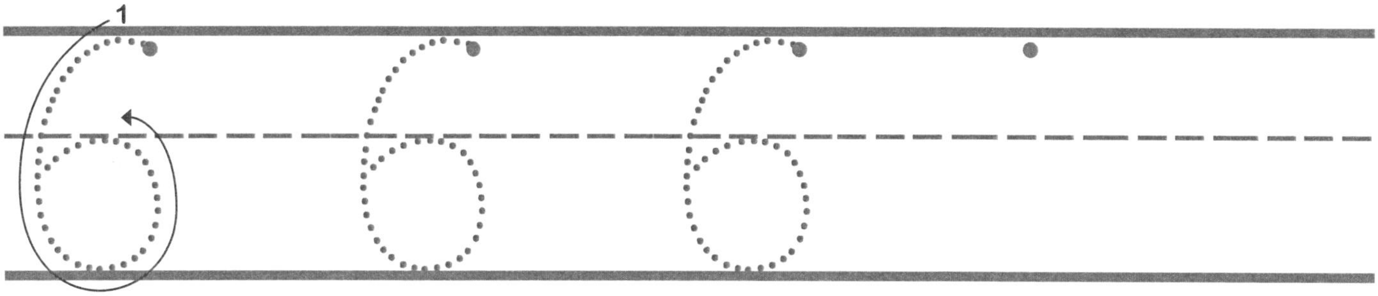

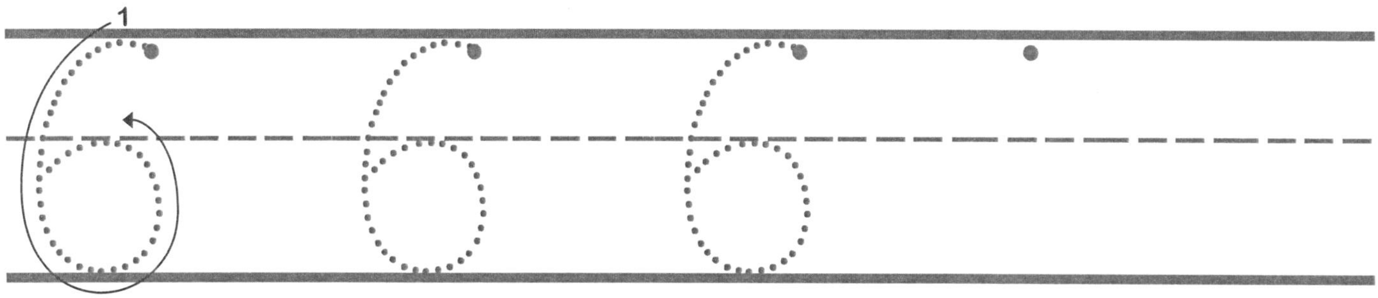

Number 6

Count the kangaroos.
Circle the correct number.

6 7 8

Draw ●s to show the number 6.

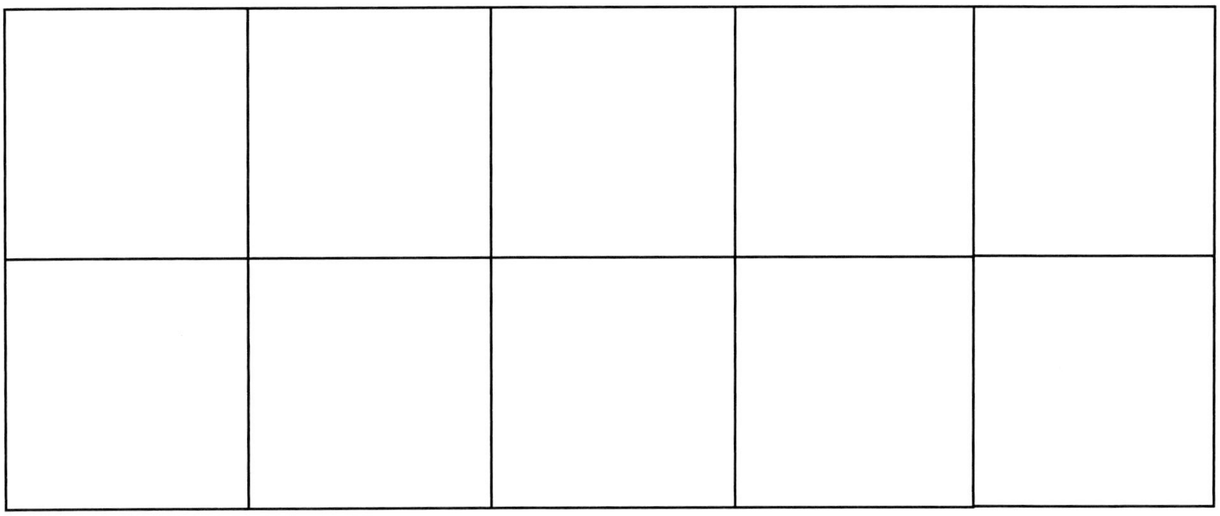

Number 7

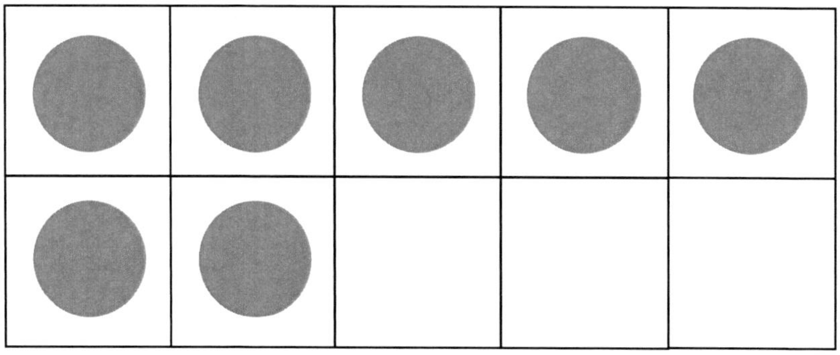

Trace and print the number.
Circle your best 7 on the line.

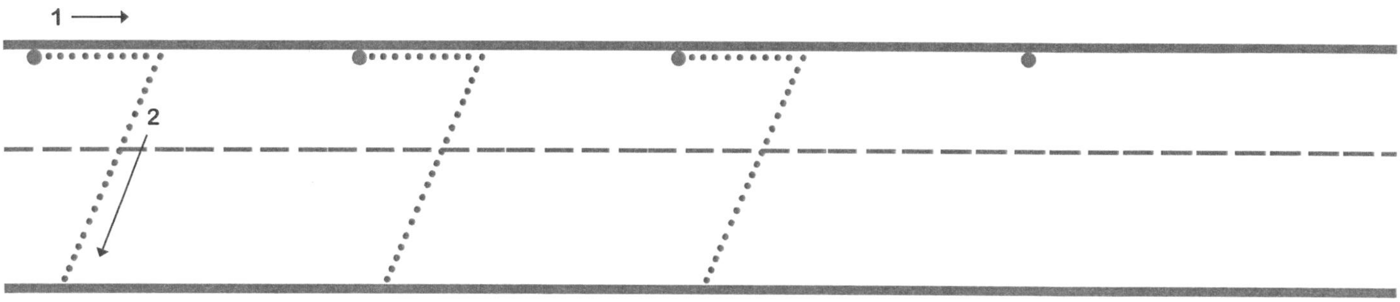

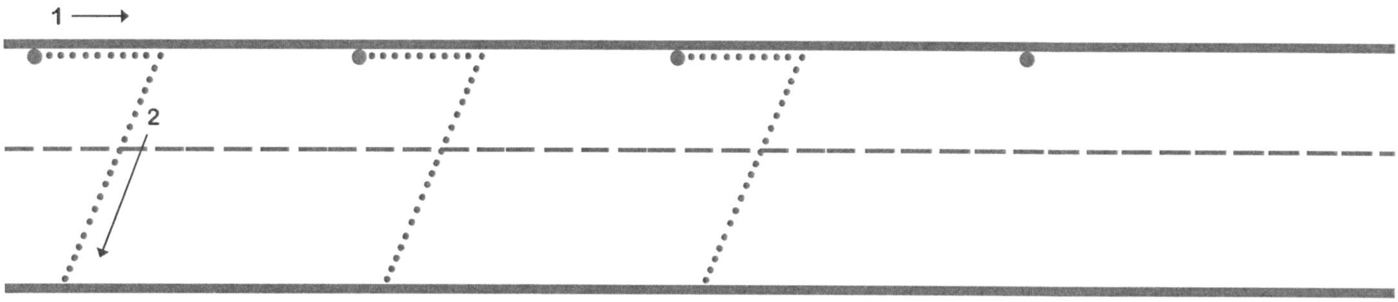

Number 7

Count the eagles.
Circle the correct number.

6 7 8

Draw ●s to show the number 7.

Number 8

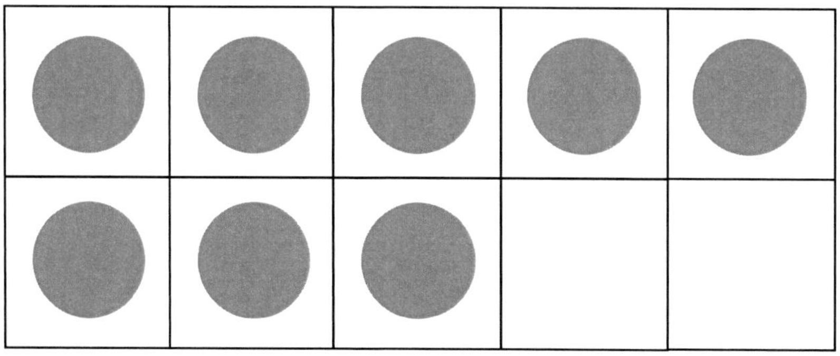

Trace and print the number.
Circle your best 8 on the line.

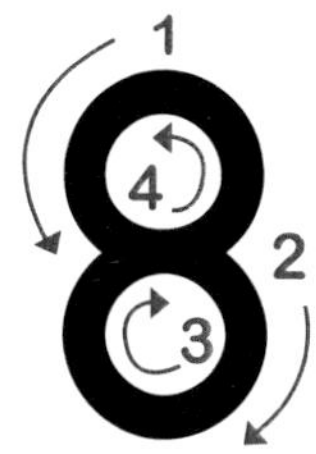

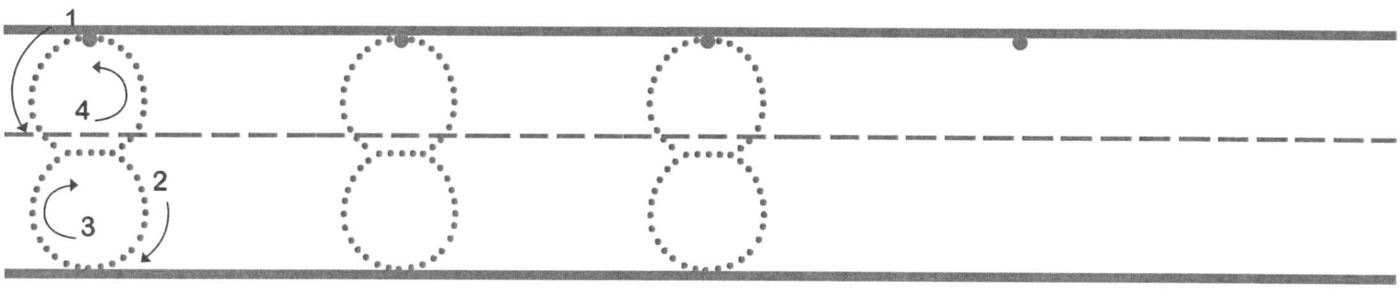

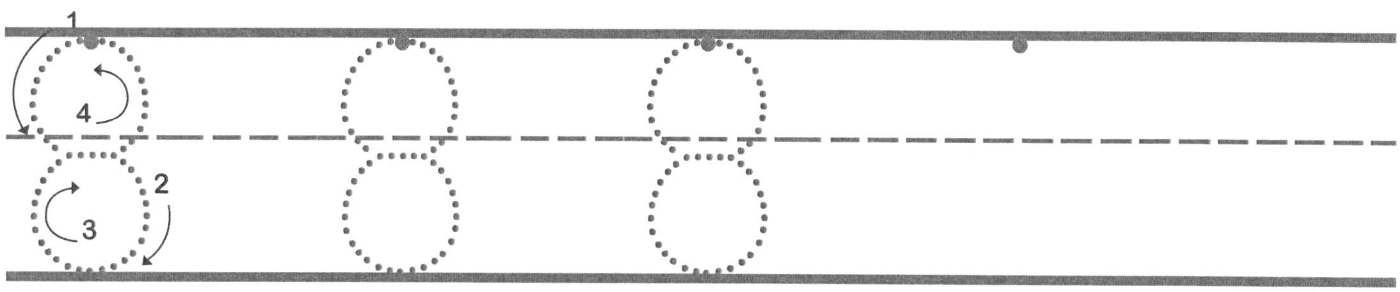

Number 8

Count the pandas.
Circle the correct number.

6 7 8

Draw s to show the number 8.

Number 9

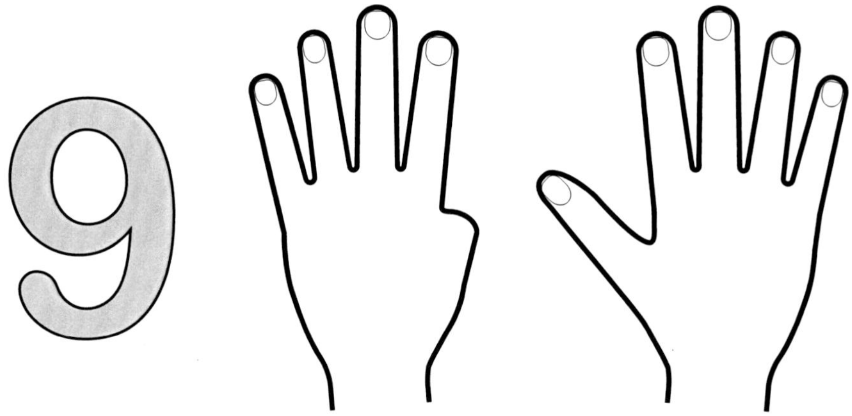

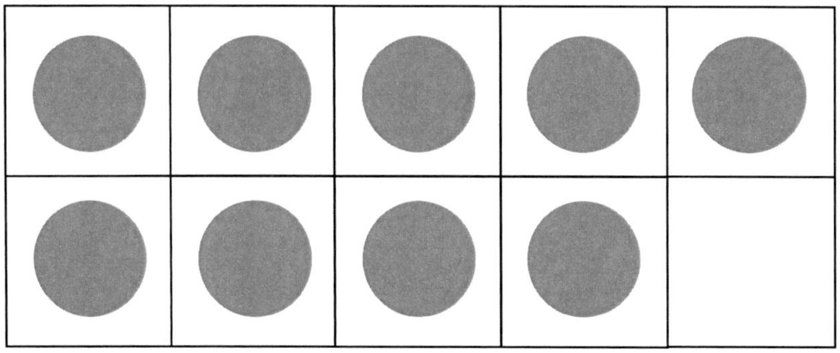

Trace and print the number.
Circle your best 9 on the line.

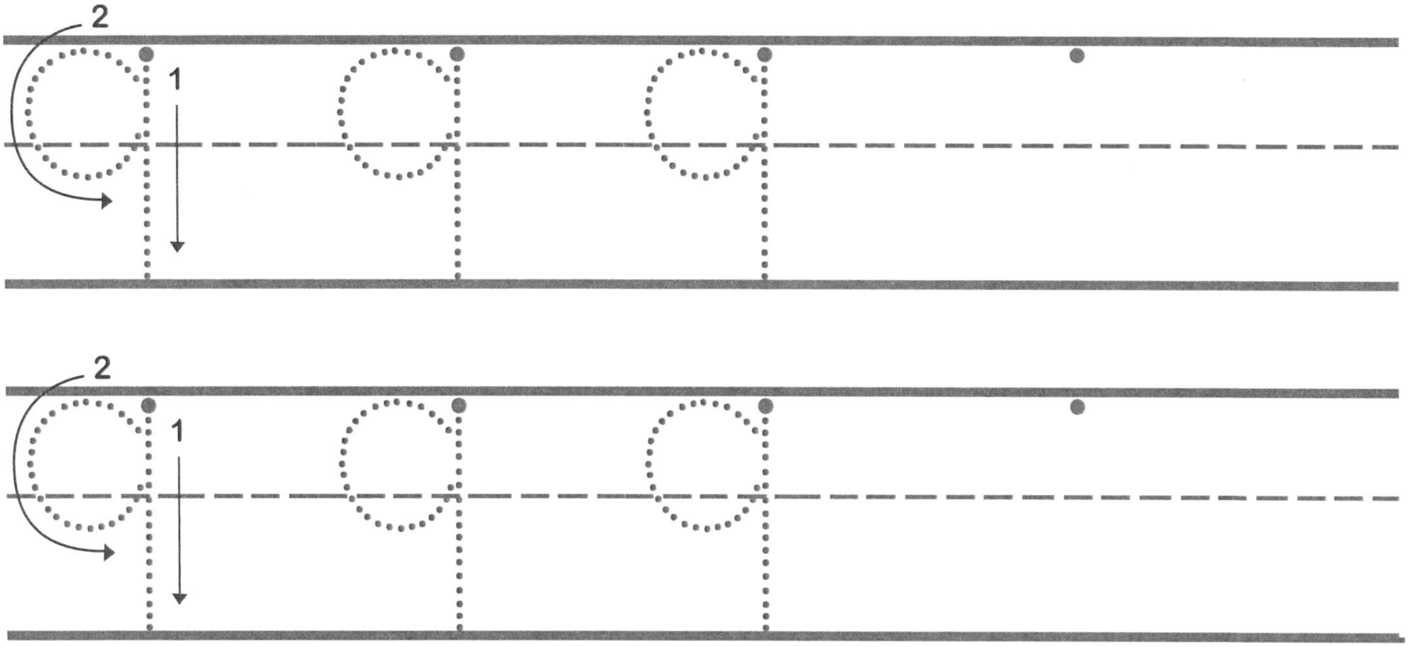

Number 9

Count the jellyfish.
Circle the correct number.

8 9 10

Draw ●s to show the number 9.

Number 10

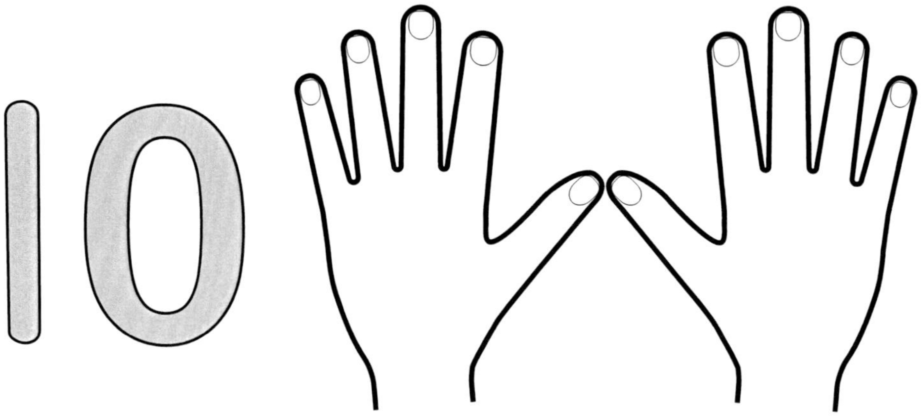

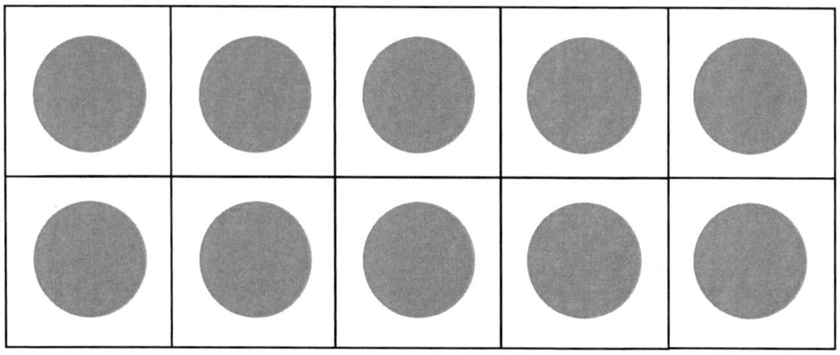

Trace and print the number.
Circle your best 10 on the line.

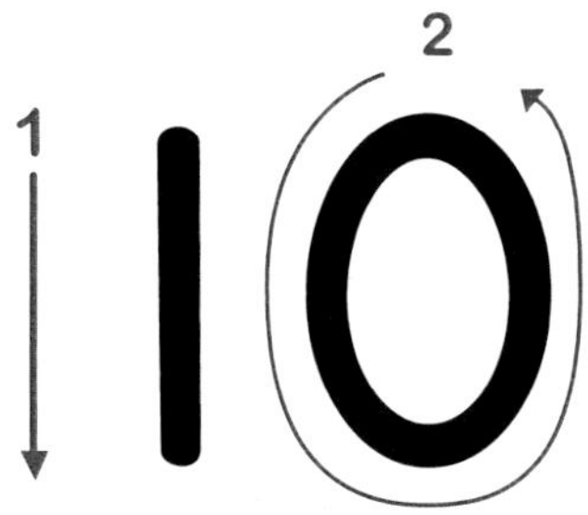

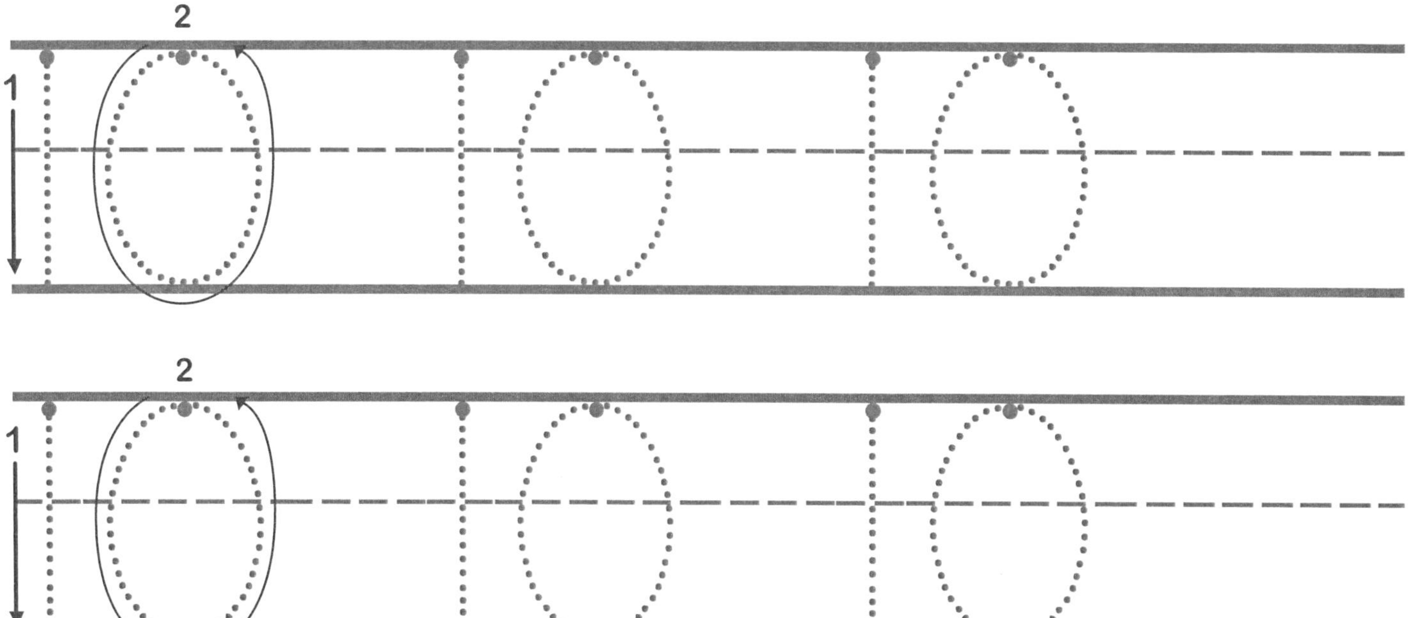

Number 10

Count the mice.
Circle the correct number.

8 9 10

Draw ●s to show the number 10.

Counting Practice to 10

How many fingers are there? Use your fingers to count.
Circle the correct number.

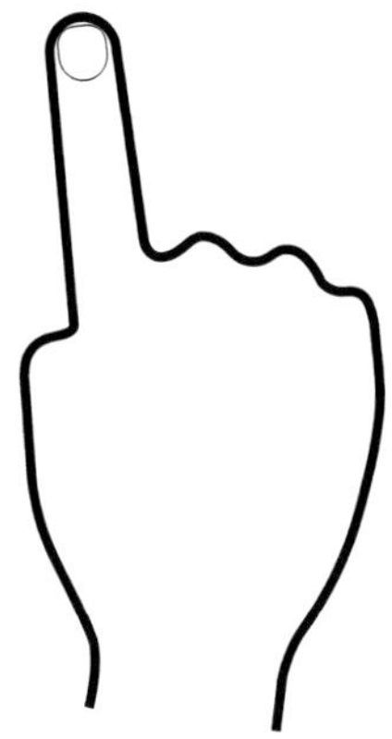

1	2	3

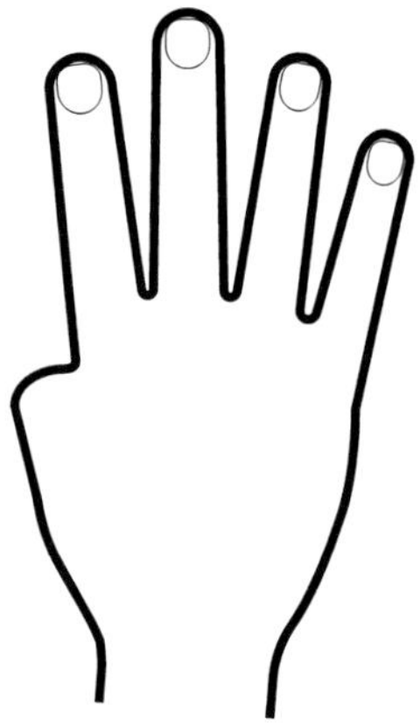

3	4	5

2	3	4

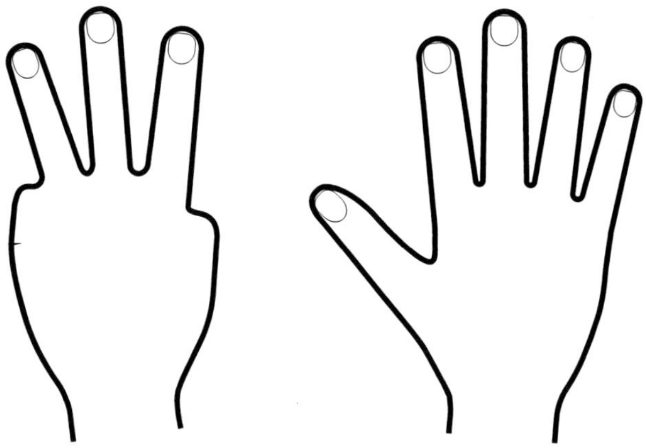

7	8	9

Counting Practice to 10

How many fingers are there? Use your fingers to count.
Circle the correct number.

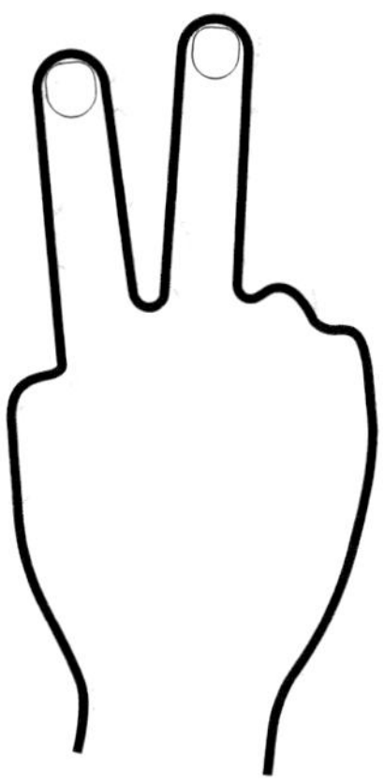

1	2	3

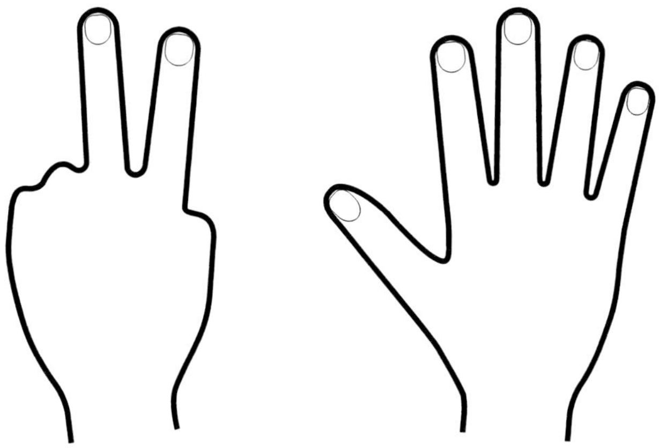

6	7	8

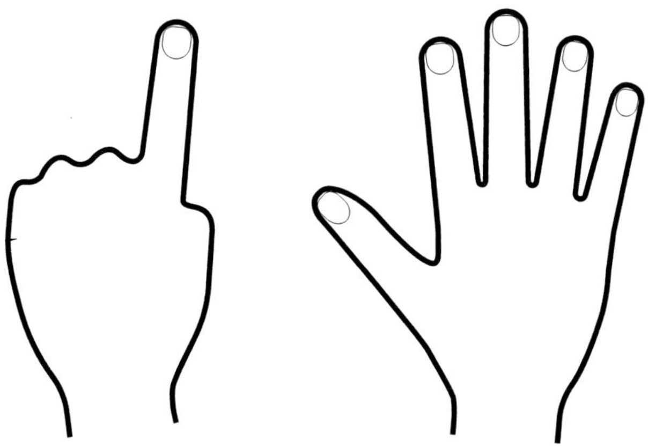

6	7	8

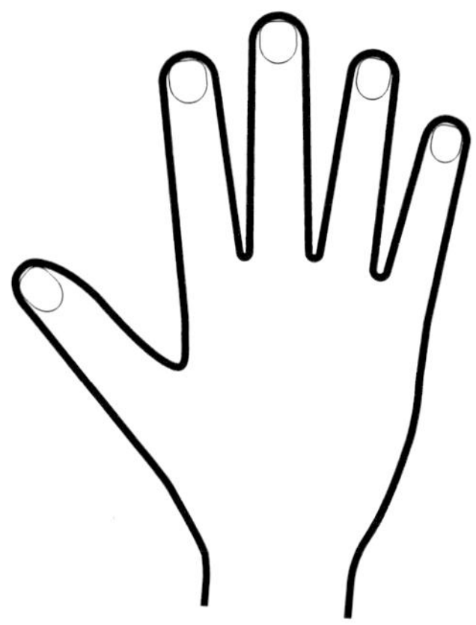

3	4	5

Counting Practice to 10

How many fingers are there? Use your fingers to count. Circle the correct number.

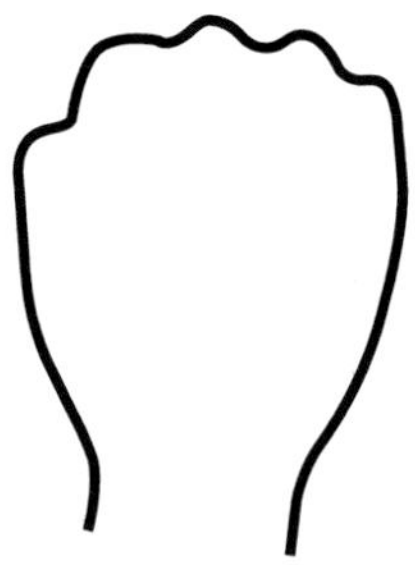

0	1	2

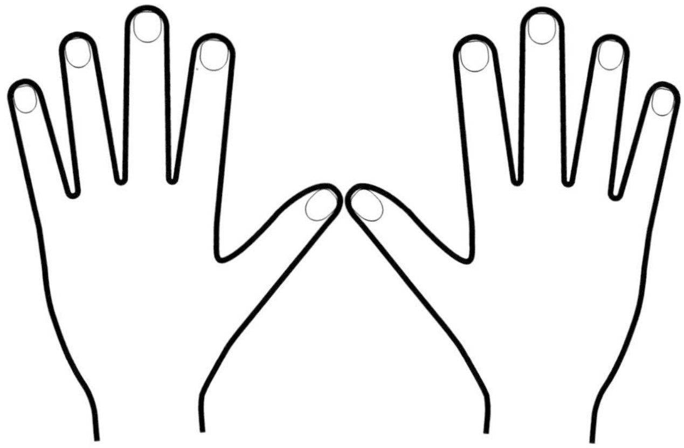

8	9	10

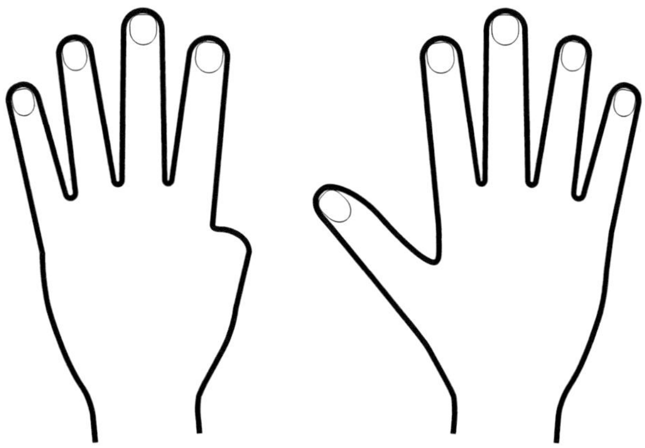

8	9	10

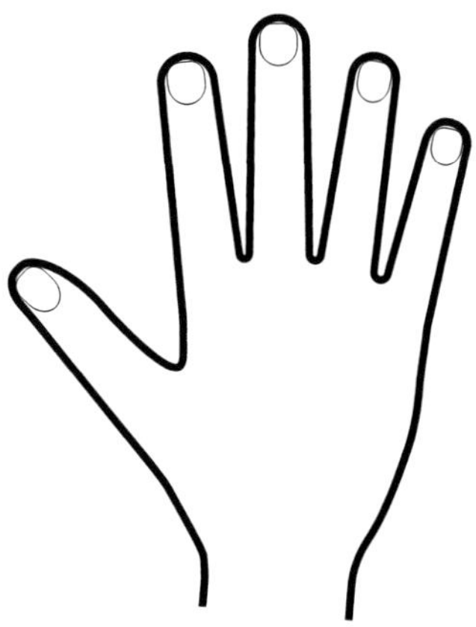

4	5	6

Counting Practice

How many shapes are there? Count the shapes and print the number below. Colour the shapes.

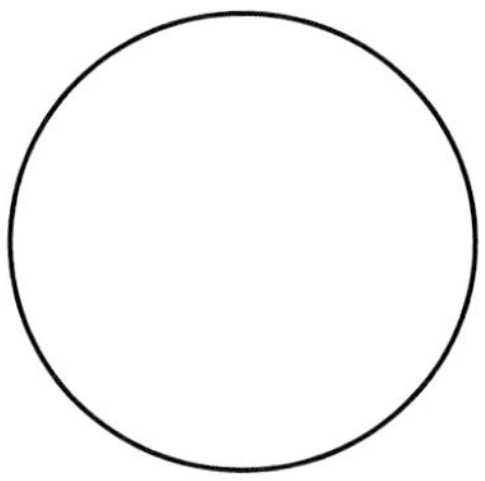

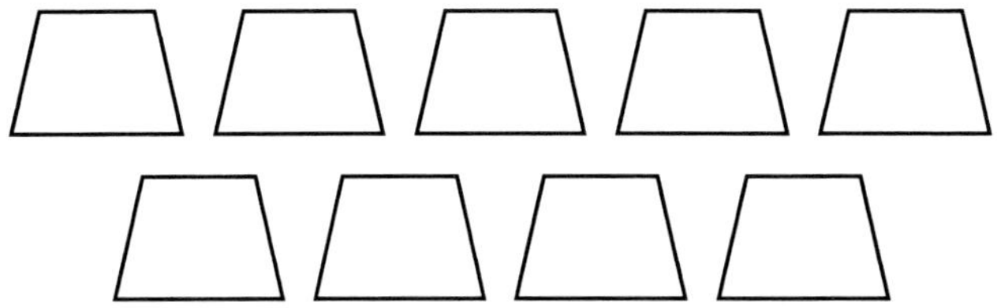

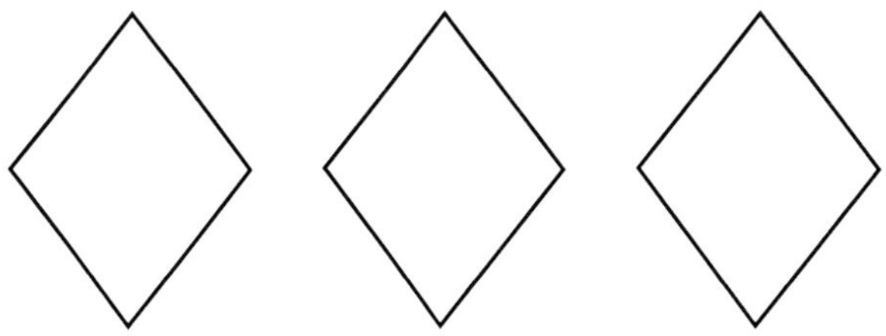

Counting Practice

How many shapes are there? Count the shapes and print the number below. Colour the shapes.

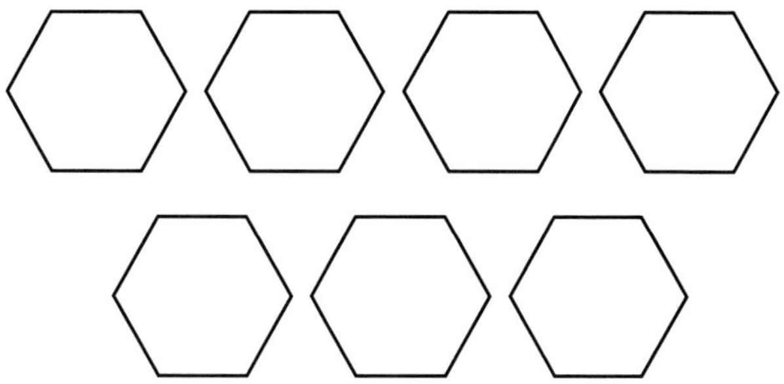

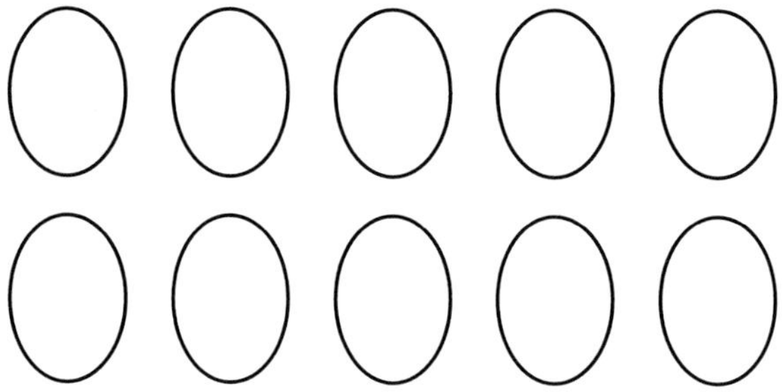

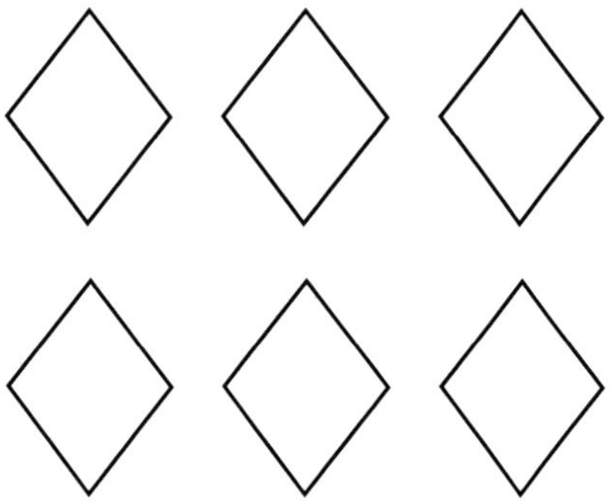

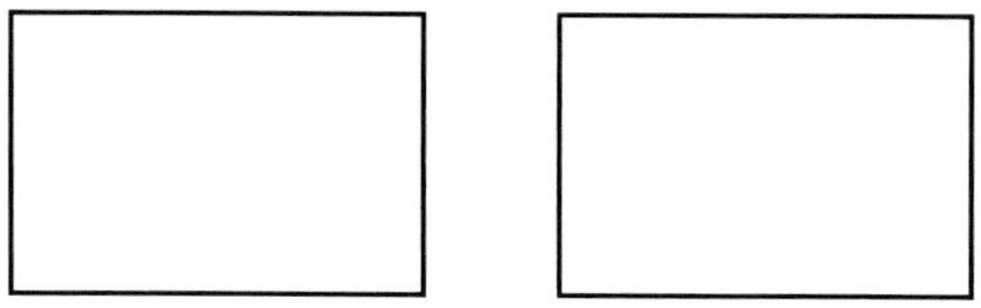

Counting Practice

How many shapes are there? Count the shapes and print the number below. Colour the shapes.

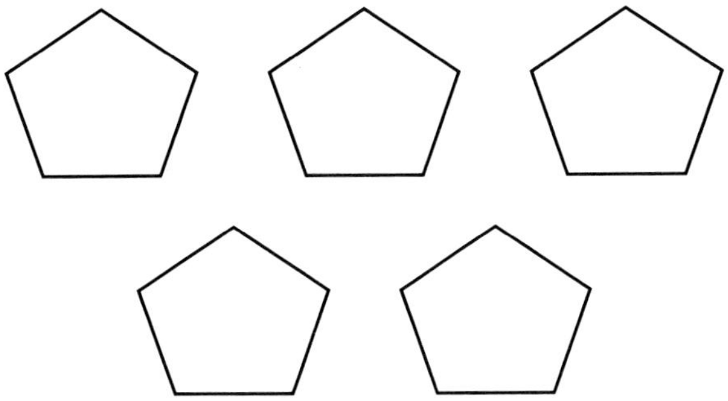

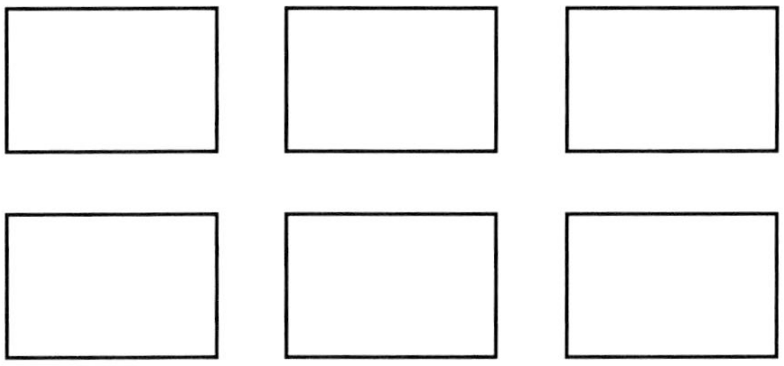

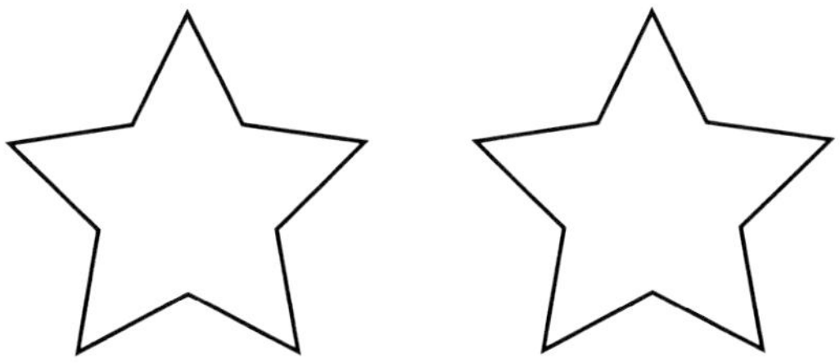

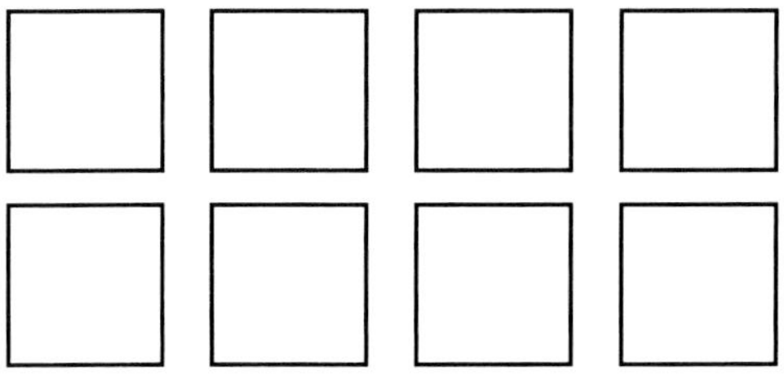

Counting Practice

Read the number. Count the shapes. Draw a line from the number to the correct number of shapes. Colour the shapes.

5

1

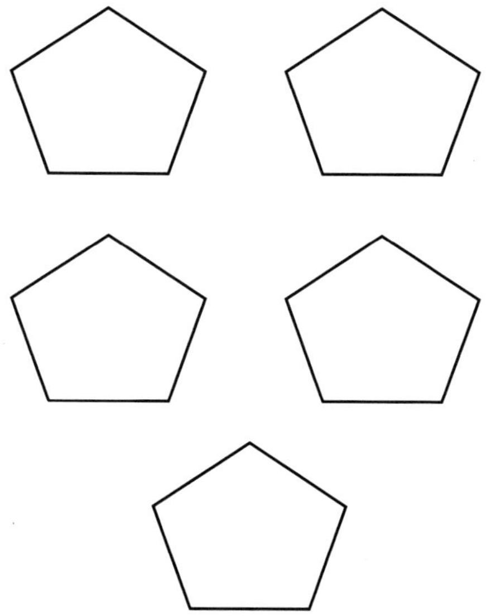

Counting Practice

Read the number. Count the shapes. Draw a line from the number to the correct number of shapes. Colour the shapes.

2

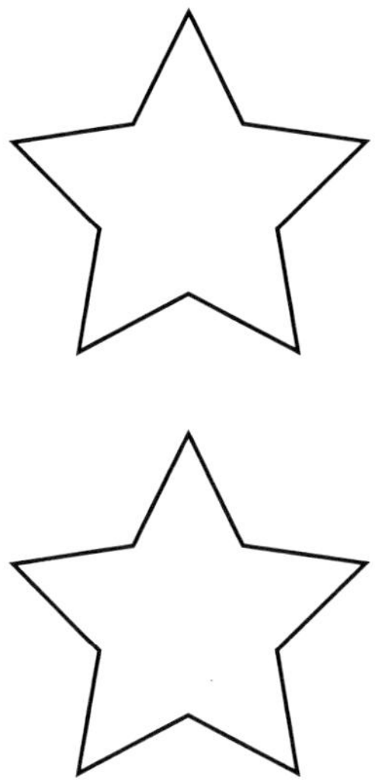

8

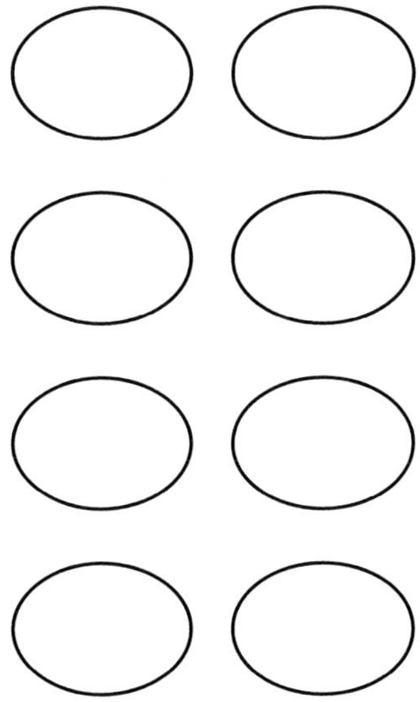

Counting Practice

Read the number. Count the shapes. Draw a line from the number to the correct number of shapes. Colour the shapes.

3

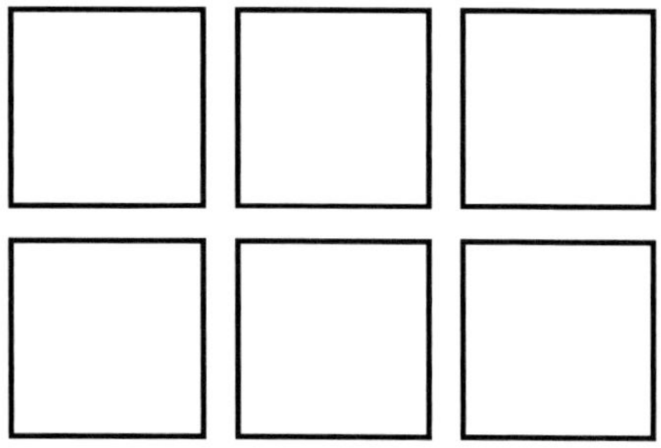

6

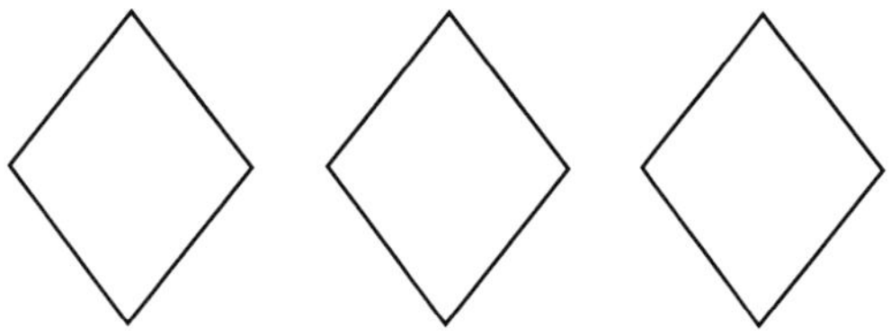

Counting Practice

Read the number. Count the shapes. Draw a line from the number to the correct number of shapes. Colour the shapes.

9

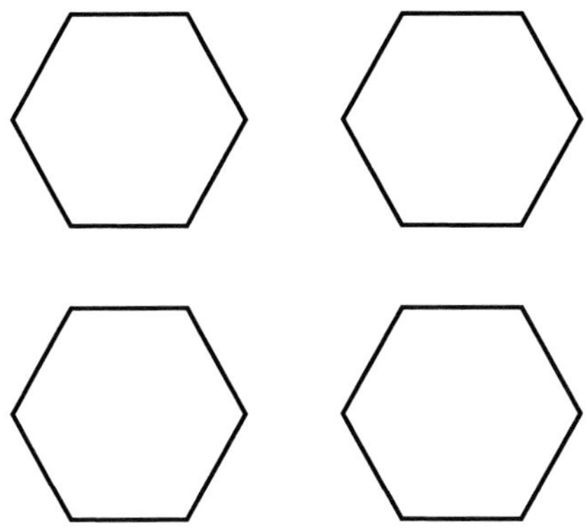

4

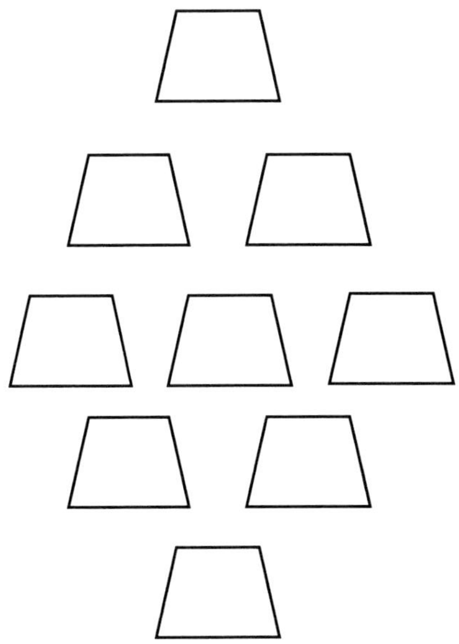

Counting Practice

Count the number of dots on each ladybug. Draw a line from the ladybug to the number of dots it has.

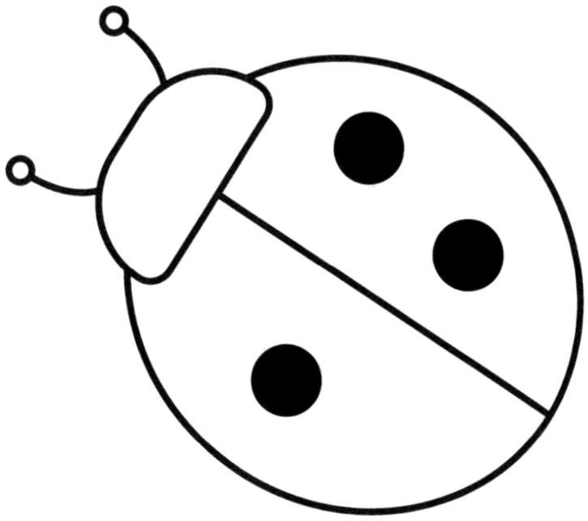

5

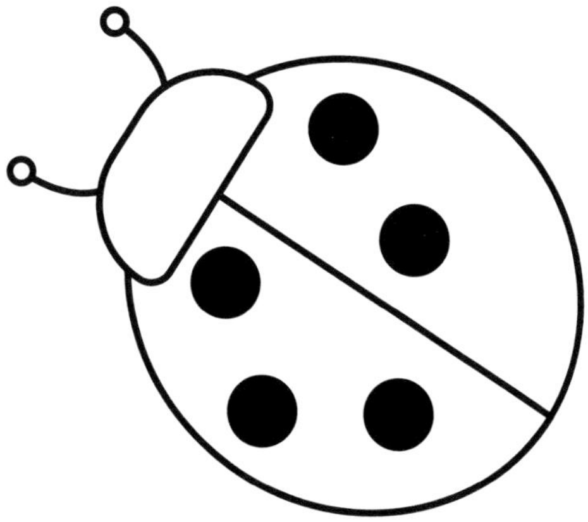

1

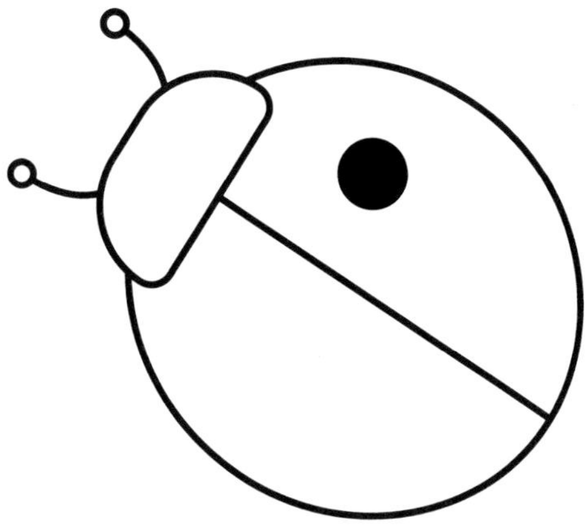

3

Counting Practice

Count the number of dots on each ladybug. Draw a line from the ladybug to the number of dots it has.

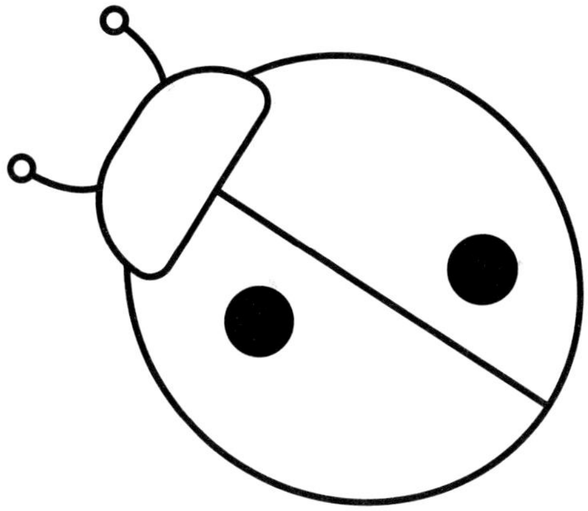

4

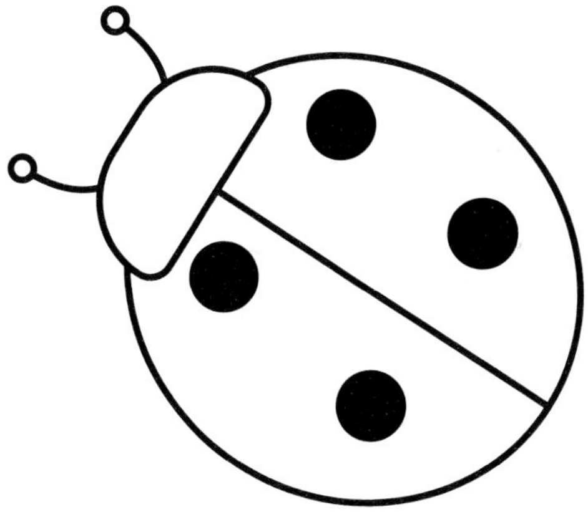

6

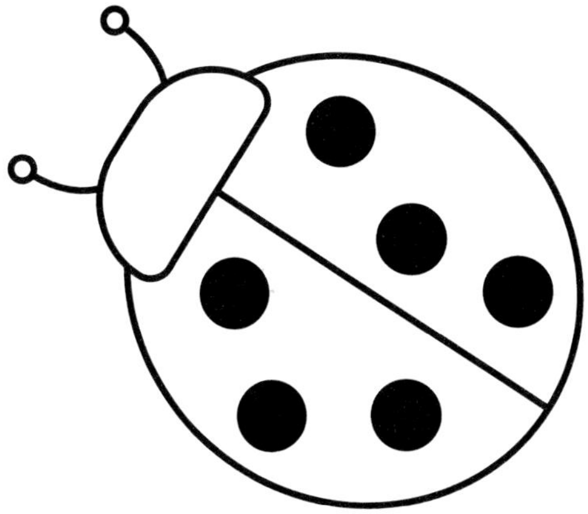

2

Connect the Dots: 0-10

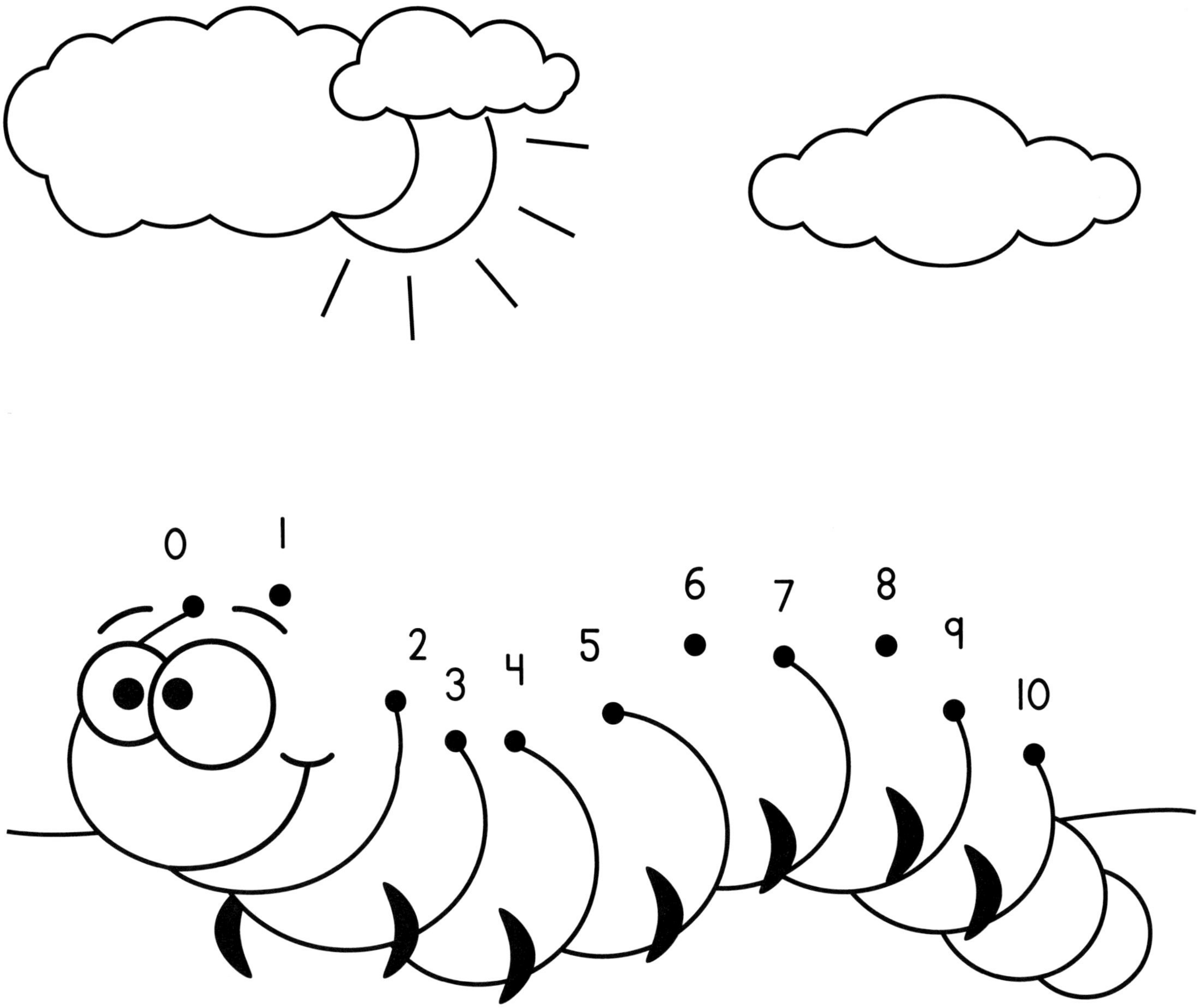

Think About It!

What does a butterfly sleep on?

A caterpillow!

Connect the Dots: 1-10

Think About It!

What's the most expensive fish?
A goldfish!

Colouring by Number

Use the colour key to colour in the picture.

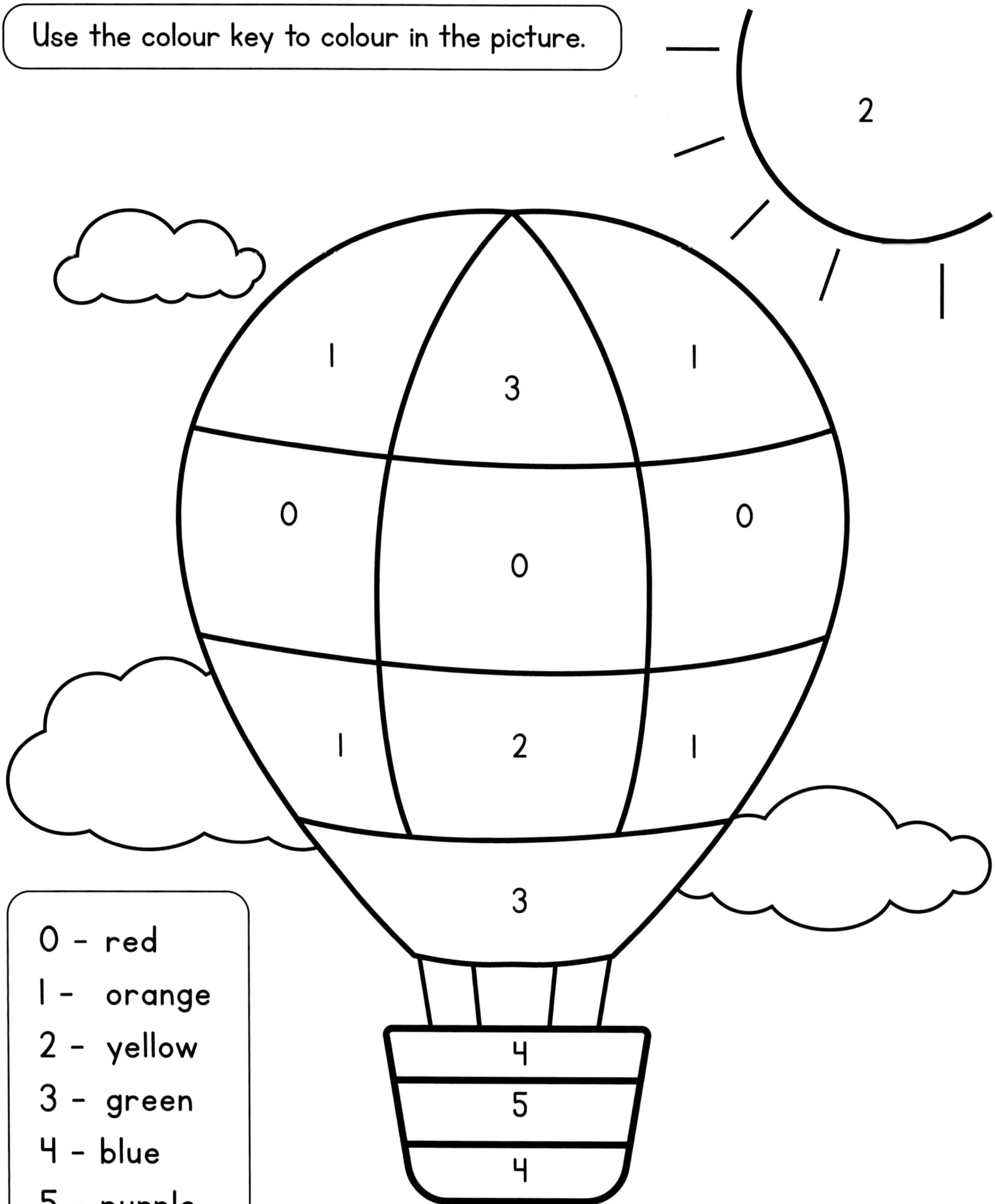

0 - red

1 - orange

2 - yellow

3 - green

4 - blue

5 - purple

Colouring by Number

Use the colour key to colour in the picture.

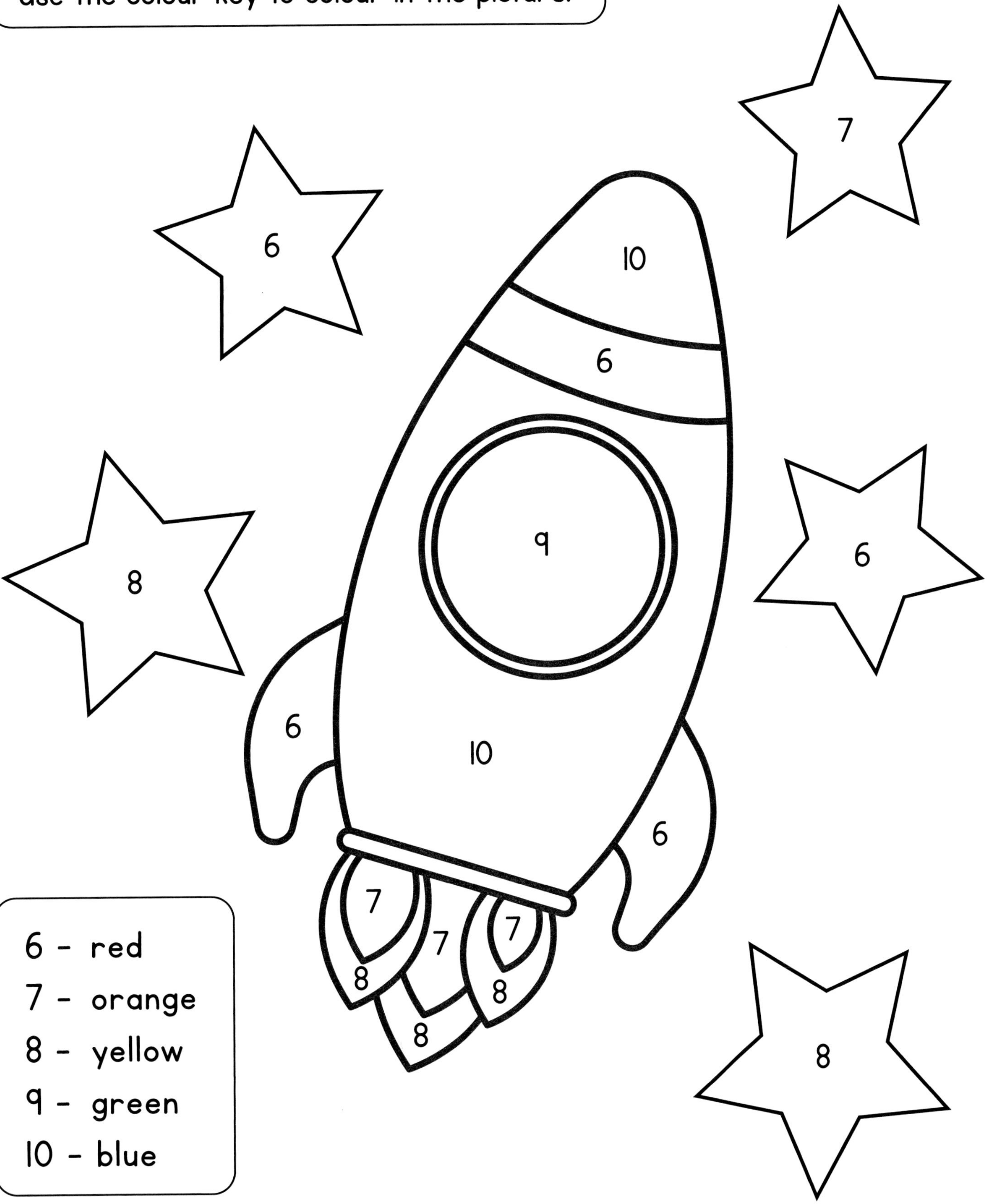

6 - red
7 - orange
8 - yellow
9 - green
10 - blue

Comparing Sets

Circle the set that has **more**. 

Circle the set that has **less**. 

Comparing Sets

Circle the set that has **more**. green

Circle the set that has **less**. yellow

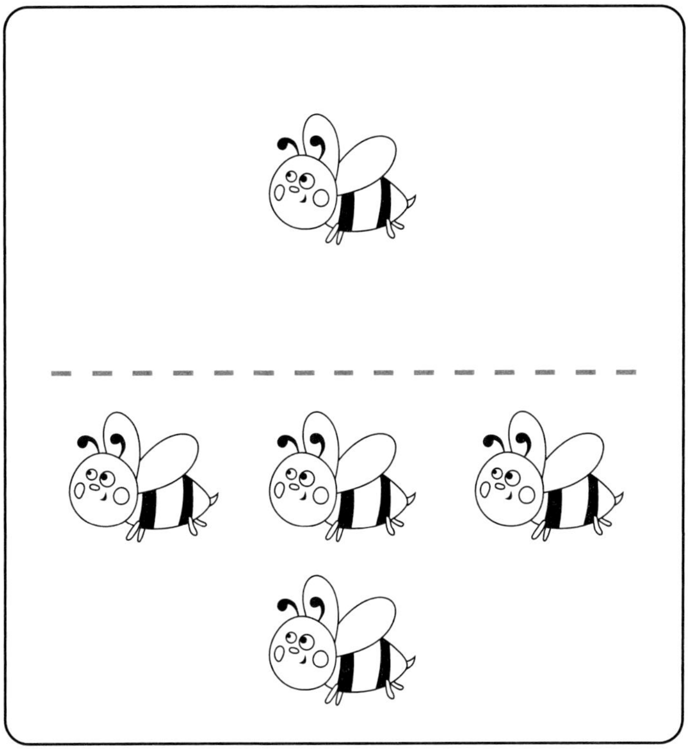

What is Your Phone Number?

Print your phone number.

Use your finger to call your phone number.

More Learning Skills

Matching Sets

Draw a line from the set of clothing to the correct weather.

hot and sunny

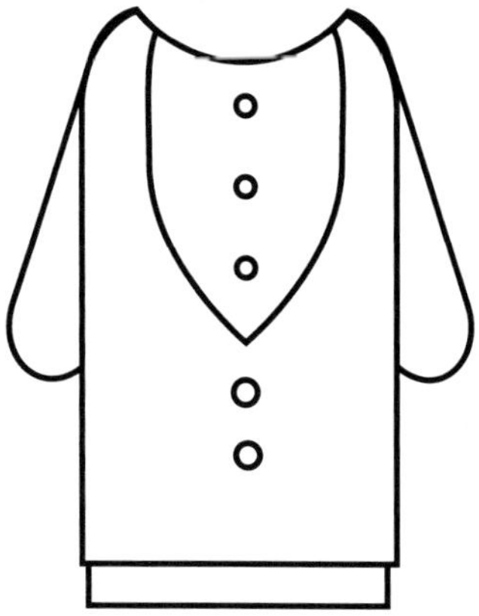

sweater

cool and cloudy

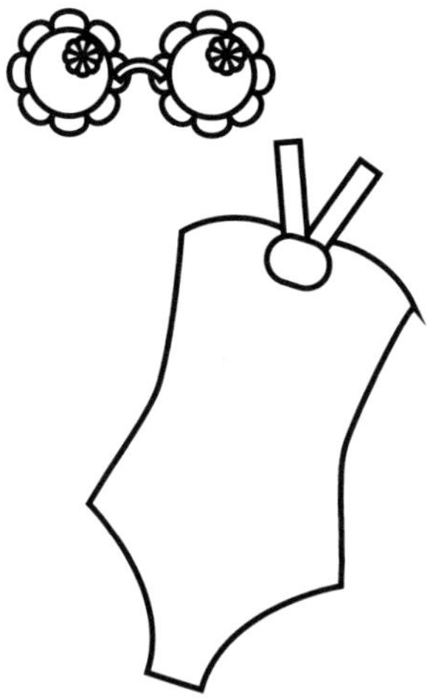

swimwear

Matching Sets

Draw a line from the set of clothing to the correct weather.

raining

coat and mittens

snowing

umbrella and boots

Matching Seasons

Draw a line from the weather picture to the thing you would use in that weather.

raining

snowing

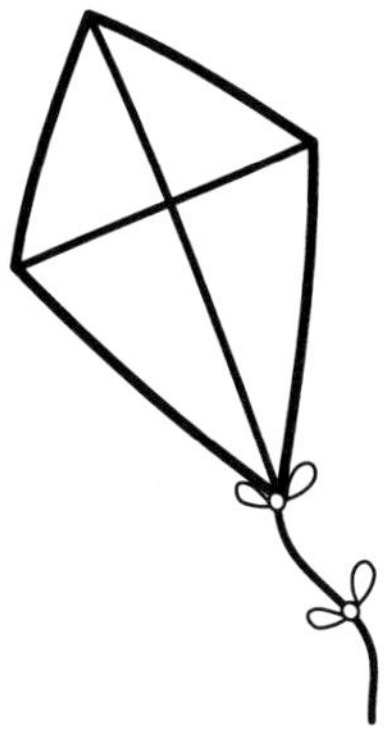

hot and sunny

windy

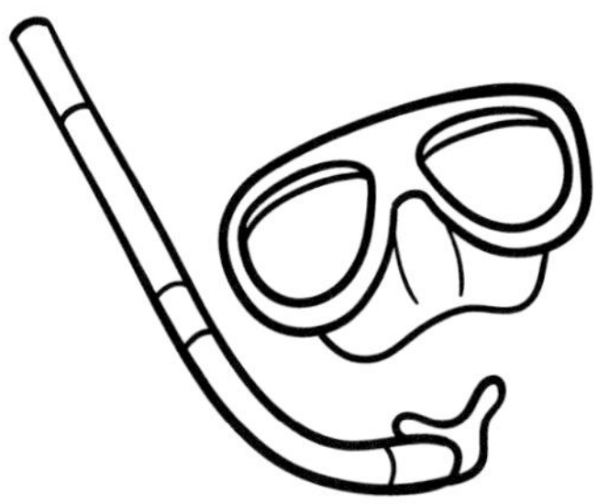

Matching Weather

Draw a line from the season to the activity you can do during that season.

Winter

Spring

Summer

Fall

Matching Animal Parents to Babies

Draw a line from the animal parent to its baby.

hen

cow

Matching Animal Parents to Babies

Draw a line from the animal parent to its baby.

sheep

rabbit

Opposites

The pairs of objects here are opposites. Draw a line from the object to its opposite. Colour the pictures.

happy

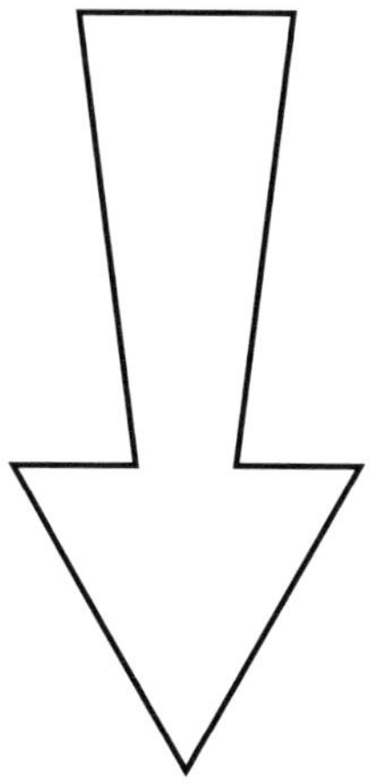

down

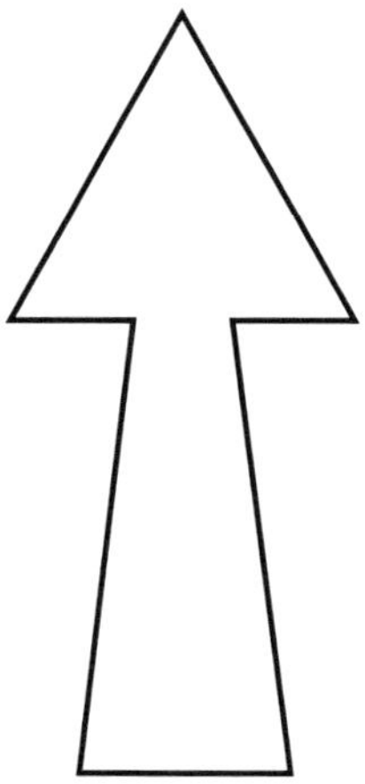

up

sad

Opposites

The pairs of objects here are opposites. Draw a line from the object to its opposite. Colour the pictures.

night

full

empty

day

More Opposites

The pairs of objects here are opposites. Draw a line from the object to its opposite. Colour the pictures.

big

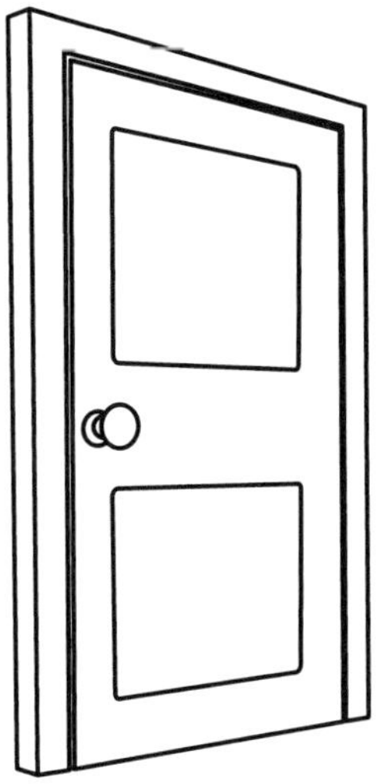

closed

open

small

More Opposites

The pairs of objects here are opposites. Draw a line from the object to its opposite. Colour the pictures.

slow

cold

hot

fast

Left to Right

Help the animals get to their homes!
Trace the lines from left to right.

left

right

quail

nest

left

right

bee

hive

left

right

cow

barn

Right to Left

Help the animals get to their homes!
Trace the lines from right to left.

left right

fishbowl fish

left right

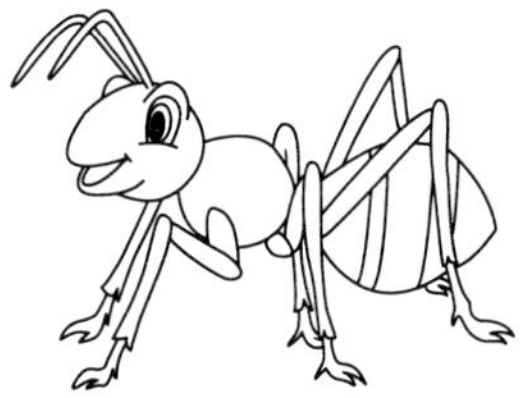

ant hill ant

left right

tree monkey

Top to Bottom

Help the spiders get down!
Trace the lines from top to bottom.

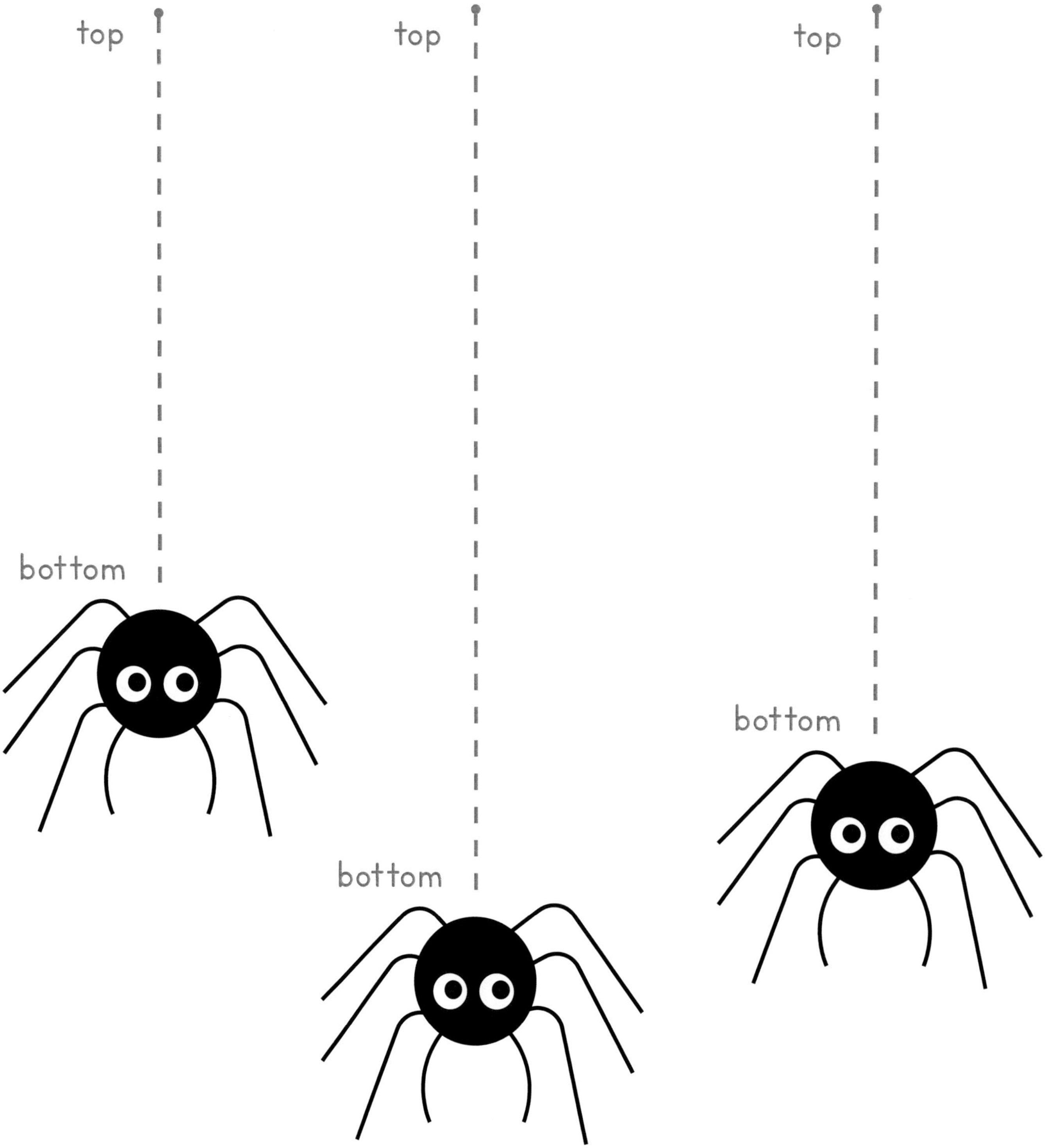

Bottom to Top

Help the butterflies fly up!
Trace the lines from bottom to top.

Pattern Fun

Look at the pattern.

Colour the next shape in the pattern.

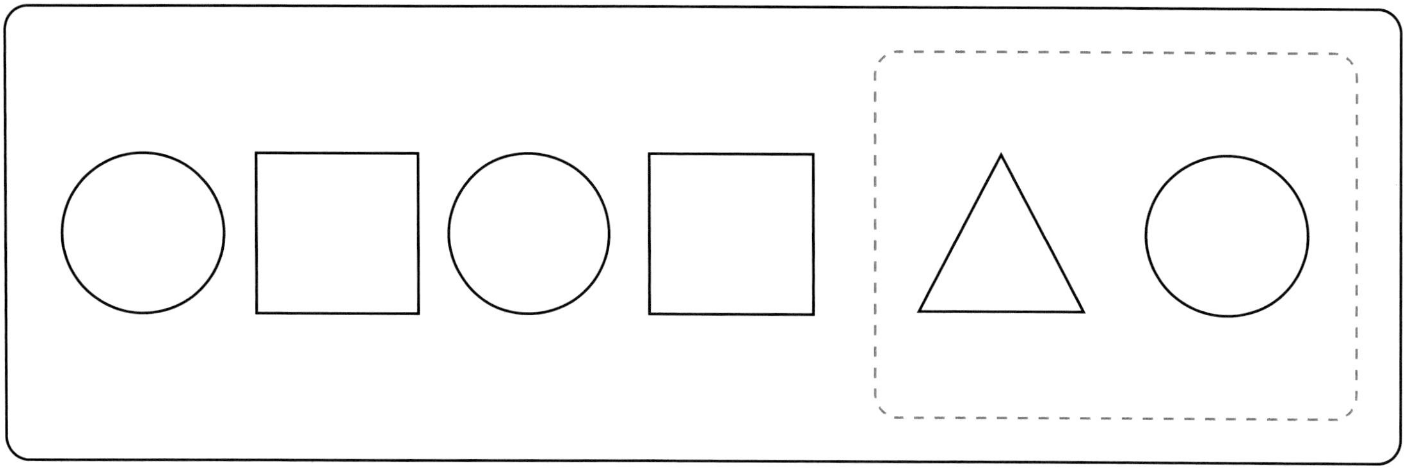

Pattern Fun

Look at the pattern.
Colour the next shape in the pattern.

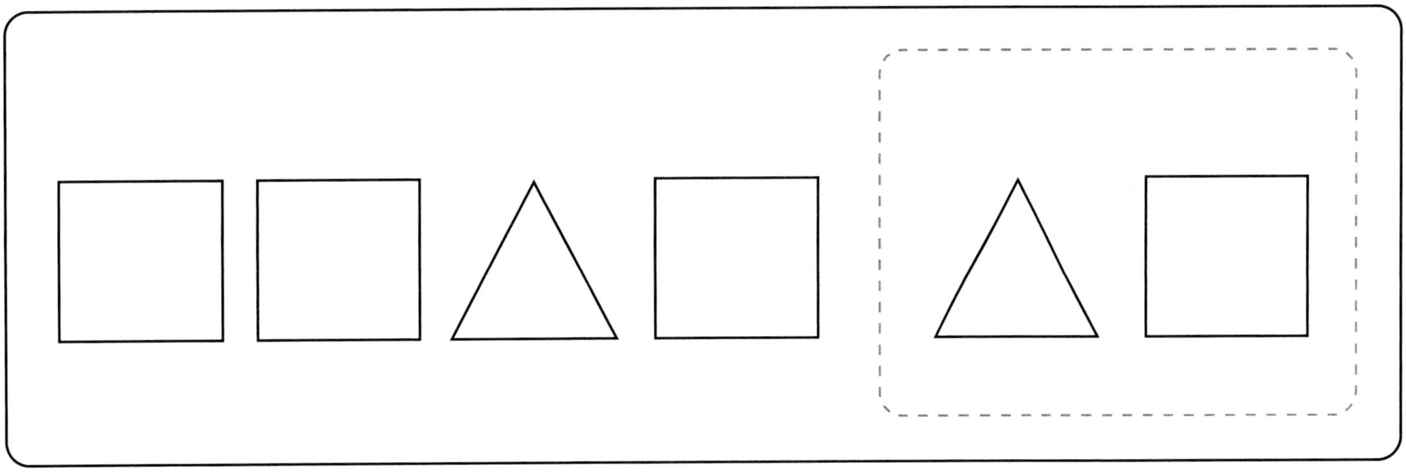

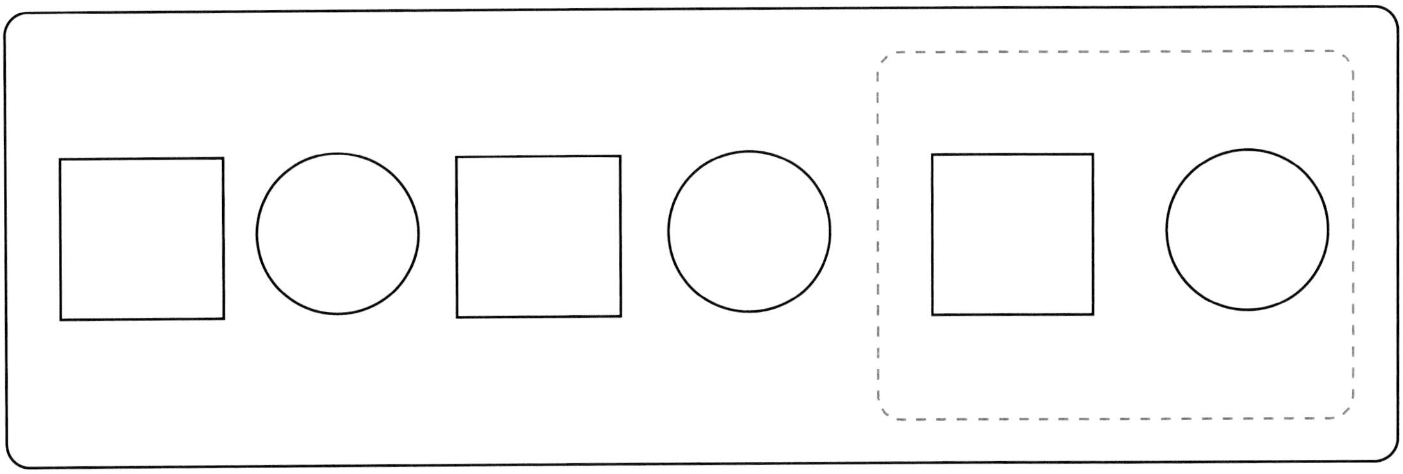

Pattern Fun

Create your own colour patterns.

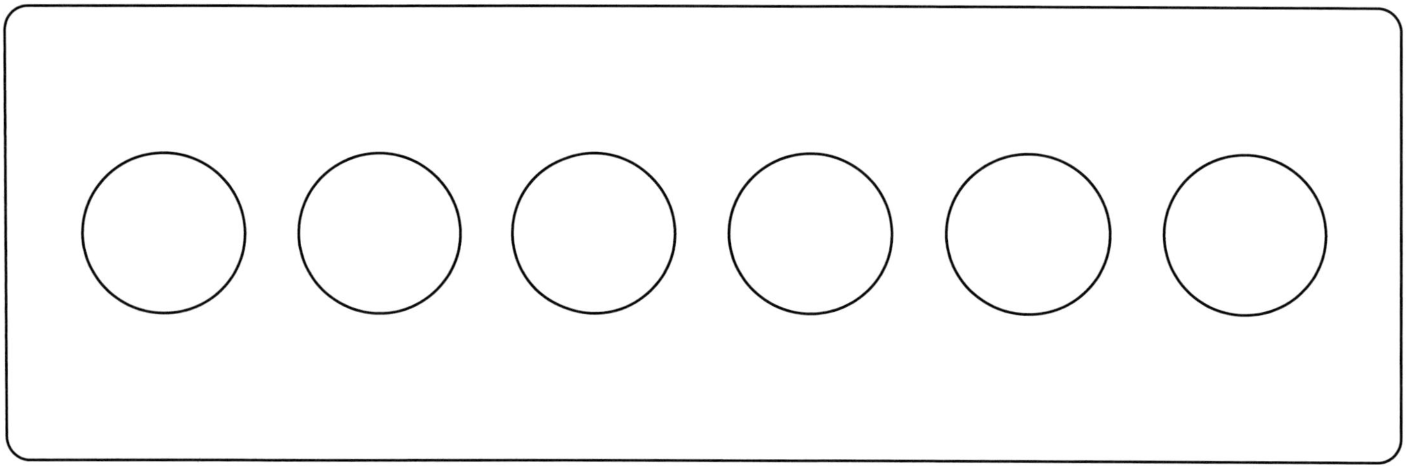

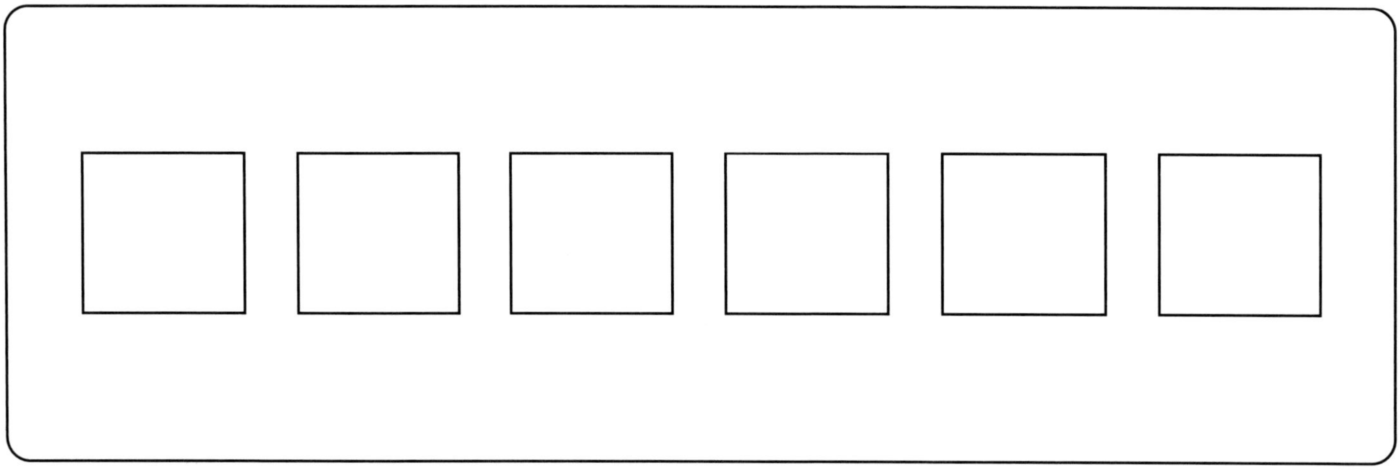

Pattern Fun

Create your own colour patterns.

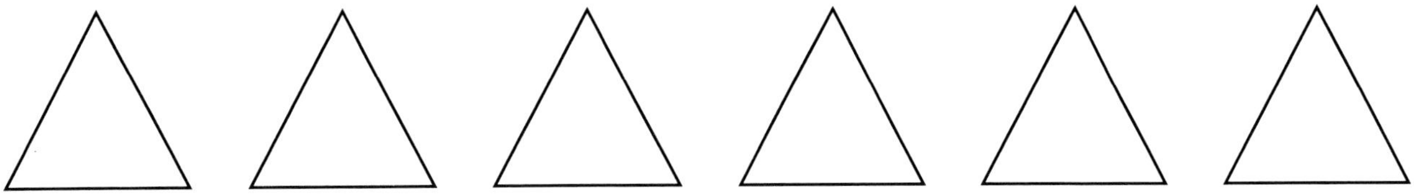

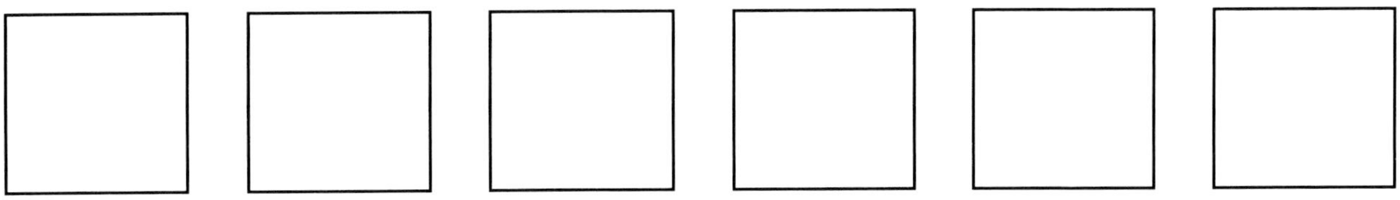

_______________'s Feelings

	I feel happy when...
	I feel sad when...
	I feel angry when...

_______________'s Feelings

	I feel excited when...
	I feel scared when...
	I feel brave when...

_________________________ 's Feelings

	I feel tired when...
	I feel proud when...
	I feel lonely when...

_______________________________ 's Feelings

	I feel silly when...
	I feel nervous when...
	I feel loved when...

What's My Temperature?

5 — furious

4 — angry, mad

3 — sad, frustrated

2 — anxious, worried

1 — calm, happy, pleased

Rhymes, Chants, and Finger Plays

Five Little Speckled Frogs

Five little speckled frogs, *(hold up five fingers)*
Sitting on a speckled log, *(sit down)*
Eating the most delicious bugs...yum, yum. *(pretend to eat)*
One jumped into the pool *(jump)*
Where it was nice and cool.
Then there were four speckled frogs.

Continue until only one frog is left.

One little speckled frog.
Sitting on a speckled log,
Eating the most delicious bugs...yum, yum.
He jumped into the pool
Where it was nice and cool.
Now there are no speckled frogs.

Hickory Dickory Dock

Hickory dickory dock,
The mouse ran up the clock.
The clock struck one,
The mouse ran down.
Hickory dickory dock.

Count to 100 Chant

Hooray! Hooray!
Count to 100 in different ways!

Count by 1s - its really fun!
1, 2, 3, 4, 5...

Count by 2s - I will count with you!
2, 4, 6, 8, 10...

Count by 5s - its easy if you try!
5, 10, 15, 20, 25...

Count by 10s, then start over again!
10, 20, 30, 40...

Rhymes, Chants, and Finger Plays

Ten Fingers

I have ten fingers *(hold up both hands showing all ten fingers)*
And they all belong to me, *(point to self)*
I can make them do things. *(wiggle fingers)*
Would you like to see? *(point to eyes)*
I can shut them up tight *(make fists)*
I can open them wide *(open hands and spread out fingers)*
I can put them together *(clasp hands together)*
I can make them all hide *(put hands behind back)*
I can make them jump high *(hold hands over head)*
I can make them jump low *(touch the floor with all ten fingers)*
I can fold them up quietly *(fold hands in lap)*
And hold them just so.

Who Stole the Cookie?

Who stole the cookie from the cookie jar?
_____________ *(child's name)* stole the cookie from the cookie jar.
(named child) Who me?
(other children) Yes you!
(named child) Couldn't be!
(other children) Then who?
Repeat above verse with the name of a new child.
Tip: The ttheer may wish to have a cookie jar filled with children's name cards. Have a child pick a name card from the cookie jar to start the rhyme.

I'm a Little Teapot

I'm a little teapot, *(place one hand on hip to imitate a handle)*
Short and stout *(position other hand in the air to imitate a spout)*
Here is my handle,
Here is my spout.
When I get all steamed up
Hear me shout!
Tip me over *(lean to the right to imitate pouring tea from the spout)*
And pour me out!

Rhymes, Chants, and Finger Plays

It's Raining, It's Pouring

It's raining; it's pouring.
The old man is snoring.
He bumped his head on the top of the bed,
And couldn't get up in the morning.

Twinkle Twinkle Little Star

Twinkle, twinkle, little star,
How I wonder what you are.
Up above the world so high,
Like a diamond in the sky.

Itsy Bitsy Spider

The itsy bitsy spider crawled up the water spout.
Down came the rain, and washed the spider out.
Out came the sun, and dried up all the rain,
and the itsy bitsy spider went up the spout again

Baa, Baa, Black Sheep

Baa, baa, black sheep,
Have you any wool?
Yes sir, yes sir,
Three bags full.
One for the master,
One for the dame,
And one for the little boy
Who lives down the lane

Congratulations!

Great Work!